Teaching Literacy Effectively in the Modern Classroom for Ages 9–12

This practical guide presents the Big 5 of literacy – decoding, comprehension, vocabulary, writing, and spelling. They are the five essential skills for success in school and in life.

Tom Nicholson offers a toolkit to help you bring your class, including those with persistent literacy learning difficulties such as dyslexia, up to typically achieving level for their age and beyond. Designed as a "one stop shop" for classroom teachers, this book covers assessment, planning and progression of writing, spelling, decoding, and comprehension, with a range of practical, easy-to-follow charts, activities, lesson plans, and posters. The final chapter is a Countdown to the Classroom, showing how to plan for a successful and explicit start to literacy, how to encourage good conduct, and how to be an effective leader. Chapters combine both the experience gleaned from a teaching career focused on literacy and countless hours of research.

The author presents solutions for the pressing problem of achieving high levels of literacy in the modern classroom for all students, not just some. Containing a wealth of resources and tips for teaching ages 9–12, this will be of great interest to all classroom teachers teaching literacy as well as parents and librarians.

Tom Nicholson is a professor emeritus in Education at Massey University who has worked as a classroom teacher, an education department researcher, a university academic, and director of a university clinic tutoring students with literacy difficulties. Awards include the International Literacy Association's doctoral dissertation award, the Mona Tobias Award, and election to the Reading Hall of Fame.

Teaching Literacy Effectively in the Modern Classroom for Ages 9–12

A Practical Guide for Teaching Reading and Writing in Diverse Learning Environments

Tom Nicholson

LONDON AND NEW YORK

Designed cover image: by Tom Nicholson, adapted from an original cartoon by Virgil Partch, with permission of Anna Partch Couch, and Special Collections and Archives, University of California, Irvine Libraries.

First published 2026
by Routledge
4 Park Square, Milton Park, Abingdon, Oxon OX14 4RN

and by Routledge
605 Third Avenue, New York, NY 10158

Routledge is an imprint of the Taylor & Francis Group, an informa business

© 2026 Tom Nicholson

The right of Tom Nicholson to be identified as author of this work has been asserted in accordance with sections 77 and 78 of the Copyright, Designs and Patents Act 1988.

All rights reserved. No part of this book may be reprinted or reproduced or utilised in any form or by any electronic, mechanical, or other means, now known or hereafter invented, including photocopying and recording, or in any information storage or retrieval system, without permission in writing from the publishers.

For Product Safety Concerns and Information please contact our EU representative GPSR@taylorandfrancis.com. Taylor & Francis Verlag GmbH, Kaufingerstraße 24, 80331 München, Germany.

Trademark notice: Product or corporate names may be trademarks or registered trademarks, and are used only for identification and explanation without intent to infringe.

British Library Cataloguing-in-Publication Data
A catalogue record for this book is available from the British Library

ISBN: 978-0-367-67319-2 (hbk)
ISBN: 978-0-367-67318-5 (pbk)
ISBN: 978-1-003-13078-9 (ebk)

DOI: 10.4324/9781003130789

Typeset in Galliard
by SPi Technologies India Pvt Ltd (Straive)

Contents

Lists of figures   viii
List of tables   xi
List of appendices   xiii
Acknowledgements   xiv

PART 1
Decoding skills   1

1   Decoding: What is it?   3
This chapter explains decoding at the higher level. It gives a scope and sequence for decoding.

2   Assessing decoding   17
This chapter assesses decoding skills and finds solutions.

3   Teaching decoding   38
This chapter shows how to learn high-level decoding skills.

PART 2
Reading comprehension   57

4   Reading comprehension: What is it?   59
This chapter explains comprehension.

5   Assessing reading comprehension   66
This chapter gives diagnostics to solve problems.

6   Teaching reading comprehension   73
This chapter shows some better ways to find the key information points in fiction and nonfiction texts.

PART 3
Reading vocabulary 95

7 Vocabulary: What is it? 97
   This chapter explains what vocabulary is and how it works.

8 Assessing vocabulary 102
   This chapter diagnoses vocabulary difficulties and gives solutions.

9 Teaching vocabulary 111
   This chapter shows how to learn vocabulary more effectively.

PART 4
Writing 125

10 Writing: What is it? 127
    This chapter explains writing.

11 Assessing writing 133
    This chapter breaks writing down and shows what works best.

12 Teaching writing 146
    This chapter shows how to write fiction and nonfiction.

PART 5
Spelling 167

13 Spelling: What is it? 169
    This chapter explains the amazing beauty of spelling.

14 Assessing spelling 185
    This chapter shows how to help students spell better.

15 Teaching spelling 206
    This chapter gives strategies to make good spelling possible.

PART 6
Countdown to the classroom   **231**

16 Countdown to the classroom   233
This chapter explains how to prepare a literate classroom. What to do 3 months before, 1 month before, 2 weeks before, and now! Plus helpful hints on what makes a happy, well-behaved classroom and an effective classroom teacher leader.

References   *241*
Author index   *245*
Topic index   *246*

Figures

1.1	Overview of Chapter 1	3
1.2	The Story of English	8
2.1	Overview of Chapter 2	17
2.2	A Lesson on the Split Digraph "Silent e" Rule	20
2.3	A Lesson on the ai-ay Vowel Digraph Pattern	21
2.4	Bryant Test of Basic Decoding Skills	26
2.5	Scope and Sequence: Decoding Skills	27
2.6	Single Consonant and Short Vowel Sounds	28
2.7	Adjacent Consonants (or Consonant Clusters)	29
2.8	Consonant Digraphs ch sh th ng	30
2.9	Consonant Digraphs, Vowel Digraphs, R- and L-Affected Vowels	31
2.10	Sounds of C, G, Y	32
2.11	Silent Letter Words gh gn st kn wr mb	33
2.12	Multisyllable Words	34
2.13	Anglo-Saxon: Prefixes, Root Words, Suffixes	35
2.14	Latin: Prefixes, Root Words, Suffixes	36
2.15	Words with Greek Origins	37
3.1	Overview of Chapter 3	38
3.2	Closed Syllable Pattern	40
3.3	Open Syllable Pattern	41
3.4	The R-Affected Syllable Pattern	42
3.5	The Split Digraph: Final E - Syllable Pattern	43
3.6	The Vowel Team Syllable Pattern	44
3.7	The -LE Syllable Pattern	45
3.8	Root Word *rupt* – To Break	51
3.9	Root Word *form* – To Shape	51
3.10	Root Word *greg* – Crowd, Assemble	52
3.11	Root Word *ped* – Foot	52
3.12	Root Word *port* – To Carry	53
3.13	Root Word *vent* – To Come	53
3.14	Root Word *struct* – To Build	54
3.15	Root Word *spect* – To See	54
3.16	Root Word *dict* – To Say	55

3.17	Root Word *scrib* – To Write	55
3.18	Root Word *ject* – To Throw	56
3.19	Root Word *tract* – To Drag	56
4.1	Overview of Chapter 4	59
4.2	Steps in the Reading Comprehension Process	61
5.1	Overview of Chapter 5	66
5.2	Simple View of Reading Difficulties	71
6.1	Overview of Chapter 6	73
6.2	Story Web for the "Hare and Tortoise" Story	78
6.3	Story Graph for the "Hare and Tortoise" Story – Timeline – Action	78
6.4	Web Structure: Snails	80
6.5	Web Structure: Dogs	81
6.6	Web Structure: Cockroaches	82
6.7	Weave/Venn Structure: Bears	83
6.8	Sequence Structure: Poverty Cycle	84
6.9	Story: "Hare and Tortoise": Blank Copy	89
6.10	Web Structure: Snails Text: Blank Copy	90
6.11	Web Structure: Dogs: Blank Copy	91
6.12	Web Structure: Cockroaches: Blank Copy	92
6.13	Venn Weave Structure: Bears: Blank Copy	93
6.14	Cyclical Text Structure: Poverty Cycle: Blank Copy	94
7.1	Overview of Chapter 7	97
8.1	Overview of Chapter 8	102
9.1	Overview of Chapter 9	111
9.2	Cartoon Showing Students Learning a Web Structure for *Tiger*	114
9.3	Web Diagram for *California*	115
9.4	Web Diagram for *Fish*	116
9.5	Web Diagram for *Chameleon*	117
9.6	Weave/Matrix Diagram to Compare Alligator, Lion, and Bear	118
9.7	Thermometer Diagram: Synonyms for *Fear*	119
9.8	Keyword Image for Spanish Word *Gata*	121
9.9	Keyword Method to Recall "Lachrymose"	121
9.10	Bookmarking Unfamiliar Words Spoken by Detective Gordon and Buffy in *A Complicated Case*	122
9.11	Blank Copy of Word Detective Bookmark	123
10.1	Overview of Chapter 10	127
10.2	Simple View of Writing	129
10.3	Scatterplot of Scores for Story Quality and Presentation	130
10.4	Students with Writing Difficulties	130
11.1	Overview of Chapter 11: Assessing Writing	133
11.2	Student Writing: "What Will Happen to Jim Jarvis?"	136
11.3	Student Writing: "Applause"	138
12.1	Overview of Chapter 12: Teaching Writing	146
12.2	Nonfiction Text Structures: List, Web, Weave/Venn, Sequence	151
12.3	Story Planner – Proficient	158

x *Figures*

12.4	Story Planner – Advanced	159
12.5	List Planner	160
12.6	Web Planner	161
12.7	Weave Planner	162
12.8	Linear String Planner	163
12.9	Problem–Solution Planner	164
12.10	Persuasion Planner	165
13.1	Overview of Chapter 13: Spelling: What Is It?	169
13.2	How Printers Changed the Rules	171
13.3	Scatterplot of Student Scores for Spelling Regular and Exception Words	175
13.4	Classification of Words for Spelling in Terms of Transfer Value	177
14.1	Overview of Chapter 14: Assessing Spelling	185
14.2	"Animals Getting Cewd"	187
14.3	Spelling Snake: Levels 1–27	191
14.4	The Big 8 Spelling Rules	195
14.5	Overview: Common Spelling Patterns	196
14.6	Long Vowel Sounds ai ay a_e	197
14.7	Long Vowel Sounds ee ea y e_e ey ie	197
14.8	Long Vowel Sounds ie y igh i_e	198
14.9	Long Vowel Sounds oa ow o_e	199
14.10	Long Vowel Sounds oo u_e ew ou ue	200
14.11	Other Vowel Sounds ow-ou oo oi-oy	200
14.12	R- and L-Affected Vowel Sounds ar or au-aw al er ir ur	201
15.1	Overview of Chapter 15: Teaching Spelling	206
15.2	Spelling -ion and -ian	210
15.3	Spelling Quiz: Consonant Sounds	213
15.4	Spelling Quiz: Short Vowel Sounds 1	214
15.5	Spelling Quiz: Short Vowel Sounds 2	215
15.6	Spelling Quiz: ch sh th ng	216
15.7	Spelling Quiz: Long Vowel Sound: Silent e Rule	217
15.8	Spelling Quiz: ar or ur	218
15.9	Spelling Quiz: all ell ill oll ull	219
15.10	Spelling Quiz: Long Vowel Sounds ai ay	220
15.11	Spelling Quiz: Long Vowel Sounds ee ea e_e	221
15.12	Spelling Quiz: Long Vowel Sounds igh ie i_e	222
15.13	Spelling Quiz: Long Vowel Sounds oa ow o_e	223
15.14	Spelling Quiz: Long Vowel Sounds ou ew	224
15.15	Spelling Quiz: Long Vowel Sounds oo ew u_e ue	225
15.16	Spelling Quiz: Long Vowel Sounds au aw	226
15.17	Spelling Quiz: Long Vowel Sounds oi oy	226
15.18	Spelling Quiz: Homophones	227
15.19	Spelling Quiz: Suffixes -s, -ed	228
15.20	Spelling Quiz: Suffixes -ian, -ion	229
16.1	Overview of Chapter 16: Countdown	233

Tables

1.1	Structural Analysis: Words with Anglo-Saxon, Latin/French, and Greek Origins	12
1.2	Common Latin Root Words	13
1.3	Common Latin Prefixes	14
1.4	Common Latin Suffixes	14
2.1	Examples of Decoding Errors while Reading Text	23
2.2	Scope and Sequence Chart for Learning Basic Decoding Skills	25
3.1	Scope and Sequence: Decoding Continuum for Ages 9–12	39
3.2	Examples of Compound Words – Write the BA Code for Each Word	46
3.3	Prefixes with a Negative Meaning: *in- im- dis- contra-*	49
3.4	Suffixes Indicating Word Class: Noun *-ity, -ion* and Adjective *-ious*	49
3.5	Student Activity: Draw a Line from Latin Prefix to its Meaning	50
3.6	Examples of Greek Combining Forms	50
5.1	Test-Taking Strategies During a Test	70
5.2	Assessment Data on Reading for Four Students	72
6.1	Narrative Lesson Plan: "Hare and Tortoise"	77
6.2	Lesson Plan: Snails	80
6.3	Lesson Plan: Dogs	81
6.4	Lesson Plan: Cockroaches	82
6.5	Lesson Plan: Bears	83
6.6	Lesson Plan: Poverty Cycle	84
7.1	A Semantic Feature Comparison of Goldfish and Rock	99
9.1	Detective Gordon's Weave Diagram to Compare Suspects	118
9.2	Prefixes and Suffixes	120
11.1	Some General Writing Expectations at Ages 9–12	135
11.2	Student Checklist for Fiction Writing	143
11.3	Student Checklist for Nonfiction Writing	144
11.4	Student Checklist for Nonfiction Writing	144
12.1	Sentence Combining Examples	156
13.1	Student Copy of Spelling Grid	173
13.2	Student Spelling Grid – Answers	179

13.3	Common Root Words with Latin Origins	182
13.4	Common Prefixes with Latin Origins	183
13.5	Common Suffixes with Latin Origins	184
14.1	The Big 14 Punctuation Tips for Writers	204
15.1	Anglo-Saxon Compound Spellings	208
15.2	Spelling Examples of -ion and -ian	209

Appendices

2	Decoding resources	26
6 A	Extension text structure activities	87
6 B	Articles and text structure diagrams	89
12	Writing planners	158
13 A	Quirky spelling patterns	180
13 B	Latin root words, prefixes, and suffixes	182
14	Spelling activities to ensure that students learn to spell well	190

Acknowledgements

Special thanks

Many thanks to Clare Midgely, editor, and to Khadijah Ebrahim and Felicia Chan, editorial assistants at Routledge.

Copyright permissions

Thanks to artist Gitte Speer for permission to reprint her original drawing of Detective Gordon and Buffy from the novel *A Complicated Case*.

Thanks to Anna Partch Couch, and Special Collections and Archives, University of California, Irvine Libraries, for permission to adapt the original cartoon by Virgil Partch.

Thanks to the UK Standards and Testing Agency for permission to reprint examples of student writing from their publication *Standards and Testing Agency teacher assessment exemplification: KS2 English writing*.

Teacher feedback

Although final responsibility for the chapters is mine, I did gain hugely from suggestions for improvement given by some amazing teachers who made time to give me feedback on early drafts of the chapters for the book:

Vicky Artavia-Brown, Matthew Astle, Lynne Bishop, Susy Carryer, Lexia Copp, Corinne Coulthard, Corinna De-Arth, Tracey Doak, Anne Grady, Olivia Graham, Don Harland, Jacqui Hopkins, Nikki Irwin, Olwyn Johnston, Stephanie Lin, Ben Ngata, Kathryn Rowe, Stephanie Thompson, and Clifford Wicks.

Part 1
Decoding skills

Chapter 1, *Decoding: What is it?*, covers the science of decoding, gives definitions of terms, explains how to crack the code, achieve fluency, help struggling students, and teach the story of English from Roman times to the 1500s.

Chapter 2, *Assessing decoding*, covers norm-referenced tests, an informal test of decoding skills, a trouble-shooting guide for decoding problems, a 23-step scope and sequence chart, and 10 phonics charts.

Chapter 3, *Teaching decoding*, covers teaching of the Big 6 rules for multi-syllable words, class activities for compound words and Latin-based words, Greek words, plus 12 teaching charts covering Latin roots.

1 Decoding

What is it?

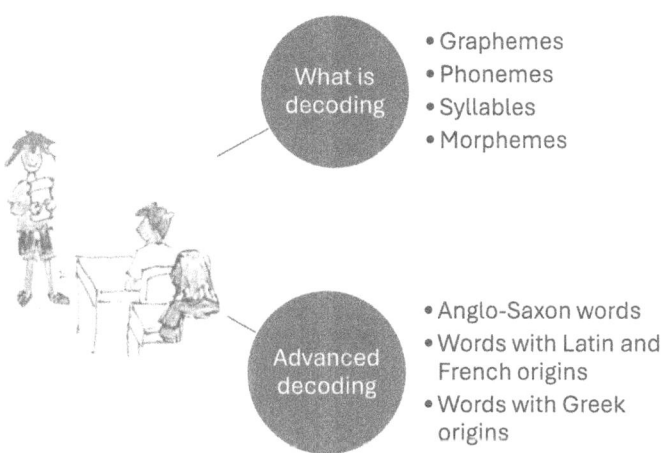

Figure 1.1 Overview of Chapter 1.

1.1 Introduction: What is decoding?

> There is a word called persevere. I know it means keep trying ... but if it was on a piece of paper, it would be too hard... unless I can read, I can't do anything.

There are many ways to define decoding, but in simple terms, it is oral reading fluency. It is the ability to read any word, real or made-up, quickly and accurately and without any context help or guessing.

Studies show that nearly four in ten students can decode but they are slow and make errors.

Why is it so difficult for them? One reason is that the texts for students at ages 9–12 have many long, multisyllable words, like *camouflage* and *bureaucratic*.

DOI: 10.4324/9781003130789-2

Another reason is that many older students have learned that they cannot learn to read. They accept that they are slow and think there must be something wrong with them. Some think they are dumb.

Students should not be stumbling and faltering in their reading. They can improve dramatically if they have a better understanding of the decoding challenges they face. If we can explain to students the nature of the code, how it works, and how it can crack open the seemingly impenetrable structure of the long words they see in their textbooks, they can conquer the challenges facing them. They do not need to fail.

The topics for this chapter are

- Defining decoding
- Beyond the basics: advanced decoding skills

1.2 Some brief definitions

In a newspaper article, a reporter lamented that their daughter was learning strange words at school (O'Neill, 2016).

> A split digraph, as my daughter (just turned six) explained to me recently, is when the "ee" or "ue" sound in a word is separated by a consonant. Words like "flute" and "complete" are examples of this grammatical phenomenon ... A few weeks on, my daughter has largely forgotten its importance. "That's because we're doing polysyllabic words now, silly," she explains.

The reporter was not convinced about these technical terms, having never had to learn them when they were at school, but school pupils are little linguists; they are designed to learn new words; they are learning them all the time. They go from knowing zero words as a baby to knowing many thousands of words by the time they leave school. This is what they do. Technical words like consonants, vowels, syllables, and morphemes are part of this.

Here are some terms that will be of use in this chapter:

Consonant: constricts the airstream (e.g., s, t, g, k, m)
Vowel: very little constriction of the airstream: *a e i o u*
Phoneme: smallest unit of sound in a word (e.g., *fish* has three phonemes: *f i sh*)
Grapheme: one or more letters for one phoneme sound (e.g., *k, th, igh, ough*)
Syllable: unit of speech with a vowel and (optionally) consonants before and/or after
Morpheme: smallest unit of meaning in a word (e.g., *s* in *cats* means more than one cat)

1.3 What is decoding?

Decoding is not just a label to describe learning the letter-sounds. It is "a truth universally acknowledged", to use Jane Austen's famous words, that English writing is a code and the student must become a codebreaker.

The label, *code breaker*, is not a metaphor; it should be taken seriously. English writing is a systematic code where the reader must convert letters into sounds (i.e., phonemes). The code is not like *007* is a code name for James Bond. It is more like saying *kbnft cpoe* is the code name. How do you decode this? First, you must know that *kbnft cpoe* is a code. Second, you must know the 26 letters in the code. Third, you must know each letter stands for a sound. Fourth, you must work out the code; in the above example, each letter-sound is the one after the one it is supposed to be (e.g., the letter *k* stands for the sound j). When you know the code, then *kbnft cpoe* becomes *James Bond*. The code is not easy. It takes most students several years to become fluent in decoding English writing.

Yet imagine a class of students where many have not fully cracked the code. They struggle to read their textbooks fluently or accurately. How can they move forward? They also want the chance to read the great playwrights and poets and popular contemporary novels like *Where the Crawdads Sing*, but many cannot do this, because they struggle to read the words.

Every class has students such as these, who have yet to reach their potential in decoding. In every class, the best readers do all the "good stuff", they are way ahead of the class, while at the other end of the spectrum, the lowest readers are left in the shallows. They are given easy readers to look at, in the hope that this will keep them happy. This is not good enough. It is not equitable.

A solid knowledge of decoding will give every student a way to succeed in school and in life. Decoding is the foundation of reading, and reading is the *sine qua non* for academic success.

1.4 What the student must do to crack the code

There is a system in English writing; letters represent sounds. The letter–sound relations are not random. The written word *cat* says "cat"; it does not say "giraffe". There are systematic links between letters and sounds. There is method.

In a classic paper, Gough and Hillinger (1980) explained the four insights needed for the student to learn this system, to learn how to decode words. Let us look at each of these:

1. Code awareness, knowing that there is a systematic code, that alphabet letters are not just squiggles
2. Alphabet awareness, the ability to identify the 26 different letter-sounds of the alphabet
3. Phoneme awareness, that spoken words are made of separate sounds
4. Decoding intent, figuring out the code

Code awareness

The student must discover that printed words are coded forms of spoken words written in a systematic code (e.g., *cat* says "cat", and the letters c-a-t represent three different sounds or phonemes). Once they know that printed words represent spoken words in a systematic way, they can start to work out the letter–sound system.

Grapheme awareness

The student must know all the alphabet letters. Learning the 26 letters is not easy, because they are abstract shapes. One writer called them *ghostly apparitions*. Orientation is important to distinguish some letters, like *b-d*, *p-q*, *u-n*. Students confuse these letters because orientation is not a distinctive feature of things in the real world (e.g., a *cup*, the thing you drink from, is still a *cup* no matter whether you turn it left or right). With letters like b and d, however, a change in orientation changes one letter into another.

Phoneme awareness

The student cannot link letters to sounds in spoken words unless they have awareness that a spoken word is usually not one sound but a sequence of different sounds. A student with phonemic awareness knows that *fish* and *dish* rhyme. They know there are two sounds in *ice* but three sounds in *nice*. They can tell you the first sound in their name. They can take the *t* out of *stand* and know it says *sand*. They can take the *d* out of road, replace it with *p*, and know it says *rope*. They know that *bug* in Pig Latin says *ugbay*.

Decoding intent

Finally, the student needs decoding intent; they must try to work out the code. We do not know the best way to do this. Some students work it out when they listen to a book being read to them, but many do not. Most students learn the code when it is explained to them, when someone says that the sound of the letter b is b or that the word cat says cat, when someone tells them the rules of the code, when someone shows them how to combine the letter-sounds to make a word (e.g., c-a-t). For most this means learning phonics, which is a method for explaining the rules. The value of knowing phonics rules is that it gives the student tools to decode for themselves and not have to ask for help or skip words; it gives a way to work out words on their own. It gives the student freedom to learn.

1.5 Fluency

Decoding is about not just working out the words but working them out very quickly, almost automatically. Slow, inaccurate decoding disrupts comprehension of text (Sabatini et al., 2019; Wang et al., 2019). This is because the mind of the reader who is a slow decoder is using valuable mental resources to read each word on the page, when those mental resources could be focused on comprehension of the text.

Are you a fluent reader? One way to check your own fluency is to read a passage and time yourself with the stopwatch function on your phone. Try the following 200-word passage from the beginning of *David Copperfield* (Dickens, 1850/1981).

"In the name of heaven," said Miss Betsey, suddenly, "Why rookery?" "The name was Mr Copperfield's choice," returned my mother. "When he bought the house, he liked to think there were rooks about it." "Where are the birds?" asked Miss Betsey. "The rooks—what has become of them?" "There have not been any since we lived here," said my mother. "We thought— Mr Copperfield thought—it was quite a large rookery; but the nests were very old ones, and the birds have deserted them a long while." "David Copperfield all over!" cried Miss Betsey. "David Copperfield from head to foot! Calls a house a rookery when there's not a rook near it, and takes the birds on trust, because he sees the nests!" "Mr Copperfield," returned my mother, "is dead, and if you dare to speak unkindly of him to me—." My poor dear mother, I suppose, had some momentary intention of committing an assault and battery upon my aunt, who could easily have settled her with one hand, even if my mother had been in far better training for such an encounter than she was that evening. But it passed with the action of rising from her chair.

How did you do? As a comparison, a 12-year-old student with dyslexia read the *David Copperfield* passage. The student had trouble with only a few words (e.g., *rookery* read as *rocky*, *momentary* as *memory*, *dare* as *dar*). It took 155 seconds to read the 200-word passage, 0.76 seconds per word, which is 77.4 words per minute (wpm). A fluent adult reader will be able to read the passage much more quickly.

Studies of oral reading show that many students are in this situation, perhaps as many as 40% (e.g., Gough, 1996; Pinnell et al., 1995; White et al., 2021). These students can decode but are slow, reading fewer than 100 wpm.

To put this into perspective, when we are talking at a normal conversational rate, the average is about 150 wpm. If students can read at that rate, then reading is like listening to the text read aloud to them. If reading rate is less than that, it will be harder to understand the text.

When students are not fluent, it is a signal that decoding words is difficult for them. It is a concern. Expectations of fluency for students depend on age.

Surveys show that the number of words read per minute increases across age levels (Hasbrouck & Tindal, 2017):

- 6 years old: 60 wpm
- 7 years old: 100 wpm
- 8 years old: 112 wpm
- 9 years old: 133 wpm
- 10 and 11 years old: 146 wpm
- 12 and 13 years old: 170 wpm

1.6 The structure of English writing

Students can learn much about decoding when they study the story of English writing. The story is shaped like a pyramid (see Figure 1.2). At the bottom of the pyramid are Anglo-Saxon words, the first words of English, the everyday words (e.g., *freedom, forgive, limestone, father, mother, wife, bread, water, cow, eat, kiss, shop, chicken*). In the middle layer are Romance words, those with French origins (e.g., *chef, beef, camouflage, justice*) and Latin origins (e.g., *nation, invent, disrupt, contract*). In the top layer are words with Greek origins (e.g., *architect, biography, geology, echo, phobia*).

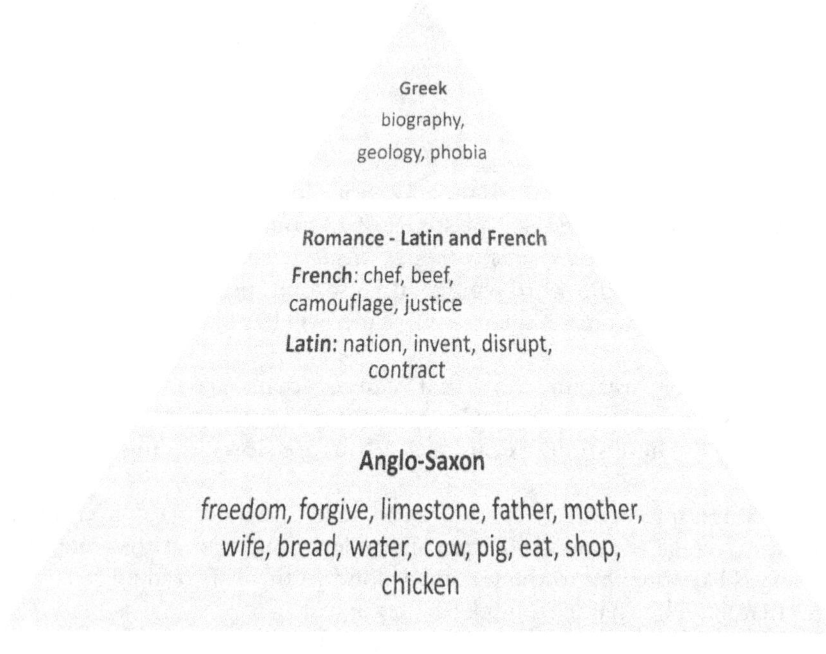

Greek
biography, geology, phobia

Romance - Latin and French
French: chef, beef, camouflage, justice
Latin: nation, invent, disrupt, contract

Anglo-Saxon
freedom, forgive, limestone, father, mother, wife, bread, water, cow, pig, eat, shop, chicken

Figure 1.2 The Story of English.

English writing has a 2,000-year history starting with the alphabet that the Roman invaders brought to England in 43 CE (Pei, 1967; Trudgill, 2023). When Roman armies left England in 400 CE, the language of new invaders, Angles and Saxons, became dominant, during the period 400–1066.

In 1066, William Duke of Normandy defeated King Harold at the Battle of Hastings, and for the next 300 years, French became the official language of England. By the 1300s, many French words found their way into English, often as synonyms (e.g., *freedom - liberty, hearty - cordial*). In the 1500s, a linguistic invasion of words used to describe scientific discoveries added many words with Latin and Greek origins.

There is origin overlap among the layers in that many French words have Latin origins, and many Latin words have Greek origins. English has words from over 100 languages but the words most used have Anglo-Saxon, Latin/French, and Greek origins.

☺ ☺**Top Tip**: Watch this 5-minute YouTube video on the story of English, https://www.youtube.com/watch?v=KbdMU64bo0Q

Or this one – 6 minutes: https://www.youtube.com/watch?v=_jsxJRoQxJw

---

English today has more than 500,000 words. The multilayered nature of English gives it a richness, a wide range of vocabulary, but it is also a challenge for the student learning to decode. Each layer has its own word structure and spelling rules. Students at ages 9–12 must learn the decoding rules for all three language layers.

1.7 Multisyllable words

There is an old saying, "Look for little words in big words", but this strategy does not work well. Some words have little words in them (e.g., *potato* = *pot* + *a* + *to*, *honey* = *h* + *one* + *y*), but the little words in these examples are the wrong sounds for the words. It is much better to decode words sound by sound, syllable by syllable.

What are syllables?

English spoken language is syllabic. Students can easily learn to clap the number of syllables in a word (e.g., *deciduous* has four syllables: *de-cid-u-ous*). For students, it is important to be able to handle multisyllable words in text. Decoding unfamiliar, long words with two or more syllables is made easier by breaking up the syllables and tackling the word syllable by syllable.

The basic building block in English writing is the one syllable, CVC (consonant–vowel–consonant) pattern, also called a closed syllable pattern. Over half of the many thousands of syllables in English have a closed pattern.

A multisyllable word has more than one syllable, and every syllable is a speech unit with one vowel sound. Knowing this makes it easier to do syllable-breaking of long words.

Key features to explain to students:

- Every syllable has *one* vowel *sound*.
- Two vowels together usually make *one* sound (e.g., *beetle*).

Why learn syllable-breaking rules?

The reason for these rules is to make it easier to decode. Studies show that students benefit from knowing how to break words into syllables (Toste et al., 2025).

It is not uncommon to find that a student can read a one-syllable word like *rain* or *coat* but will say they cannot read a word like *raincoat*, which is two syllables. Many students baulk if the word is more than one syllable.

To make *raincoat* easier to decode, the student needs to break this two-syllable word into manageable chunks, and the best way to do this is to split *raincoat* into two syllables.

It is easier to decode a two- or three-syllable word if it is divided into single syllables. The student must especially learn the two most common syllable types: the closed and open syllable patterns. They make up 75% of all the syllables in words (Stanback, 1992).

To remind the reader of the meaning of the term *syllable*, see the definition below.

> Definition: A **syllable** is a unit of speech that contains **one** vowel sound (e.g., *dog* is one syllable, and it has one vowel sound).
>
> In written form, **every syllable has a vowel**, either a single vowel (e.g., *e*) or a vowel team (e.g., *ea*). The vowel is usually bounded by a consonant before, after, or before and after it (e.g., *at, go, cat*).

Here are the six syllable types:

- Closed: VC or CVC, there is a consonant C after the vowel V (e.g., *mag/net*)
- Open: V or CV, no consonant after the vowel (e.g., *open*)
- Split digraph: CVCe final e pattern (e.g., *e/vac/u/ate*)
- Vowel + r or + l, when a vowel is followed by *r* or *l* (e.g., *car/pen/ter*)
- Vowel team syllable: two or occasionally three vowels (e.g., *sea/son*)
- -LE syllable: a consonant + -le (e.g., *scru/ple*)

Decoding 11

> ☺☺**Top Tip**: Watch these two 5-minute videos on multisyllable words.
>
> Syllables – part 1
> https://www.youtube.com/watch?v=fQg2M0eNTWk&list= PLvmDzSqKe9JC2McuLoYnWhOPsyOzSbWcV&index=20
>
> Syllables – part 2
> https://www.youtube.com/watch?v=XIB6jo7-xxM&list= PLvmDzSqKe9JC2McuLoYnWhOPsyOzSbWcV&index=20

1.8 Anglo-Saxon words

Compound words

A compound word is two words joined together. Usually, one part of the word contains the core of the word's meaning. In the word *boathouse*, the core part is part B, *boat*; it is a house for boats.

Some compound words are slightly puzzling in meaning, but they keep to that pattern, where the core meaning is in part B of the word. A *strawberry* is not a straw, but it is a kind of berry; a *foxglove* is not a fox, but the flower looks like a glove.

Compound words, although they contain two real words, should form a new word that is different in meaning.

There are different compound word patterns. Here are some:

1. B is of A: a *footstep* is a step of the foot; a *raindrop* a drop of rain.
2. B is from A: a *moonbeam* is a beam from the moon; a *sunshade* is shade from the sun.
3. B is A: a *blackbird* is a type of bird that is black; a *goldfish* is a fish that is gold.
4. B is for A: a *sunhat* is a hat for the sun; a *footstool* is a low stool for the foot.
5. B does A: a *handcuff* is a cuff that does up hands; a *farmhand* is a hand that does farming.

Prefix–root word–suffix structures

By analysing Anglo-Saxon word structures, one can work out their meanings. Some root word, prefix and suffix structures for words of Anglo-Saxon origin are shown in Table 1.1.

The root word is the core meaning. Prefixes and suffixes change or add to the core meaning.

Table 1.1 Structural Analysis: Words with Anglo-Saxon, Latin/French, and Greek Origins

Language	Root words	Prefixes	Suffixes	Examples
Anglo-Saxon	bid, get, give, like, love, place, read, slow	by, for, in, over, with, be, un, dis, under	-ed, -er, -ing, -ly, -s, -es, -able, -ful, -hood, -less, -ship	like, dislike, likeable, unlikely, likelihood
Latin/French	dict, duct, flect, form, ject, mit, pend, port, rupt, spect, struct, script, tract, vent	dis, ex, inter, intro, mis, pre, pro, re, trans, uni	-age, -ance, -ence, -ism, -ist, -ity, -ive	tract, contract, traction, distract, protract, retract
Greek	chrono, graph, meter, phono, phys, psych, sphere, thermo	auto, biblio, hemi, hex, tri, hydro, hyper, octo, peri, quad, semi, tele	-archy, -crat, -cracy, -logy, -phile, -phobia, -scope	graph, autograph, graphology, seismograph, telegraph

- Root words in Anglo-Saxon can be almost any word (e.g., *bid, get, give, like, love, place, read*).
- Prefixes, nearly always prepositions, go in front of the root word and change the meaning (e.g., *for + bid - forbid, un + just - unjust, be + hold - behold, over + see - oversee, with + hold - withhold, under + go – undergo, out + last - outlast*).
- *Suffixes* come after the root word and can change the word's part of speech or meaning (e.g., *like + -ly, ask + -ed, walk + -ing, small +-er, big + -est, rabbit + -s, peach + -es, like + able, help + ful, false + hood, luck + less, hard + ship, wis + dom, kind + ness*).

1.9 Latin/French words: Root word–prefix–suffix structures

> ☺ ☺ **Top Tip**: Watch this 5-minute YouTube video on Latin words: https://www.youtube.com/watch?v=OnUQIX3r-8k&list=PLvmDzSqKe9JC2McuLoYnWhOPsyOzSbWcV&index=23
> Or this 19 minute one: https://www.youtube.com/watch?v=_7kQQGsfn5k

In the *Harry Potter* novels, the magic spell *petrificus totalus* stopped Neville in the Forbidden Corridor and he did not move at all. In Latin, *petra* means stone and *totalus* means total. The magic spell figuratively turned Neville totally into stone.

Words with Latin origins

By analysing Latin word structures, one can work out their meanings. Some root word, prefix, and suffix structures for words of Latin origin are shown in Table 1.1.

Root words

Latin root words carry the core meaning of the word but cannot stand on their own. For example, *spect* means to see but needs a prefix or suffix or both to become a real word.

Common root words: *dict* - say, *duc* - lead, *flec* - bend, *form* - shape, *ject* - throw, *mit* - send, *pend* - hang, *port* - carry, *struct*- build, *rupt* - break, *spec* - see, *tract* - drag, *vent* - come (see also Table 1.2).

Prefixes

Prefixes come before the root word, and carry meaning (e.g., re-*spect*, to see again; retro-*spect*, to see back; e-*rupt*, to break out; *interrupt*, to break between).

Common prefixes are *re, dis, ex, inter, intro, pre, pro, anti, trans, retro, uni, ad (ap), con (com), in (im), ob, sub,* and *syn (sym)*. See also Table 1.3.

Table 1.2 Common Latin Root Words

Root word	Meaning	Examples
scrib/script	write	describe
spect	see	disrespect
dict	say/tell	diction
flect	bend	reflect
mit	send	admit, dismiss
fer	carry	fertilize, transfer
duct	lead	conductor
pend	hang	pendulum
fac	make	benefactor, artificial
tend	stretch	tension
capt	seize	captive, captor
tain	hold	container
fide	trust	confide, affidavit
sist/sta/stat/stit	stand	statue, resist, substitute
pose	put	dispose, exposure

Table 1.3 Common Latin Prefixes

Prefix	Meaning
re-	back, again
in- [im-, il-, ir]	not, absence of
dis-	not, away, undo
en-, em-	to put into, make
non-	not
in- [il, im, ir]	in, on, toward
sub-	under, beneath, below
pre-	before, earlier
inter-	among, between
de-	removal, reversal, away
trans-	across or beneath
anti-	against, opposed to

Table 1.4 Common Latin Suffixes

Suffix	Word class	Example word
-able, -ible	adjective	comprehensible
-tion, -sion, -ation	noun	compensation
-ity, -ty	adjective to noun	alacrity
-ment	verb to noun	adjustment
-ify, -fy	verb	justify
-al, -ical	adjective	historical
-ent, -ant	adjective or noun	resistant
-ary, -arium	noun	aquarium
-ure	noun	structure
-ous, -eous, -ious	adjective	magnanimous
-ence, -ance	noun	resistance
-ian, -an	noun or adjective	urban, magician

Suffixes

Suffixes come after the root word and usually indicate word class, such as *-ion* a noun (e.g., *erupt-ion*), *-ive* an adjective (e.g., *disruptive*), and *-ate* a verb (e.g., *dictate*). The suffix *-ian* refers to a person, but *-ion* does not. Common suffixes are *age, ance, ence, ism, ist, ity, ive, ial, ian, ion, ible, ist, ium, ous,* and *ure* (see also Table 1.4).

French and Latin spellings

French-based words have different letter-sounds (e.g., *ch* in *chamois, champagne, chalet, chauffeur; et* in *ballet, bouquet; qu* in *quiche, antique, boutique*).

Latin-based words have some new letter–sound rules: *-ti, -si, -ci* before *-ion, -ial, -ous* have a *sh* sound (e.g., *commercial, suspicious, national, elevation, extension*).

Decoding   15

1.10 Greek words: root word, prefix, suffix structures

> ☺☺**Top Tip**: Watch this 5-minute YouTube video on Greek words: https://www.youtube.com/watch?v=8WOxANqtoaQ&list=PLvmDzSqKe9JC2McuLoYnWhOPsyOzSbWcV&index=25
> Or this 12-minute one: https://www.youtube.com/watch?v=jKYzAANCdOI

Words with Greek origins usually consist of two parts: prefix + root word (e.g., *graph* - *autograph*) or root word + suffix e (e.g., graph<u>ology</u>).

By analysing Greek word structures, one can work out their meanings. Some root word, prefix, and suffix structures for words of Greek origin are shown in Table 1.1.

Common Greek root words, prefixes, and suffixes
root words (e.g., chron, meter, sphere, thermo, graph)
prefixes (e.g., auto, hemi, hex, semi, tele, hydro, hyper, octo, peri, quad)
suffixes (e.g., archy, cracy, ology, phile, scope, phobia, scope)

Examples of Greek words
- *archaeology*: *archaeo* means ancient and *logy* means study of: the study of ancient things.
- *architect*: *arch* means chief and *tect* means builder, an expert who designs buildings.
- *philosopher*: *philo* means love and *sophy* means wisdom: a thinker, someone who seeks wisdom.
- *octo/pus* means eight feet.
- *tri/pod* means three feet.
- *dino/saur* means terrible lizard.
- *galaxy* is from *galaxia* in Greek, refers to *Milky Way*.
- *monochrome*: mono + chrome means one coloration.
- *astronaut*: star + sailor: a star sailor, person who has flown in space.
- *agoraphobia*: public place + fear: fear of public places.
- *aerophobia*: flying + fear: fear of flying.
- *arachnophobia*: spiders + fear: fear of spiders.
- *acrophobia*: heights + fear: fear of heights.
- *spectrophobia*: mirrors + fear: fear of mirrors.

Greek spellings
ph: f sound (e.g., *phobia*)
ch: k sound (e.g., *chorus*)
y: short and long *i* (e.g., *gym*, *hyper*)

ps: s sound (e.g., _**ps**ychology_)
rh: r sound (e.g., _**rh**ododendron_)
pn: n sound (e.g., _**pn**eumatic_)

1.11 Conclusion

Decoding is essential for reading success. It is knowledge of how to decipher words. Studies show that decoding difficulties will disrupt the comprehension process.

It is easy to assume that students at ages 9–12 will not have decoding difficulties, but this is not so. Decoding is an issue for many students; they read slowly and make decoding errors. Slow decoding disrupts comprehension. Even a small number of decoding errors can take comprehension down the wrong path. It does not make sense for the student to ignore these difficulties. They must do something.

Students with decoding difficulties are likely to benefit from following a clear scope and sequence of learning, not stopping until they are decoding at the highest level, multisyllable words and words with Latin/French and Greek origins.

Students will know when they have a high level of decoding skill because they will be able to decode in an instant every word on the page. Decoding will feel like fun, not hard work.

2 Assessing decoding

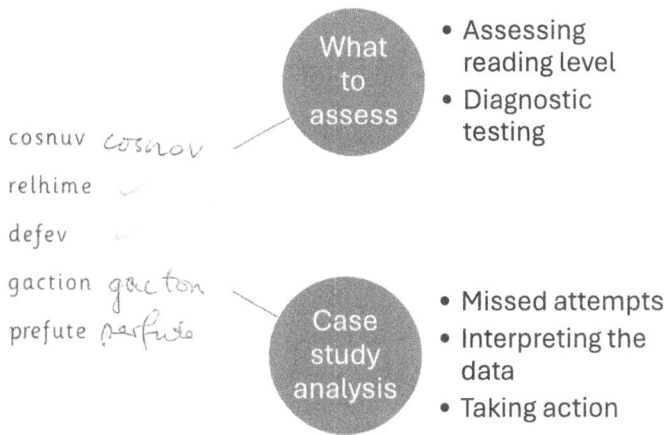

Figure 2.1 Overview of Chapter 2.

> I feel unequipped to teach students who are still struggling with literacy.

2.1 Introduction

The best assessment tip is to assess, carry out a series of lessons, and then re-assess to see if the lessons made a difference. There are some questions, though. Whom will the assessment help? Will the assessment diagnose difficulties? Will the lessons that follow the assessment address those difficulties?

Often the assessments do not give a clear direction as to what a follow-up lesson might be. They explain what is obvious, that the student is not decoding to their potential. What now?

What is needed is a trouble-shooting guide, a way of looking at the errors the student makes and being able to diagnose what they mean and what action to take.

DOI: 10.4324/9781003130789-3

In this chapter, assessment is a two-step process. The first step is to find the student's decoding status. Are they able to decode as well as other students of the same age? This requires a norm-referenced measure. Step 2 is to look at the kinds of decoding errors that the student makes, work out what the problems are, and decide on what lessons are needed.

The chapter covers the following topics:

- Assessing current decoding level using a norm-referenced assessment
- Diagnostic assessments – what do the reports mean?
- Case study analysis

2.2   Norm-referenced tests: assessing current reading level

There are many decoding or word-reading assessments available online, but a small number of tried-and-true measures may be sufficient to assess decoding skills.

A suggestion is to use a norm-referenced test that you are familiar with and comfortable using. This is the most accurate way to assess decoding status.

There are many tests available from educational publishers (e.g., *Wide Range Achievement Tests*). The school may need to get advice on which test to use from a specialist assessor, such as a psychologist or speech language therapist.

A free-to-use test is the *Motif* decoding test, called *CC2*. For the free version, you need to download *Motif* in PDF form and administer and score it yourself. It has 40 regular words, 40 irregular words, and 40 non-words. It is a norm-referenced assessment for ages 6 to 11 (see the website: https://www.motif.org.au/). The results will indicate whether the student is able to decode real words and non-words to their potential.

2.3   Informal assessment and resources

If norm-referenced data show the student is not decoding to their potential, the next step is to follow up with informal, diagnostic assessments to find out why this is happening. Non-words are a well-tried way to assess these skills, because the student cannot rely on memory for words they have seen before. The non-words are new words that they have never seen and the only way to decode them is to sound them out.

Some students may struggle with simple non-words such as *zeg*. At the next level, it may be consonant + h patterns like ch - *chu*, or split digraph patterns like *zute*, or consonant clusters and long vowel patterns like *scoon*. At the next level, it may be multisyllable non-words like *chuzeg* and Latin-based non-words like *rezutable*.

Exactly why a student is not reading to their potential becomes clearer with diagnostic assessment using non-words. This is the best way to assess decoding.

For those students not decoding at their potential, a recommended assessment is the *Bryant Test of Basic Decoding Skills* (Bryant, 1975; Nicholson, 2005; Nicholson & Dymock, 2023) (see Figure 2.4 in the chapter Appendix). This test of basic decoding skills is not a norm-referenced test, but it does have diagnostic information. Student errors on the test reveal what skills they need to review or re-learn.

2.4 Trouble-shooting guide

The next section of the chapter looks at different kinds of decoding errors on a diagnostic test – and what to do about them. This section will be helpful if the teacher has students who struggle with decoding. For each decoding "problem", the "things to do" section refers to the chapter Appendix for teaching charts.

Problem 1: CVC (consonant-vowel-consonant) patterns

Test words	Student attempt	Strong points	Confusion	Things to do
gac	jac	Most vowel sounds correct	Consonant sounds Short vowel sound – *a* Pronounced as *u*	Review consonant and short vowel sounds and patterns – see chapter Appendix
dit	bit			
yeg	weg			
san	sun			

Problem 2: Consonant digraphs – ch, sh, th, wh, ph

Test words	Student attempt	Strong points	Confusion	Things to do
cho	coe	Vowel sounds correct	ch, sh, wh	Review sounds *ch, sh, th, ng, wh* - See practice chart in the chapter Appendix
shi	sky			
whe	we			

Problem 3: Vowel sounds affected by r and l

Test words	Student attempts	Strong points	Confusion	Things to do
blor	blow	Consonant clusters correct	r-affected vowel sounds	Review the main vowel sounds, e.g., ar, or, ur, ir, er, al - see the relevant practice chart in the chapter Appendix
fler	flor			
smar	smair			

20 *Teaching Literacy Effectively in Modern Classroom for Ages 9–12*

Problem 4: Split digraph "silent e" pattern

Test words	Student attempt	Strong points	Confusion	Things to do
fute yode	futtee yod	Consonant sounds correct	Silent e rule	Review the "silent e" rule, e.g., *gate, note* - see the relevant practice chart in the chapter Appendix - see Figure 2.2 below

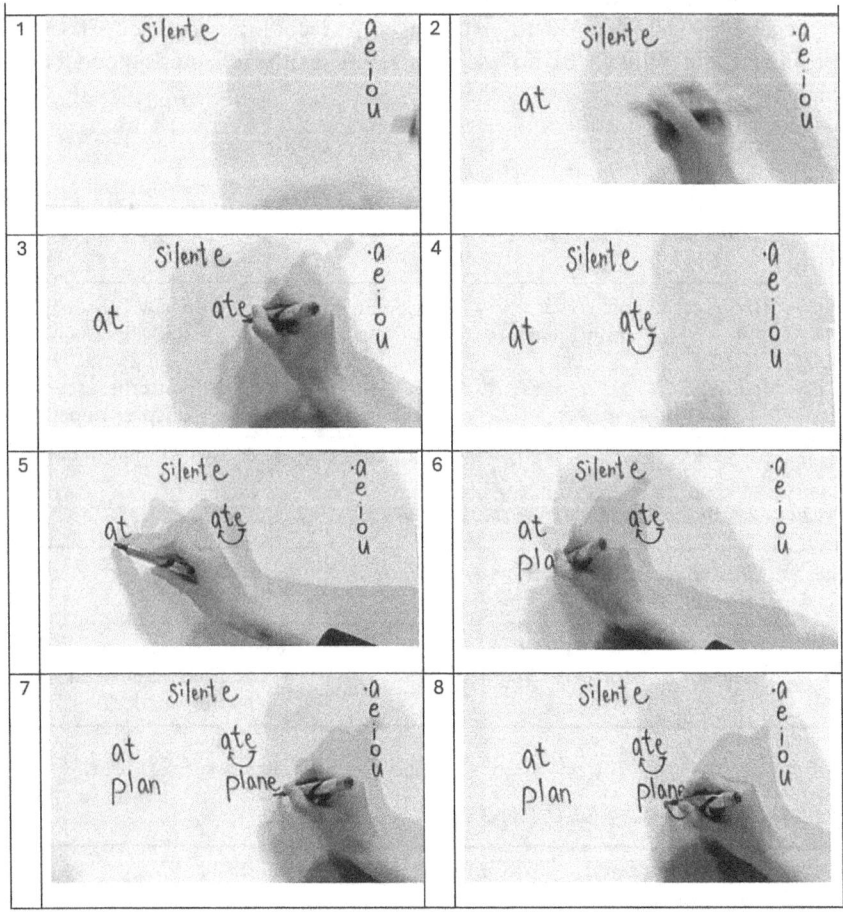

Figure 2.2 A Lesson on the Split Digraph "Silent e" Rule.

Assessing decoding 21

Figure 2.3 A Lesson on the ai-ay Vowel Digraph Pattern.

Problem 5: Vowel digraph long vowel sounds and consonant clusters

Test words	Student attempts	Strong points	Confusion	Things to do
troob	trob	Consonant clusters correct	Vowel digraph sounds	Review – ai, ee, igh, oa, au, eu/ue
spail	spill			see Figure 2.3 below
groaf	gruff			Review – ea, oo, ow, ou, ei, ie
cleef	cliff			Review one-sound vowel digraphs in final position: – ay, ew, aw, oy.
staw	stair			- see the relevant vowel practice chart in the chapter Appendix
plew	plen			
groy	grow			

Problem 6: Multisyllable words

Test word	Student attempts	Strong points	Confusion	Things to do
vomazful	vome-	Some sounds pronounced correctly	Syllable breaking	Review the 6 syllable rules
cosnuv	√			- see the relevant practice chart in the chapter Appendix
relhime	rel-			

Problem 7: Words with prefix–root word–suffix structure

Test words	Student attempts	Strong points	Confusion	Things to do
sanwixable	snake	Some single sounds correct	Prefix–root word–suffix pattern	Review words with prefix, root word, and suffix patterns
bufkibber	buf-			
vomazful	vom-		Latin prefix, *pre-*	- see the relevant practice charts in the chapter Appendix for Anglo-Saxon, Latin, and Greek words
uncabeness	uncr-			
prefute	perfit		*ti sound	
gaction	gakiton			

* ti in *gaction* has a sh sound.

Problem 8: Chameleon sounds of C, G, Y

- see the relevant practice chart in the chapter Appendix

Problem 9: Silent letter words KN, GH, GN ...

- see the relevant practice chart in the chapter Appendix

Table 2.1 Examples of Decoding Errors while Reading Text

Word	Errors	Meaning	Word origin
accustomed	accusetend	used to it	French/Latin *custum*
despairing	despering	lose hope	Old French *desespoir*
necessity	nesety	not to be done without	French/Latin *necessaire*
initial	initile	the beginning	Latin *initium*
essential	esenal	necessary, very important	Latin/French *essentia*
attaining	antaning	to reach	Latin *at* + *tangere*
mishap	mish-ap	unlucky accident, bad luck	Anglo-Saxon *mis* + *hap*
plateau	plat-yew	tableland	Old French *plat*, meaning dish
incessant	incestance	does not cease	Latin *in* + *cess* + *ant*
unconquered	unconkewerd	not yet overcome	Old French *un* + *conquerre* + *ed*

2.5 Case study

Looking at the decoding errors of the student, as shown in Table 2.1, what information is there as to what lessons are needed?

Using the problem analyses above, we can see that this student's errors seemed to be mainly due to difficulty in decoding multisyllable words with Latin/French origins. The student needs to focus on how to deconstruct these words in terms of their prefix–root word–suffix structure.

For example, *accustomed* is of Latin origin, has a prefix–root word–suffix structure, and means customary ways, the ways things usually get done.

2.6 Students who need extra help with decoding

What is stopping these students from progressing like their peers? There are four hurdles that these students must overcome.

Avoiding the code

Some students fear the code and try hard to avoid it. They do not see that the spoken word is encoded using letters. They know that each letter in the word encodes a sound, but they cannot break the code. It seems too hard. Instead, they treat each word as if it is Chinese; they remember each word as a sight word. This can work for a while, and if they make some good guesses, they get by, but eventually this way of reading words breaks down. There are too many words to remember. Words get jumbled and look the same, and their reading grinds to a stop. Students need to break the code, but often they persist in trying to remember the words as whole units. They persist with this failing strategy because it is all they know.

Alphabet confusion

Amazingly, some students after several years of school still do not know the 26 letter-sounds, yet these are crucial to start decoding words. They confuse the name of the letter with its sound, and they persist in thinking that the g says j, that the c says s, and that the y says w. They confuse the a with u. The b is a d. The solution is to practise the letter-sounds and only the sounds, forget the letter names, and focus on the sounds. Students can get confused when they must learn letter names and sounds at the same time, they dutifully recite *ay apple a, bee butterfly b, see cat k*, but this is terribly confusing and kills any learning opportunity.

Phonemic awareness

Some students lack phonemic awareness. Phonemes glue themselves together in words so that a word seems like one sound, not many, e.g., *box* has four sounds, but it is hard to hear all four. So, the student tries to bypass the sounds and remember the look of the word. They avoid sounding out the word – too hard.

Decoding intent

The next-to-last hurdle is breaking the code. Despite years of instruction, they do not get it. They are not experts, they do not know how the writing system works, all they see is lots of tiny little squiggles, they see words on flashcards, they see books with lines of squiggles, but it is like looking at Japanese. They need to start slow, with a few letters at a time, like SATP, and see how you can make words out of those letters and even sentences: *sat, pat, tap, at, pats, taps, spat – Pat sat at tap*. Use plastic letters like the Smart Kids product, move the letters around, and make words until the light goes on, and they can see that this is how words work; they have the insight that you can decipher words. It is a slow at first, but they must be persistent.

Set for diversity

Successful decoders have a set for diversity. When a word has an irregular part, they try different options until they work it out. Too many students lack this set for diversity. They make one attempt at the word and then stop. If they use the set for diversity principle, they will try another sound. This is called TOTO (Try One, Try Other): try one sound, then another until something works.

When a student has a set for diversity, they will juggle the ambiguous sound and try different options; for example, *yacht* looks like *yatch*, but in sentence context, they know it is a kind of *boat*, so they juggle the vowel sound slightly, say *o* instead of *a*, now it says yocht, and they juggle a little more and they work out the word. This is the last hurdle. It is hard to do set for diversity until the student has a good grasp of the basic decoding skills. This must be firmly in place. Set for diversity is not taking a wild guess. The student needs good skills to make set for diversity work. It is the final step on the road to literacy. This is what good readers do.

2.7 How do students who need extra help learn basic decoding skills?

Set for diversity works only if the student has good basic decoding skills. These skills are what they must learn. The scope and sequence rules for learning these basic decoding skills are shown in Table 2.2; see also the scope and sequence chart in Figure 2.5 in the chapter Appendix.

This is the path that the aspiring decoder must follow. The chapter Appendix has a series of learning charts that follow the scope and sequence chart. The charts have been field-tested many times. The key to success for the student is regular practice until the charts are read fluently.

> ☺ ☺**Top Tip**: The spelling charts in Chapters 14 and 15 are closely linked to decoding skills covered in the Appendix to this chapter. The student can easily link spelling and decoding practice together. It is a win-win.

Table 2.2 Scope and Sequence Chart for Learning Basic Decoding Skills

	Single consonants and short vowel sounds	
Single letters	*Consonant clusters*	*Consonant digraphs*
26 letter-sounds: two- and three-letter words (e.g., *at, in, up, on, cat, log, sun, big*)	Consonant clusters (e.g., cr in *crab*, -mp in *lamp*)	Consonant digraphs ch sh th wh ng (e.g., *fish*)
	Long vowel sounds	
Split digraphs Final e rule (e.g., *o_e* in *bone*) Doubling rule (e.g., *hoping hopping hopped*)	r- and l-affected vowel sounds ar - park, er - fern, or - corn, ir - bird, ur - surf, al - call, walk	Vowel digraphs One-sound vowel digraphs (e.g., *ee - bee*) Two-sound vowel digraphs (e.g., *oo-book, oo-roof*)
	Advanced rules	
Two sounds of *c, g* and the two sounds of final *y* Silent letter words (e.g., *gh-ghost*) Multisyllable words (e.g., *napkin*)	**Anglo-Saxon** - compound forms (e.g., *rain/coat*) prefixes (e.g., *by, for, over*) root words (e.g., *like*) suffixes (e.g., *ed, ing, ly, hood*) **Latin** - prefixes (e.g., *pre-, com-, trans-*) root words (e.g., *struct, tract*) suffixes (e.g., *-ion, -ial, -ious, -ive*)	**Greek** - root words (e.g., *chron, graph*) prefixes (e.g., *semi, hydro, hyper*) suffixes (e.g., *scope, cracy, phile*)

2.8 Conclusion

There should be a two-step process of assessment. In step 1, assess the student's current decoding status using a norm-referenced test.

In step 2, analyse the decoding errors of the student and check which problem types seem to be prevalent.

Assessment will give some specific information on what is happening and what to do about it. Assessment of decoding misses is a cross check on intuitions, to avoid "confirmation bias". It is a check whether observational impressions are, in fact, correct.

Using assessment data effectively means gathering diagnostic information that will move the student forward in their skill set. Assessment data give a nuanced picture of the student's decoding skills.

Appendix: Decoding resources (Figures 2.4–2.15)

Alien Words

buf	fute	cosnuv
cos	yode	relhime
dit	bime	defev
fev	nepe	gaction
gac	cabe	prefute
huz	phune	uncabeness
jod	cho	exyoded
kib	shi	sanwixable
lek	whe	bufkibber
maz	thade	vomazful
nuv	staw	
pof	plew	
quig	fler	
rel	smar	
san	blor	
tup	cleef	
vom	troob	
wix	spail	
yeg	groy	
zad	groaf	

Figure 2.4 Bryant Test of Basic Decoding Skills.

Assessing decoding 27

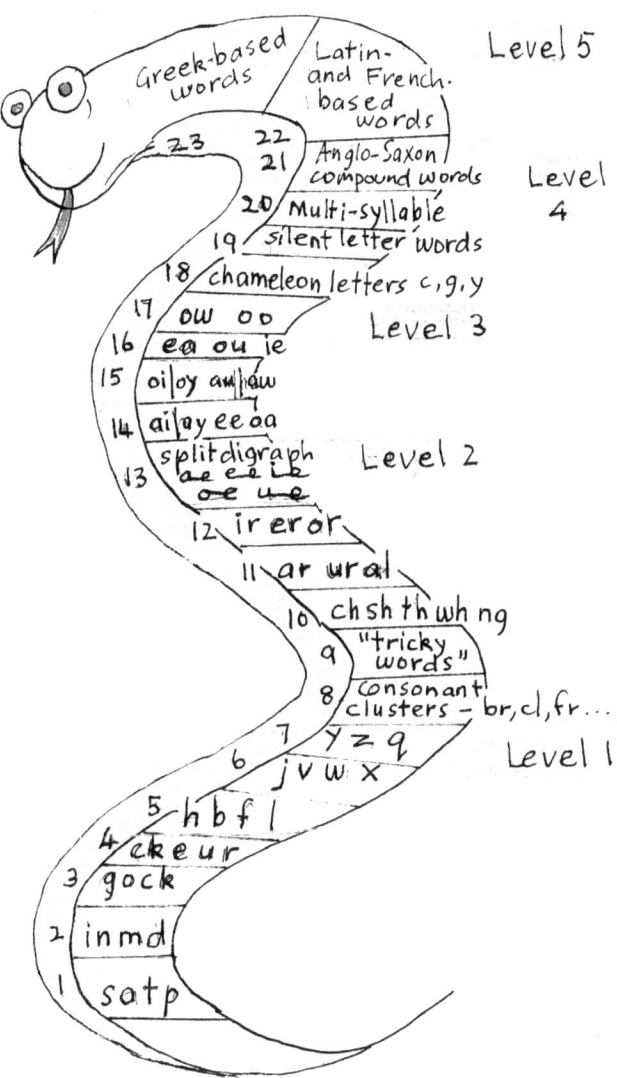

Figure 2.5 Scope and Sequence: Decoding Skills.

Figure 2.6 Single Consonant and Short Vowel Sounds.

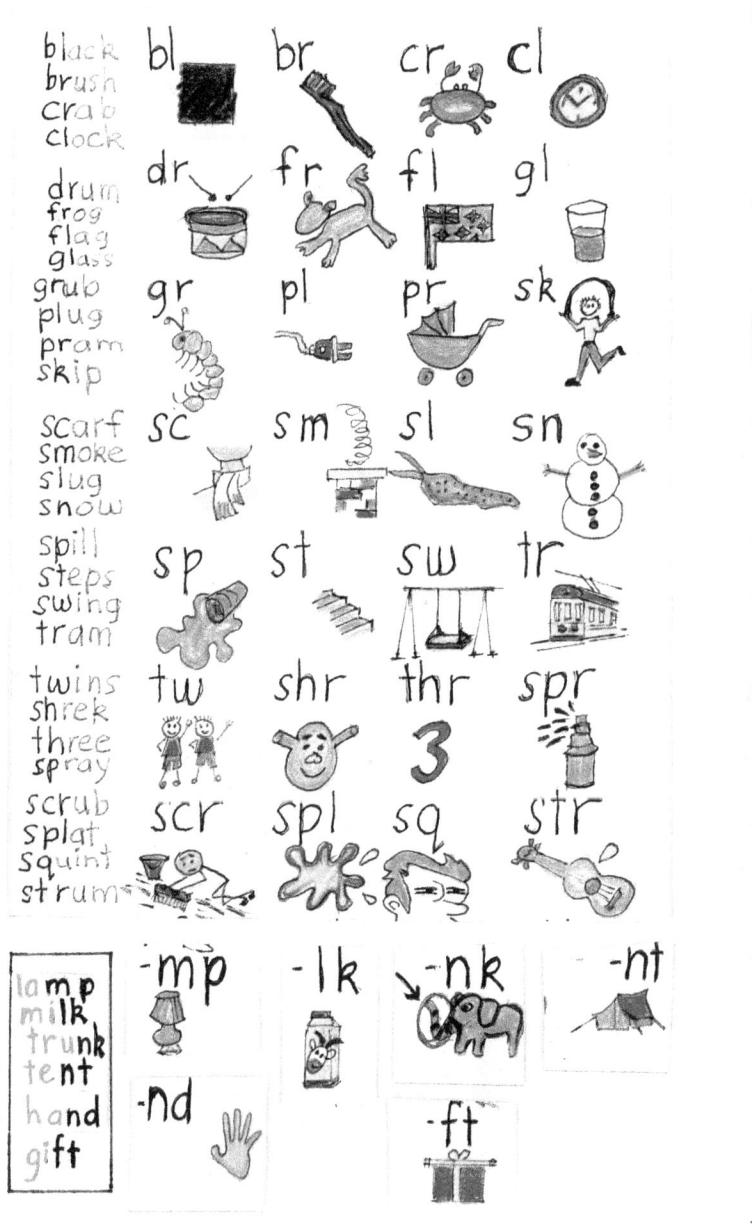

Figure 2.7 Adjacent Consonants (or Consonant Clusters).

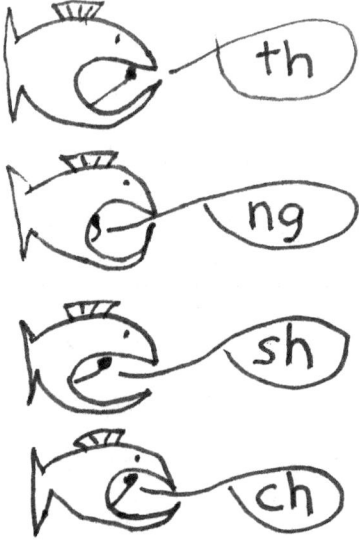

Figure 2.8 Consonant Digraphs ch sh th ng.

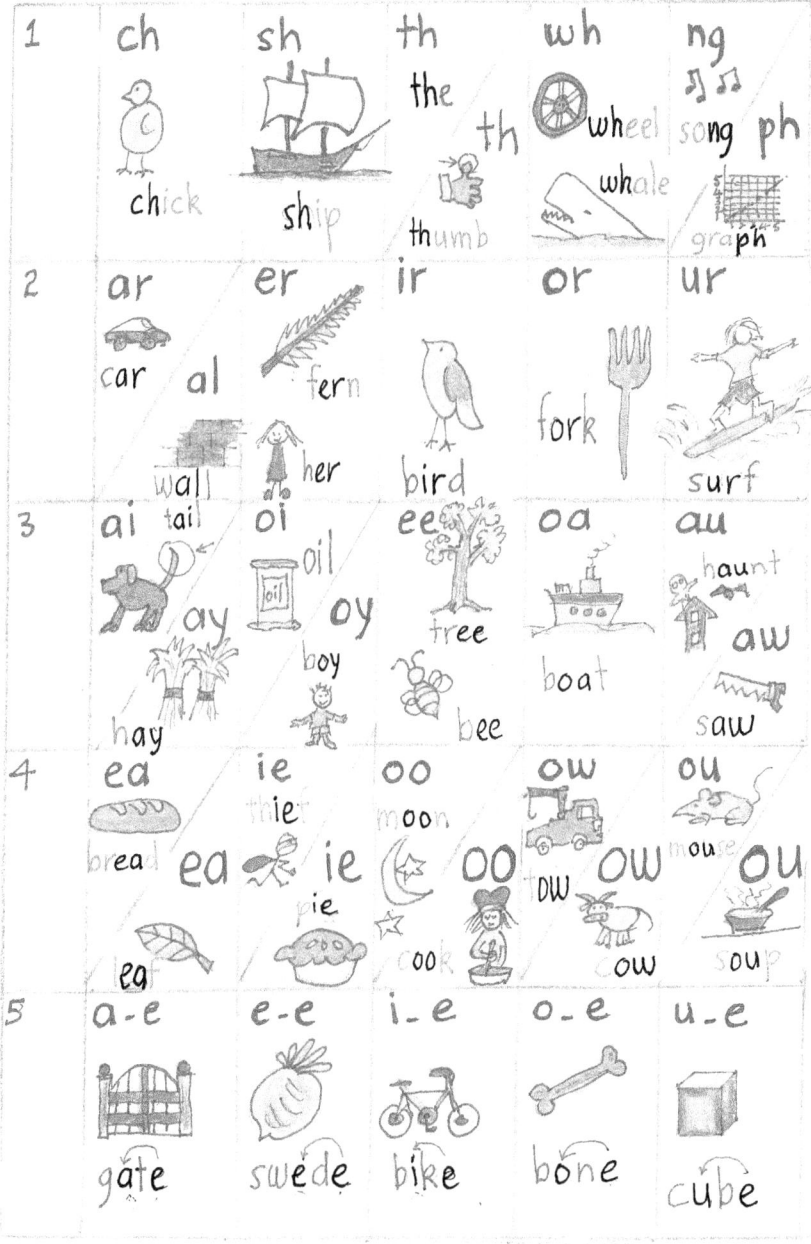

Figure 2.9 Consonant Digraphs, Vowel Digraphs, R- and L-Affected Vowels.

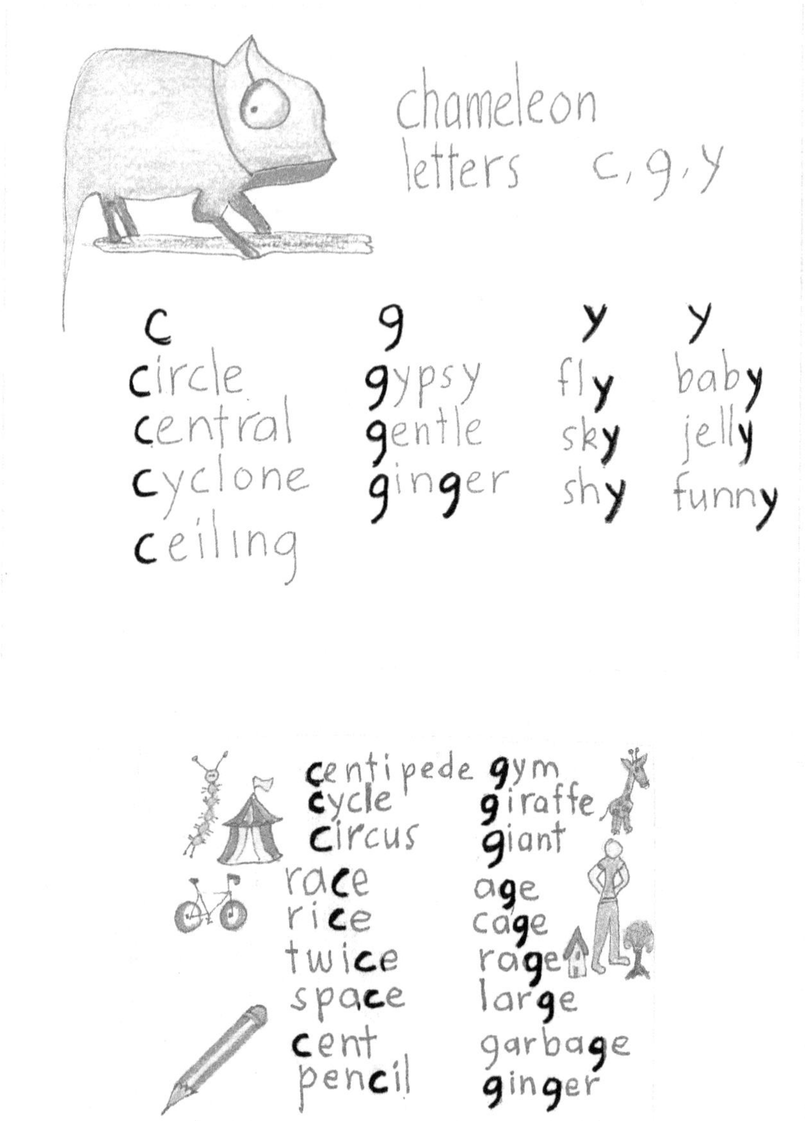

chameleon
letters c, g, y

c	g	y	y
circle	gypsy	fly	baby
central	gentle	sky	jelly
cyclone	ginger	shy	funny
ceiling			

centipede gym
cycle   giraffe
circus   giant
race   age
rice   cage
twice   rage
space   large
cent   garbage
pencil   ginger

Figure 2.10 Sounds of C, G, Y.

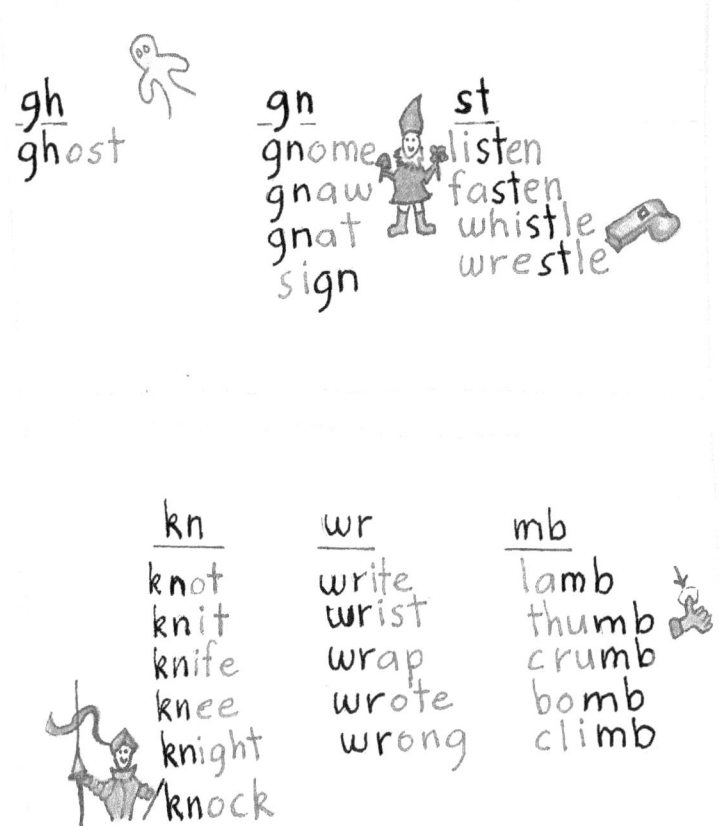

Figure 2.11 Silent Letter Words gh gn st kn wr mb.

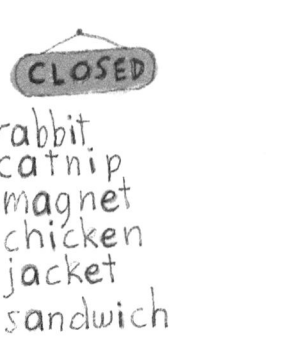
rabbit
catnip
magnet
chicken
jacket
sandwich

robot
super
bacon
frozen
donut
driver
pilot

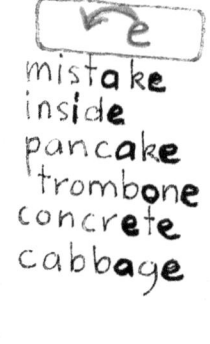
mistake
inside
pancake
trombone
concrete
cabbage

ar or er ur ir

farmer
corner
hermit
murder
thirsty
garden

ai ee igh oa ue

coffee
raincoat
shampoo
booster
painter
mountain

-LE

apple
juggle
paddle
cattle
table
turtle
middle

Figure 2.12 Multisyllable Words.

Figure 2.13 Anglo-Saxon: Prefixes, Root Words, Suffixes.

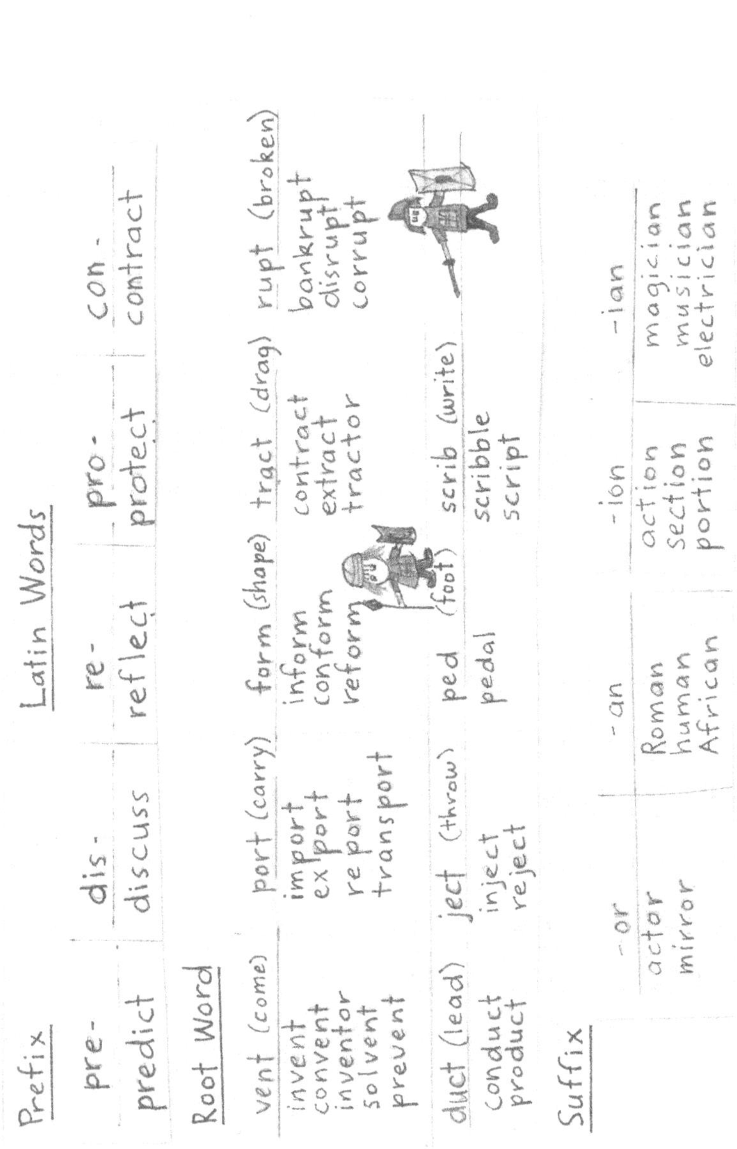

Latin Words

Prefix

pre-	dis-	re-	pro-	con-
predict	discuss	reflect	protect	contract

Root Word

vent (come)	port (carry)	form (shape)	tract (drag)	rupt (broken)
invent	import	inform	contract	bankrupt
convent	export	conform	extract	disrupt
inventor	report	reform	tractor	corrupt
solvent	transport			
prevent				

duct (lead)	ject (throw)	ped (foot)	scrib (write)	
conduct	inject	pedal	scribble	
product	reject		script	

Suffix

-or	-an	-ion	-ian
actor	Roman	action	magician
mirror	human	section	musician
	African	portion	electrician

Figure 2.14 Latin: Prefixes, Root Words, Suffixes.

Figure 2.15 Words with Greek Origins.

3 Teaching decoding

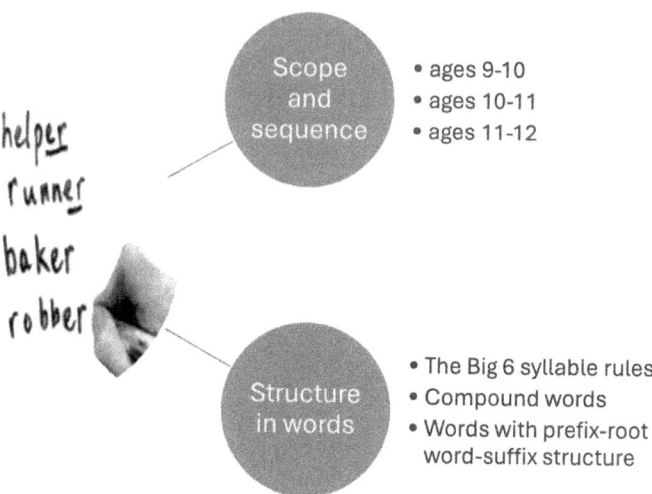

Figure 3.1 Overview of Chapter 3.

3.1 Introduction

> I've got a class this year where half the kids can't even pronounce the words. They make all sorts of wrong guesses and panic. It's hard to know where to start when they're at that level.

If you are a fan of the *Detective Gordon* book series, you will know that Buffy, the trainee police mouse, could not read the *Book of Law* because she did not know how to read. She could not decipher the "teeny-tiny" marks in the *Book of Law*.

DOI: 10.4324/9781003130789-4

Advanced decoding skills are necessary to absorb and digest the thousands of borrowed words that have come into English with Latin/French and Greek origins. Texts in the middle grades and junior high school have many of these words. Students need advanced decoding skills to decipher them quickly and accurately. It is important to know and use the Big 6 syllable rules to work out difficult, multisyllable words. Another key skill is knowing how to unpack the prefix–root word–suffix patterns of words with Anglo-Saxon, Latin/French, and Greek origins.

For students not yet at this level of proficiency, review the instructional diagnostics and charts in the assessment chapter. These students need lots of quick daily reviews using the charts to brush up their skills.

The chapter covers the following topics:

- Scope and sequence
- Big 6 syllable rules
- Words with Anglo-Saxon origins
- Words with Latin origins
- Words with Greek origins

3.2 Scope and sequence

At ages 9–12, the scope and sequence chart below will help students with what they need to learn (see Table 3.1).

Table 3.1 Scope and Sequence: Decoding Continuum for Ages 9–12

Age	Topic			
9	"Big 6" syllable rules for multisyllable words: closed, open, r- and l-affected vowel sounds, split digraph, vowel digraphs, LE			
10	Words with Anglo-Saxon origins	Prefixes (e.g., un, in, over, with, by, under)	Root words (e.g., get, give, like, love, place, put, read, red, slow)	Suffixes (e.g., s, ed, ing, ly, er, able, ful, less)
11	Words with Latin/French origins	Prefixes (e.g., dis, ex, inter, intro, mis, pre, re, trans, uni, in)	Root words (e.g., dict, flect, form, ject, mit, pend, port, rupt, spect, struct, script, tract, vent)	Suffixes (e.g., ion, ous, ial, ist, ance, ence, ive, ity)
12	Words with Greek origins	Prefixes (e.g., semi, hemi, auto, octo, tele, hydro, hyper)	Root words (e.g., chron, graph, sphere, phys, thermo)	Suffixes (e.g., scope, phobia, phile, cracy, ology)

40 *Teaching Literacy Effectively in Modern Classroom for Ages 9–12*

3.3 The Big 6 syllable rules

In the following, we explain the six syllable rules and how to identify the different syllable rules in words.

Rule 1: Closed syllable pattern VC and CVC

Say something like
1. Today we are learning how to decode words with closed syllables. Look at the word on the board: *possum* (see Figure 3.2).
2. A closed syllable has a consonant after the vowel (e.g., *at*).
3. Here is an example, *possum*; it has two closed syllables: *pos + sum*.
4. Tick the vowels (check there are two vowels).
5. Divide between the two consonants, *ss*.
6. Say the two syllables: pos sum.
7. Say the word: possum.
8. Write *possum* in a sentence.

Activity for students to complete

For the sidebar words, students tick the vowels and divide the syllables. Answers: *rab/bit, cat/nip, mag/net, chic/ken, jac/ket, sand/wich.*

A follow-up is to read aloud the sidebar words several times as fast as they can. An extended follow-up is to write each word in a sentence (e.g., *Our pet rabbit is eating lettuce way down the back of its hutch*).

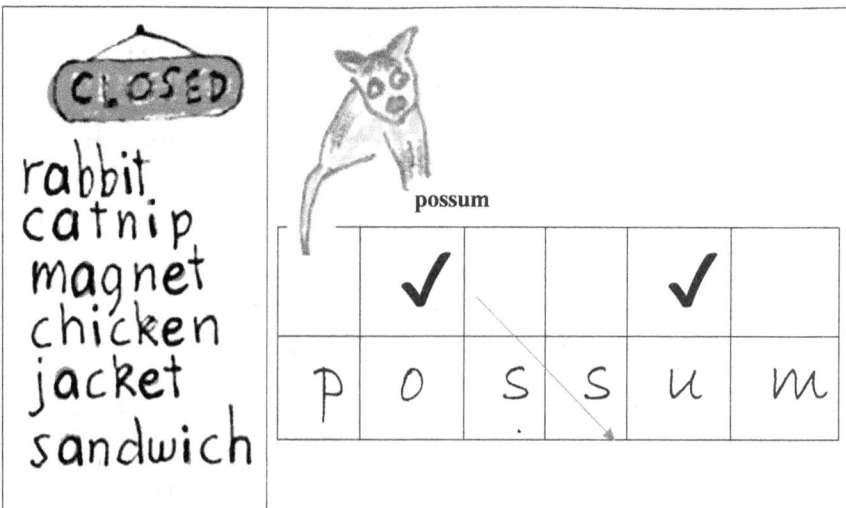

Figure 3.2 Closed Syllable Pattern.

Teaching decoding 41

Rule 2: Open syllable V or CV

Say something like
1. Today we are learning how to decode words with open syllables. Look at the word on the board: *robot* (see Figure 3.3).
2. In an open syllable, the vowel has a long sound. There is no consonant after it. In *robot*, the open syllable is *ro*.
3. *Robot* has one open syllable and one closed: *ro* + *bot*.
4. Tick the vowels (check there are two vowels).
5. Divide after the first vowel, *ro*.
6. Say the two syllables: *ro bot*.
7. Say the word: *robot*.
8. Write *robot* in a sentence.

Activity for students to complete

For the sidebar words, students tick the vowels and divide the syllables. Answers are *ro/bot, su/per, ba/con, fro/zen, do/nut, dri/ver*.

Notes

Definition: An **open** syllable does not have a consonant after it (e.g., *tu/lip*).

The open syllable rule can help to read some tricky words (e.g., *joking*). It is not uncommon for a student to read it as *jocking*.

Figure 3.3 Open Syllable Pattern.

42 *Teaching Literacy Effectively in Modern Classroom for Ages 9–12*

Rule 3: The -r and -l syllable pattern

Say something like
1. Today we are learning how to decode words with words with r- and l-affected vowel sounds.
2. Look at the word on the board: *starling* (see Figure 3.4).
3. In this syllable pattern, the r and l after the vowel change the vowel sound (e.g., *ar or er ir ur al*).
4. *Starling* has one r-affected syllable and one closed: *star + ling*.
5. Tick the vowels (check there are two vowels).
6. Divide after the first vowel, *ro*.
7. Say the two syllables: *star ling*.
8. Say the word: *starling*.
9. Write *starling* in a sentence.

Activity for students to complete

For the sidebar words, students tick the vowels and divide the syllables. Answers are far/mer, cor/ner, her/mit, mur/der, thir/sty, gar/den.

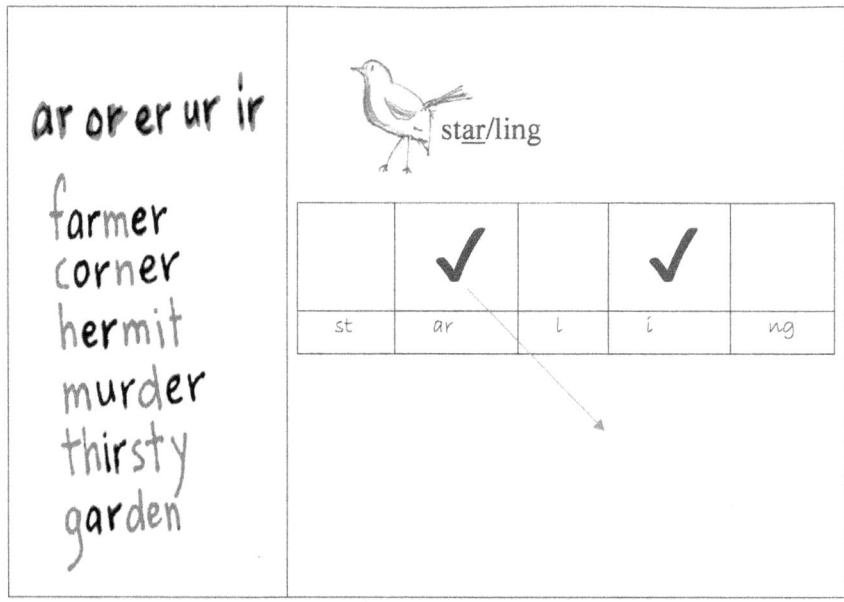

Figure 3.4 The R-Affected Syllable Pattern.

Rule 4: Split digraph: final e pattern CVCe

Say something like
1. Today we are learning how to decode words with words with a split digraph vowel pattern.
2. Look at the word on the board: *trombone* (see Figure 3.5).
3. In this syllable pattern, the final e at the end of the word is silent and means the vowel before it has a long sound, *bone*.
4. Check off each vowel sound √ but do not count final e as a vowel sound.
5. Split between the two middle consonants, *trom/bone*.

Question: "What about *cupcake*, does it have three syllables?"

Answer: "No, it has two vowel sounds so it has two syllables, the final e is silent, it does not have a sound."

Activity

For the sidebar words, students tick the vowels and divide the syllables. Answers are *mis/take, in/side, pan/cake, trom/bone, con/crete, cab-bage.*

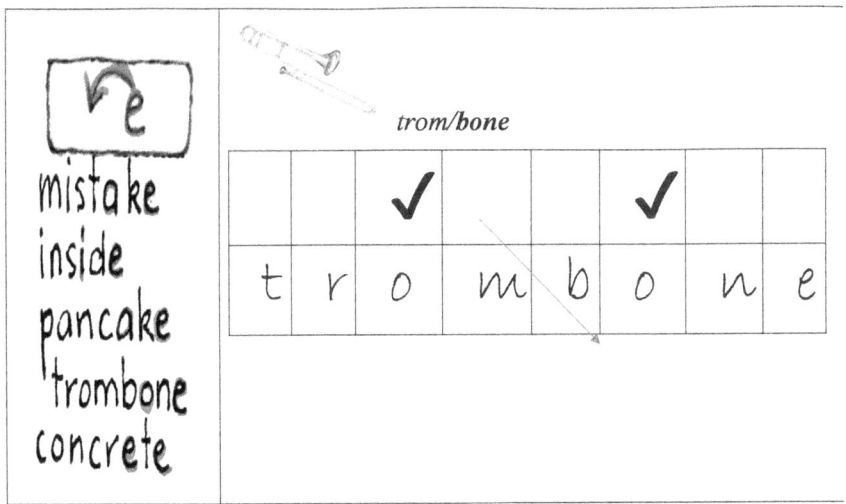

Figure 3.5 The Split Digraph: Final E - Syllable Pattern.

Rule 5: Vowel VV vowel team syllable pattern

Say something like
1. Today we are learning how to decode words with words with a vowel team – or vowel digraph – pattern.
2. A vowel team syllable pattern is two vowels together making one sound. A vowel digraph syllable has two vowels together inside the syllable.
3. Look at the word on the board: *coffee* (see Figure 3.6).
4. Watch what I do. I check off each vowel sound √ and split between the two consonants, *ff*.
5. If there are two vowel letters is in the middle of the word, remember it is ONE sound (e.g., *rain*: one team, one vowel sound; *rain/coat*: two teams, two vowel sounds).

Activity

For the sidebar words, students tick the vowels and divide the syllables. Answers are *cof/fee, rain/coat, sham/poo, boo/ster, pain/ter, moun/tain*.

Rule 6: Consonant plus -LE syllable pattern

Say something like
1. Today we are learning how to decode words with words with -LE syllable pattern (see Figure 3.7).
2. An -LE syllable pattern is where the syllable has a consonant sound + -LE. The rule is to keep the consonant and -LE together.

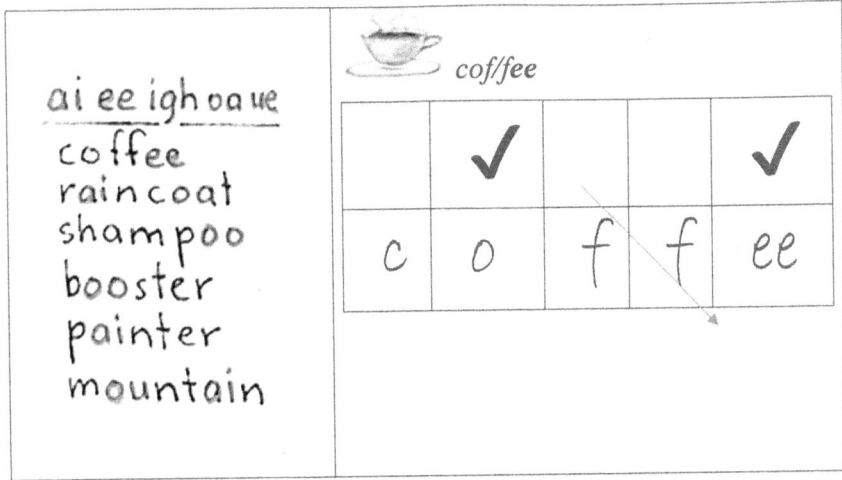

Figure 3.6 The Vowel Team Syllable Pattern.

Teaching decoding 45

Figure 3.7 The -LE Syllable Pattern.

3. Look at the word on the board: *apple*.
4. Watch what I do. I check off each vowel sound √ and split between the two consonants, *pp*, so it becomes *ap-ple*.

Activity

For the sidebar words, students tick the vowels and divide the syllables. Answers are *ap/ple, jug/gle, pad/dle, cat/tle, ta/ble, tur/tle, mid/dle*.

3.4 Words with Anglo-Saxon origins

Compound structures

Many Anglo-Saxon words are compounds of two words. To explain *compound word*, you could say

- A compound word is made of two real words.
- Usually, the two words will tell you the meaning (e.g., *raincoat* is a coat for the rain).
- Sometimes only one part of the word has the meaning (e.g., *strawberry* is not straw, but it is a kind of berry).

Table 3.2 Examples of Compound Words – Write the BA Code for Each Word

Compound words	Code: B is A, etc.
bird/bath	B is for A
black/bird	
blue/bird	
gold/fish	
jail/bird	
jelly/fish	
king/fish	
moon/beam	
moon/light	
moon/shine	
moon/stone	
rain/bow	
rain/coat	
rain/drop	
rain/fall	

Activity for students to complete

Hand out the list of words in Table 3.2. In each compound word, the first word is A, and the second word is B. Students must write the code for each word; it will be one of the following:

B is A (e.g., goldfish, a fish that is gold).
B is for A (e.g., fishhook, a hook for fish).
B is from A (e.g., moonbeam, a beam from the moon).
B is of A (e.g., raindrop, a drop of rain).
B does A (e.g., jailbird, a bird that does jail).

Answers
B is A: goldfish, jellyfish, kingfish, blackbird, bluebird
B is for A: fishhook, birdbath, raincoat
B is from A: moonbeam, moonlight, moonshine, moonstone
B is of A: raindrop, rainfall, rainbow
B does A: jailbird

Follow-up activity for students to complete

Students must think of a meaning for each made-up word

ducknet:
hatvan:
catcup:
jamjug:
foxhut:
yesfrog:
ratrug:
fingerhut:

Answers: possible meanings for each made up word
ducknet: a net to catch ducks, hatvan: a van that carries hats, catcup: a cup to put the cat's milk in, jamjug: a jug to hold jam, foxhut: a house for a fox, yesfrog: a frog who talks, ratrug: a rug for rats, fingerhut: a hut for the finger or thimble

Anglo-Saxon Root words, prefixes, and suffixes

Some Anglo-Saxon words have a prefix–root word–suffix structure. Root words can be almost any word (e.g., *like, give*). A prefix at the start of a word is usually a preposition (e.g., *for, over*). A suffix at the end of a word indicates form class: verb and so on (e.g., *-ed, -s, -ship*).

> prefix = start of a word
> suffix = end of a word

Activity

MAKE AN ANGLO-SAXON WORD

Students cut out the Anglo-Saxon prefix–root word–suffix patterns from the lists below and put them into three piles (e.g., prefixes in red, root words in blue, suffixes in yellow). The goal is to make as many new words as they can (e.g., *overbid, unlikely, beginning*).

Prefixes

for	un	be	over	with	under

Root words

bid	just	gin	see	hold	go
wise	free	false	hard	lord	like

Suffixes

dom	hood	ship	ly	ed	ing	s

3.5 Words with Latin/French origins

> ☺☺**Top Tip**: This short video is on Latin words.
> https://www.youtube.com/watch?v=OnUQIX3r-8k&list=PLvmDzSq Ke9JC2McuLoYnWhOPsyOzSbWcV&index=24

Latin Root words, prefixes, and suffixes

Latin root words carry the core meaning of the word. Prefixes are placed before the root word. Suffixes are placed after it. Some examples are below.

Latin prefixes

pre	dis	re	pro	con
im	in	ex	sub	pro

Latin root words

vent - come	port - carry	form - shape	tract - drag	rupt - break
duct - lead	ject - throw	ped - foot	script - write	mit - send

Latin suffixes

or	al	ion/ian	ious	ence
able	ure	or	ive	ity

Invent a Latin word

Instructions: Choose one prefix, one root word, and one suffix from the lists above. Create a new word. Write what it means. Use the word in a sentence.

Example: *exportable*

ex = out, port = carry, able = able to

Meaning: something you can send overseas; for example,, a product like bananas is exportable; you can send it to another country for sale.

Activities

PREFIXES

The prefixes *in, im, un, dis, contra* mean *not* or *against*. Look at each example word and underline the prefix. Select five of the words in Table 3.3 and write each one in a sentence to show its meaning.

SUFFIXES

The suffixes -ity, -ion, and -ious change the part of speech (e.g., to a noun or an adjective). Select five of the words with a suffix in Table 3.4 and write each one in a sentence to show its meaning.

Match the Latin prefix to its meaning

Draw a line to match the Latin prefix with its meaning (e.g., *sub-* means under) (see Table 3.5).

Answers: <u>sub</u> - under, <u>de</u> - away, <u>dis</u> - away, <u>in</u> - not, <u>re</u> - again, <u>tri</u> - three, <u>post</u> - after, <u>trans</u> - across, <u>contra</u> - against, <u>inter</u> - between, <u>ex</u> - out.

Table 3.3 Prefixes with a Negative Meaning: *in- im- dis- contra-*

in	im	dis	contra
inept: <u>not</u> having the aptitude for something	immune: <u>not</u> susceptible	distrust: <u>no</u> trust	contradict: <u>goes against</u> what is said
inertia: not alive, not moving	impasse not passable, like a cul-de-sac	dissemble: not what it seems	contraband: goes against what is banned
inevitable: not avoidable	immense: not measurable)	disparity: not the same, not on a par	contravene: goes against what people come to believe in
	impeccable: no faults	dissonant: not sounding right, out of harmony	controversy: turns against

Table 3.4 Suffixes Indicating Word Class: Noun *-ity, -ion* and Adjective *-ious*

Root word	Root word meaning	Noun suffix -ity, -ion	Adjective suffix -ious
cautio: take heed	word of warning	caution	cautious
audere: bold	daring, defiant	audacity	audacious
ostendere: stretch	display, conspicuous	ostentation	ostentatious
fractura: break	peevish	fraction	fractious
locutio: talk, speak	talking too much	locution, loquacity	loquacious
ob + sequio: follow	servile, fawning	–	obsequious
malus: bad, ill will	mischievous intent	–	malicious

3.6 Words with Greek origins

> ☺ ☺ **Top Tip**: This video is on words with Greek origins.
> https://www.youtube.com/watch?v=8WOxANqtoaQ&list=PLvm
> DzSqKe9JC2McuLoYnWhOPsyOzSbWcV&index=25

Greek words usually have two parts, and both parts are important for working out the meaning of the word. There are root words, prefixes, and suffixes, but they are basically combining forms. Some root words can combine (e.g., *thermometer*); a prefix and suffix can combine (e.g., *bibliophile*) (see also Table 3.6).

Table 3.5 Student Activity: Draw a Line from Latin Prefix to Its Meaning

Prefix	Meaning
sub	out
de	three
dis	against
in	across
re	away
tri	between
post	away
trans	under
trans	not
contra	after
inter	again

Table 3.6 Examples of Greek Combining Forms

Root word	Meaning	Combining forms
auto	self	automatic
astro	star	astronomy
bio	life	biohazard
chrono	time	synchrony
cratia	rule	democracy
geo	earth	geography
graph	write	autograph
logos	study	ecology
micro	small	microscope
tele	far	telescope
therm	heat	thermometer
hyd	water	hydrology

- Greek root words (e.g., *chron, graph, meter, phono, photo/phos, phys, psych, sphere, thermo*)
- Greek prefixes (e.g., *auto-, biblio-, hemi-, hex-, tri-, hydro-, hyper-, octo-, peri-, quad-, semi-, tele-*)
- Greek suffixes (e.g., -archy, -crat, -cracy, -logy, -phile, -phobia, -scope)

3.7 Conclusion

The secret of decoding success in the modern classroom is to follow a logical scope and sequence for everyone. Even if for some students there is no need, they will still benefit from revision. Regular assessment will ensure that no one is falling behind.

Teaching decoding 51

Further exercises: words with Latin origins

The exercises below are opportunities to discuss different root words, suffixes, and prefixes and what the words mean (Figures 3.8–3.19).

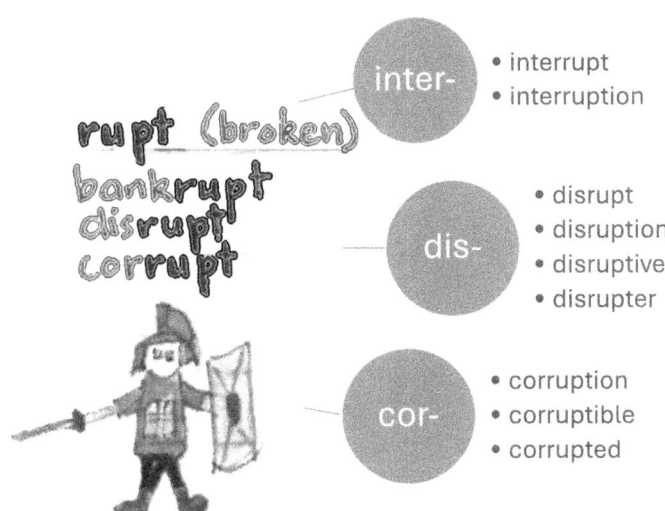

Figure 3.8 Root Word *rupt* – To Break.

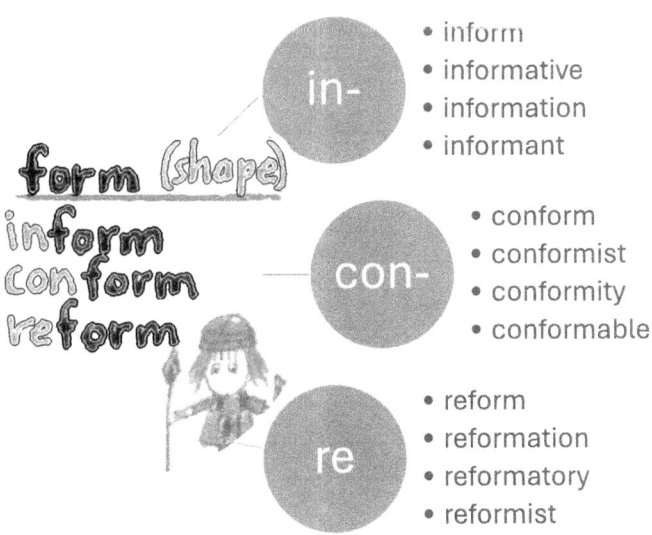

Figure 3.9 Root Word *form* – To Shape.

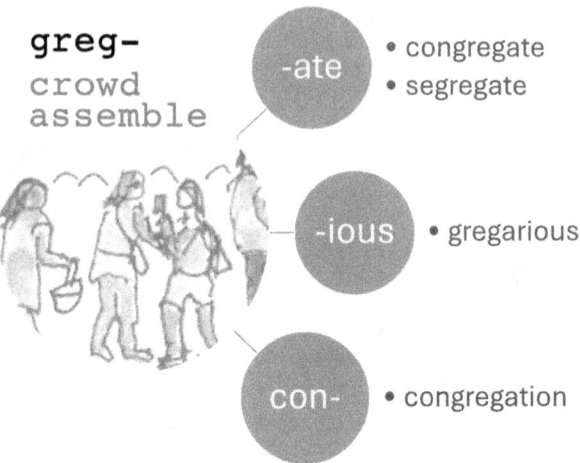

Figure 3.10 Root Word *greg* – Crowd, Assemble.

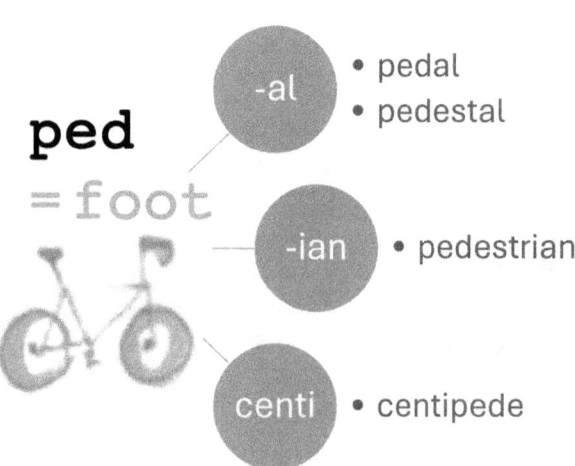

Figure 3.11 Root Word *ped* – Foot.

Teaching decoding 53

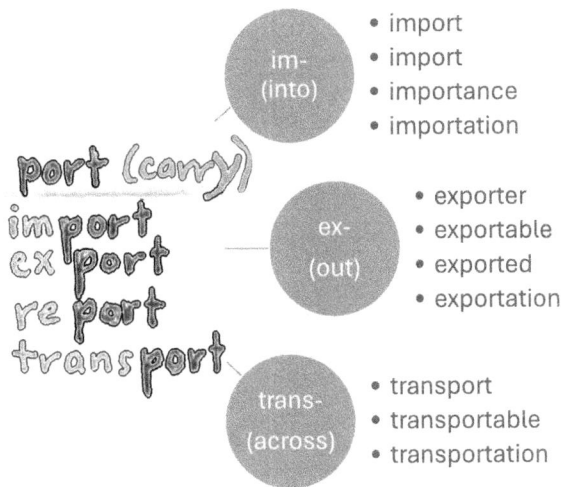

Figure 3.12 Root Word *port* – To Carry.

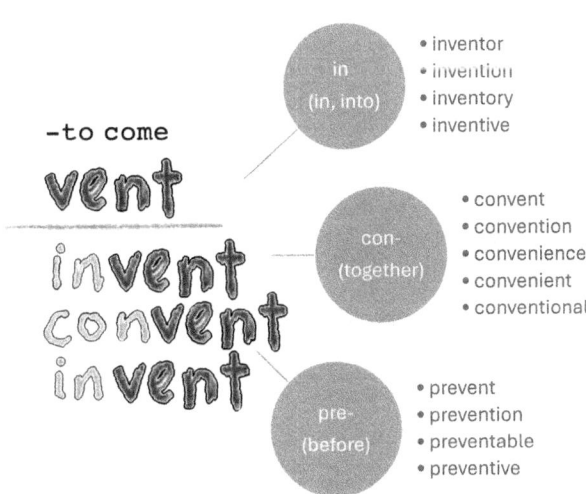

Figure 3.13 Root Word *vent* – To Come.

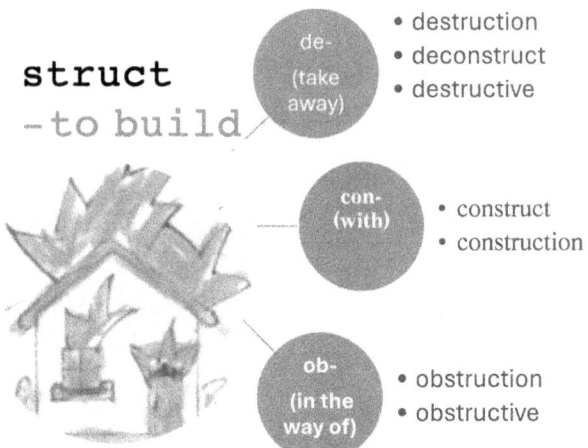

Figure 3.14 Root Word *struct* – To Build.

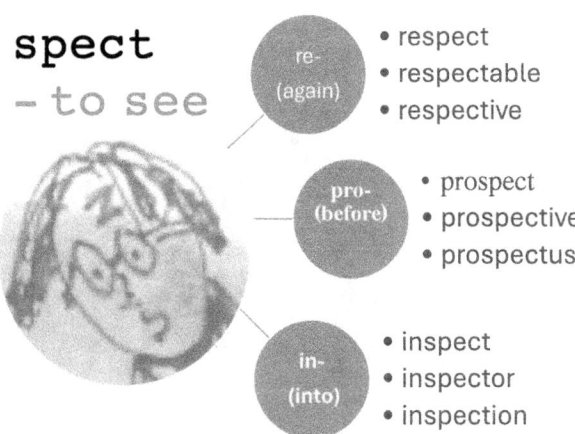

Figure 3.15 Root Word *spect* – To See.

Teaching decoding   55

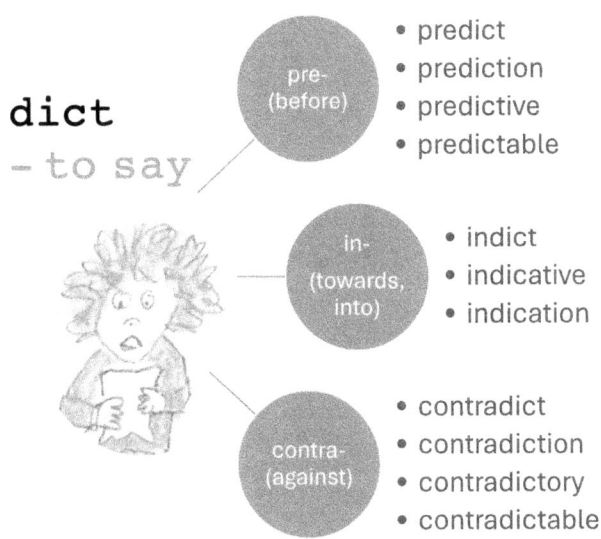

Figure 3.16 Root Word *dict* – To Say.

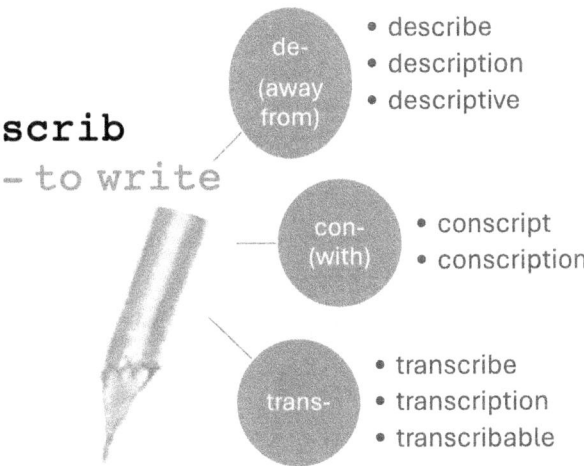

Figure 3.17 Root Word *scrib* – To Write.

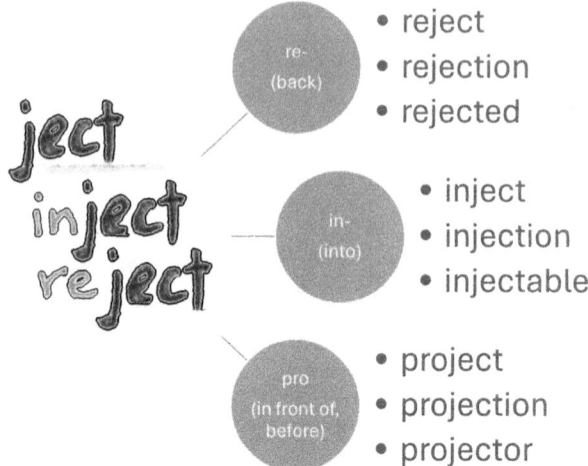

Figure 3.18 Root Word *ject* – To Throw.

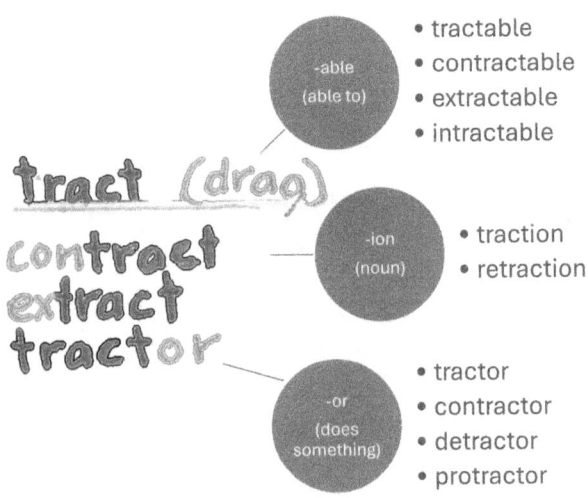

Figure 3.19 Root Word *tract* – To Drag.

Part 2
Reading comprehension

Chapter 4, *Reading comprehension: What is it?*, explains the science of reading, gives definitions, explains top down and bottom-up theories, and shows how fiction, nonfiction, and persuasion texts differ.

Chapter 5, *Assessing reading comprehension*, covers norm-referenced tests, expectations for ages 9-12, why students fail to answer exam questions, gives a list of test-taking strategies, and shows how the simple view explains comprehension problems.

Chapter 6, *Teaching reading comprehension*, shows students how to answer comprehension questions, provides 12 practice text passages plus activities, and advocates whole class teaching to replace the segregation effects of ability grouping.

4 Reading comprehension
What is it?

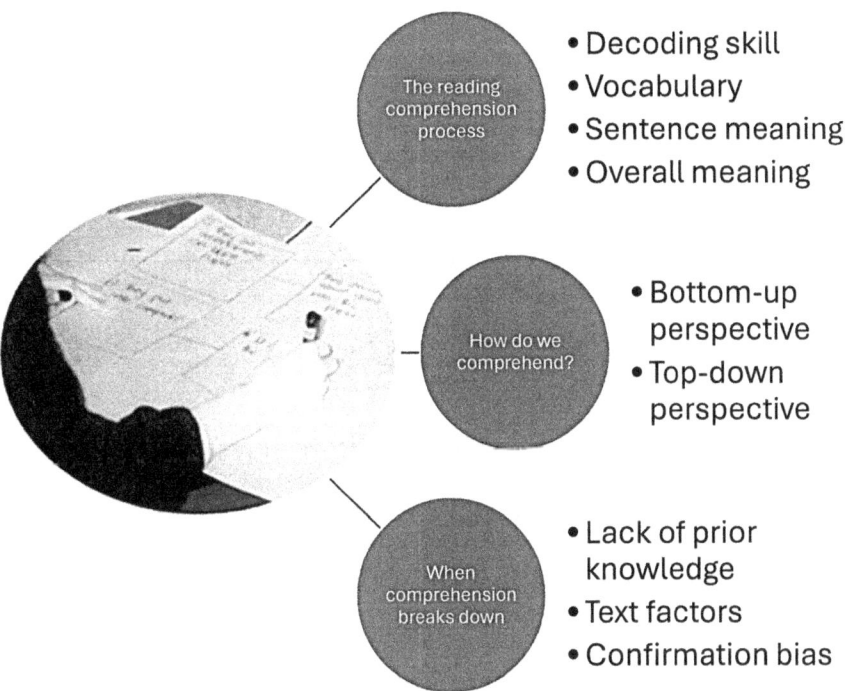

Figure 4.1 Overview of Chapter 4.

4.1 Introduction

> When you've got a real long page, very long story to read, and then you answer questions. You read it through and then you start to forget different parts of the story … and then you go and answer the questions and can't even answer them properly because you can't remember it.

DOI: 10.4324/9781003130789-6

Many students feel overwhelmed by the texts they must read. It is not as if they do not understand the language. Most native speakers have a good grasp of their language. What is it then that makes comprehension difficult? The students' day is filled with reading activities, but it is worth pausing to ask whether these activities are improving student comprehension.

The key messages of this chapter are

1. Comprehension is difficult because many writers do not write very well. Students need study strategies to restructure the text and make it comprehensible, but they do not know what strategies to use.
2. Students must be confident in how to capture in diagram form the key ideas in the author's text.
3. Students spend most of their time answering comprehension questions, doing busy work, rather than standing back and looking at the design and overall message of texts. They do not use their time to best effect. They work in the dark, with very few glimmers of light.
4. Comprehension requires the reader to create a mental discourse structure and make it their own. Many students do not know how to do this.
5. Students are not blank slates. They can already comprehend spoken language. What they do not have are effective study skills to untangle the byzantine writing of their school texts.

The topics covered in this chapter

1. Defining reading comprehension
2. The difference between fiction, non-fiction, and argument texts
3. Comprehension theory
4. Why does comprehension break down?

4.2 What is reading comprehension?

A simple definition is that reading comprehension is the process of understanding any communication that is in writing, whether it be books, letters, Twitter/X, Facebook, Instagram, billboards, road signs, package labels, and so on.

A more in-depth definition of reading comprehension might be that it is the process of extracting information from text and constructing meaning from it. This process will involve both the literal information in the text (i.e., the lines) and the unstated but implied meaning (i.e., between the lines).

Reading comprehension is decoding the words and making sense of them. The reader decodes words letter by letter, mapping letter-sounds to stored vocabulary in their mental dictionary. Sentences are parsed grammatically, and finally the text is understood. The reader moves through text this way, processing one word at a time, one sentence at a time, one idea at a time, until the text is finished.

Reading comprehension: What is it? 61

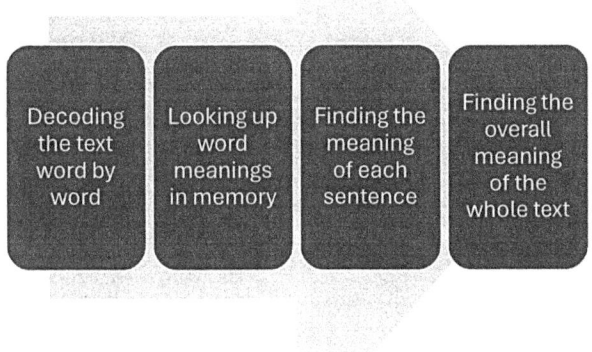

Figure 4.2 Steps in the Reading Comprehension Process.

Reading comprehension requires several things to happen, as shown in Figure 4.2.

- Decoding each word
- Accessing the meaning of each word
- Parsing the grammar of each sentence and paragraph
- Understanding the message of the whole text

Comprehension happens very quickly. The reader makes decisions about the meanings of words and sentences virtually on-line, while reading. Comprehension is such a complex concept and not completely understood. It is so mysterious that one researcher, slightly tongue in cheek, called it "The place where sentences go when they are understood."

Even though comprehension is hard to define, most readers can understand what they hear or read almost as soon as it happens. The native speaker's innate ability to process language is just there within the reader. Comprehension is a mysterious cerebral activity. The big question is, why does it happen for some but not others?

4.3 Comprehension theory

Bottom-up theory

Some argue that comprehension is what is in the text. It is text-driven. Comprehension is not skimming the text or guessing without reading it. Studies of speed readers show that they remember almost nothing of what they read. The text information is important.

Eye movement studies show that the reader looks at nearly every word of the text. If the reader processes every word, the text must be important for comprehension.

It seems natural that the language of the text is the source of meaning. Our language system is designed to process language, whether spoken or written, to figure out what words and sentences mean, and to store the meaning in memory.

Top-down theory

On the other hand, some argue that reading comprehension is what we think it is. It is driven by knowledge. To understand a text, you need knowledge. If you do not have knowledge, you will not understand. Knowledge makes it easier to comprehend; for example, a student with depth of knowledge of computers will understand a text on that topic much better than someone who has no knowledge of computers.

Knowledge about spiders, kangaroos, coyotes, or platypuses helps comprehension when we read texts about these animals. Without relevant knowledge, comprehension will be disrupted. Knowledge is important.

Interactive "in the middle" view

The text provides relevant information for comprehension, some would say most of the information, but knowledge is relevant, too. The reader integrates text information with their own subject or general knowledge to comprehend.

4.4 Why does comprehension break down?

Why is it that some students do well on comprehension tasks and others do not? The comprehension process is multifaceted, which means the comprehension process can break down at any point: decoding, vocabulary, grammar, or interpreting the meaning.

In this book, these topics get specific attention. If words in the text are hard to decode accurately, if word meanings are unknown, if sentences are hard to work out, or if the overall meaning is unclear, any of these can cause problems for comprehension. Students must be skilled in all these areas.

4.5 The structure of texts – what is fiction, non-fiction, and argument?

Here are two different texts. How are they different? Yes, text A is fiction, or narrative. Text B is non-fiction, or expository. The question is, why is one fiction and the other non-fiction? Students need to know the similarities and differences.

Reading comprehension: What is it? 63

Text A	Text B
Once upon a time on a shelf in a junk shop, there was a dusty green bottle. Inside it lived a genie named Gaga, who was scrawny, all skin and bones. Gaga was like this because Gaga was a worrier.	What is a door for? Doors are for keeping in or out. There are French doors, folding doors, oven doors, etc. There are revolving doors, sliding doors, and roller doors. Early doors were hung on pivots. Later came hinged doors. In China, doors had a solid lower half and a top half of lattice panel to let air through. Some doors are to keep things safe and secure...

Why is Text A fiction?

Fiction texts, like Text A about Gaga the genie, tell an imaginary story. They have a setting, characters, plot, and theme as the main parts of their structure. Text A introduces the setting and the main character in the story, Gaga, a genie who lives on a shelf in a junk shop, inside a bottle.

What is fiction?

Fiction is an imaginary series of events involving characters. A narrative text is not true. What you did on the weekend is not a story because it is true. Narratives are not true; they are made up.

Narrative structure has a set design that applies to all imaginary stories that authors write. The text must have

- Setting: the setting can be summed up in terms of when, where, and atmosphere or mood.
- Characters – major and minor – can be described in terms of features, personality, aspirations, faults, and so on. They can be compared.
- Plot: action in the story. The action consists of one or more episodes. In each episode, the main character has a problem, a reaction to the problem, actions to solve the problem, and an outcome. The plot can be drawn using a story graph that shows the events over time. Students looking for structure will design a story graph to show the sequence of actions, including the high and low points in the action.

Why is text B a non-fiction text?

Text B is a non-fiction text because it is about real things that really exist or have existed. It is not an imaginary story. Text B is about a real concept in the world, doors, and the uses they have in real life. The *doors* text is descriptive of real things. It explains about types of doors, history of doors, and specific door designs.

What is non-fiction?

Non-fiction texts are not stories. They are not imaginary; they are real. A recount, biography, interview, film review, news report, or article, they seem like narrative and are often called *stories*, but they are not stories. They are not imaginary; they are real. Non-fiction text is information about real things. Non-fiction writing can be descriptive, sequential, or persuasive.

Descriptive non-fiction text gives key points about a person, place, event, state of mind, or thing. The main structures for descriptive texts are

a) lists – like a "to do" list – a random list of items (e.g., a list of what can go into your recycling bin or a list of products of Japan)
b) webs: they are spider web-like diagrams that explain the attributes and other aspects of ONE thing (e.g., the yak)
c) weaves: they have a matrix or tapestry design, with interlocking threads to compare more than one thing (e.g., kiwis and seagulls)
d) hierarchy: they are like an upside-down tree structure, with the main category at the top and subcategories below; for example, gemstones can be divided into two types of stones, precious, like a *diamond* and semi-precious, like a *garnet*.

Sequential non-fiction text shows the process in carrying out an action or series of actions. A sequence text is step by step. There are different kinds of sequential text structures. For example:

a) Linear: a string of events (e.g., how to make butter, a history of …, biography of …)
b) Cause and effect (e.g., earthquake causes X … effects are Y …)
c) Problem-solution (e.g., six ways [solution] to lose weight [problem], highway will go through church [problem], move the church [solution])
d) cyclical, where the events recapitulate (e.g., life cycle of a butterfly)

What is persuasive text?

Persuasive text is a different kind of writing. It is not fiction or non-fiction. It presents arguments. It has an argument structure. It presents one or more arguments for and against a topic. It has a for–against text structure.

A persuasive text musters a series of arguments to support a claim or thesis. It will give a clear position. It will give arguments to support the thesis and refute arguments that go against the thesis. The arguments are designed to persuade. Advertisements persuade. The arguments may or may not be true. The arguments may be fake. The arguments may be overstated or misleading.

In today's world, it is difficult to distinguish accurate and misleading information, which is why many writers have to fact-check.

There are different kinds of persuasive text structures, including podcasts, news stories, advertising scripts, billboards, speeches, debates, and opinion articles.

4.6 Conclusion

In schools, students often encounter texts that seem hard, but these texts can be seen as learning opportunities, even though the texts may be poorly written. Effective comprehension strategies can help. Students want to do well; this is why they attend school purposefully, to gain necessary knowledge and leave equipped for success.

Comprehension must be made visible; it is about getting inside the mind of the writer, to *see* the design of the text, its skeleton, its bones. It is about creating a diagram that is a summary of the text and gives the main points. The diagram shows the bones of the text and the weight of information. Comprehension is about seeing text as a forest, not a jumble of trees. It is about seeing structure where others see a bunch of words. Effective text comprehension is about reading a text today and remembering it tomorrow.

5 Assessing reading comprehension

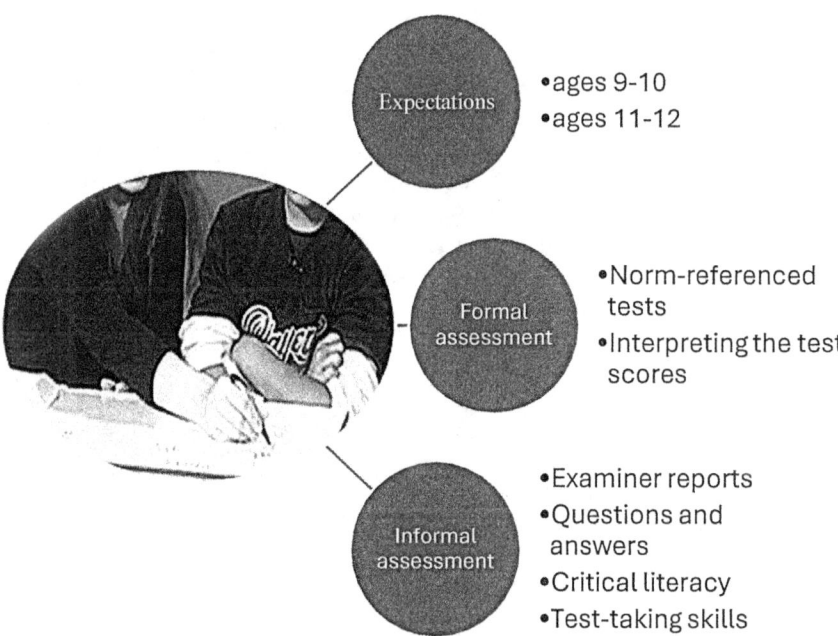

Figure 5.1 Overview of Chapter 5.

> I am a very lousy reader... It's mainly my comprehension is down.

5.1 Introduction

The value of assessing reading comprehension is to give direction for helping those not achieving at their potential. Assessment is a description of performance. It is a source of information. If done at regular test points during the school year, assessment will show whether students are learning. An assessment is not a value rating; it is a description to indicate what skills are secure

DOI: 10.4324/9781003130789-7

and what skills need assistance. The data help in designing better learning opportunities. Assessing reading comprehension shows where the class is at and what kinds of material the class can properly understand.

This chapter covers the following topics:

- Expectations
- Norm-referenced assessment
- Test-taking skills
- Examiner comments
- Question-answering skills
- Critical literacy
- The "simple view" of reading difficulties

5.2 Age-related expectations in reading comprehension

Inspection of curriculum and learning progression documents shows a wide range of comprehension skill expectations. Students, when they discuss these lists of skills, will see clearly that the focus is on three things: (a) building general knowledge and vocabulary, (b) understanding the structures of different texts, and (c) building their ability to be "savvy" and use critical thinking when answering test questions. Below is a summary of skill expectations in some curriculum and learning progression documents.

Ages 9–10
- quick and accurate decoding
- wide and deep vocabulary
- able to read the text carefully and get the facts
- make inferences that fit with the text data
- ask questions and see gaps
- construct a summary of the text
- know the two main types of questions: literal and inferential
- figurative language (e.g., metaphor)
- multiple meanings (e.g., idioms and homonyms)
- sustained attention to longer texts like novels

Ages 11–12
- read complex texts
- understand complex plots and themes
- identify text structures (e.g., compare/contrast and cyclical)
- read critically
- understand abstract ideas
- question whether the text is credible and factual
- identify author bias and self-interest
- see the text from different points of view – uncritical and critical

5.3 Norm-referenced tests

The most accurate way to assess reading comprehension is to use a norm-referenced test. There are many published tests available, and the school may want to consult a specialist to select which to use.

According to the *simple view of reading* (Hoover & Tunmer, 2020), students not reading to their potential will have difficulty with word decoding, listening comprehension, or both. Reading comprehension is the product of word decoding and listening comprehension. Students need to be assessed in both of these components to have a clear idea of their ability.

Reading comprehension

The tests to use will differ according to jurisdiction. There are many norm-referenced tests. One suggestion is the *Progressive Achievement Test of Reading* (*PAT-R*). It can be used with individuals or groups of students. Individual tests are the *York Assessment of Reading for Comprehension* (*YARC*) and the *Neale Assessment of Reading Ability* (*NARA*).

Decoding

The tests to use will differ according to jurisdiction. Individual tests of oral reading are *NARA* and *YARC*. The *Burt Word Reading Test* is an individual test that gives a reading age (there are copies of the test in Nicholson, 2005; Nicholson & Dymock, 2023). A similar test to the *Burt* is the *Schonell Word Reading Test*. It may be available online.

Listening comprehension

The tests to use will differ according to jurisdiction. The norm-referenced *Progressive Achievement Test of Listening Comprehension* (*PAT-L*) can be used with individuals or groups of students. *The British Picture Vocabulary Scale* (*BPVS*) is an individual test of receptive vocabulary.

5.4 Examiner reports on student test-taking strategies

Examiner reports on student performance in literacy exams highlight certain test-taking skills that students seem not to have under control. Reports mention that students must consider what the best answers to questions are. They should not just put a check mark on the most plausible answer.

Examiner reports from national examinations of reading achievement highlight key strengths and weaknesses of students:

Students at or exceeding expectation

1. Use their skills to understand the text
2. Unpack each question, evaluate options, and select the correct answer

3. Work out *why* the author wrote the text (the purpose)
4. Work out *who* the writer was writing for (the audience)
5. Work out the writer's strategies
6. Determine the credibility of the information in a text

Students approaching expectation or needing extra help

1. Do not understand the text
2. Do not pick out the best answer option
3. Do not understand why the text was written (the purpose)
4. Do not understand who the text was written for (the audience)
5. Do not determine the credibility of information in the text

Examiner suggestions for students to improve

1. Decide *what* the text is about
2. Decide *why* the author wrote the text
3. Decide *how* the author wrote the text
4. Decide how to work out meanings of unfamiliar words in the text
5. Decide on the nature of the text – is it to explain, persuade, narrate, entertain, and so on?
6. Make sure answers to comprehension questions can be verified in the text
7. Check whether the text information is credible

Questions and answers

Students can do better if they know how to use strategies for answering questions. The key strategy is to assume that most questions will require the reader to read between the lines. In exams, answers are not usually stated explicitly in the text. There will be text clues to the answer, but the student must make inferences from their own knowledge of the topic. Students can make a calculated guess from context clues and their own knowledge, but they need to verify their guess in the text. The text must explicitly support their guess about the best answer.

Critical literacy skills

The student must apply critical literacy skills, asking themselves whom is this for, why did the author write this, and what is the purpose of it. The student must question the purpose of the test questions, what the examiners are looking for, and what is in their minds as to the best answer. It involves thinking not just about what the author wrote but the audience they wrote for, what the author wanted to achieve in writing it, and what the examiners are looking for in a "best" answer.

Test-taking skills

Students can do better in tests if they use test-taking skills. Every student will have their own study strategies. The class can discuss their personal strategies. Students will learn new strategies by sharing and learning about the strategies that others use. Students must keep a list of test-taking strategies to use.

Students must look at previous exam questions and decide how they can improve (a) their question-answering skills and (b) their decisions as to the most likely answers to multiple options. Students can do mock-tests, using past examples, to strengthen their skills.

Sometimes the answer to the question is explicitly stated in the text. The words in the question and the words in the text are an exact match. Not many questions are like this, but they do happen. Most test questions are implicit; they require a combination of text information and the student's own knowledge. The student, in the end, must integrate text information with their own knowledge but must always check that they can verify their choice of answer with data explicitly stated in the text. Test-taking ideas for students to consider are shown in Table 5.1.

5.5 Why do students have difficulty with reading comprehension?

For most students with difficulties, the answer to this question is that they are struggling either with decoding the words on the page or with the language of the text; they just cannot understand it.

If you cannot decode the words on the page, you are not going to understand what the text is about. Likewise, if you cannot understand what the words mean, then you will not understand. Most poor readers are stuck with

Table 5.1 Test-Taking Strategies During a Test

Following directions	*Question-answering strategies*
– Read the test passage closely. – Read the questions closely. – Answer all the questions.	– Find the answer options that are clearly not right and avoid them. – Read the question options closely and assume that the answer will be partly but not completely in the text. – Use personal knowledge combined with text information to figure out the best answer.
If you cannot answer the question …	*Final check*
– Guess the most likely option. – Skip the question and come back later. – See if a later question in the test has clues to answering the present question.	– Read through the test again. – Change answers but only if you are sure.

Assessing reading comprehension 71

poor decoding skills (e.g., dyslexia) or with language issues (e.g., English language learners [ELLs]) or both.

This is what the *simple view of reading* predicts. It states that comprehension difficulties will be due to decoding or language or both.

How does the simple view work? It says that reading comprehension has two parts:

- decoding, as measured by the ability to read printed words fluently
- listening, as measured by the ability to understand spoken language

The simple view had its origins in the 1980s when Gough (1983) wrote that reading comprehension, or R, was the product of decoding skill, or D, and listening comprehension, or C. The simple view stated that $R = D \times C$.

The simple view (Hoover & Tunmer, 2020) predicts that students not reading to their potential must have difficulties with decoding or listening or both.

In the *simple view*, students with no difficulties are *Readers* while students with reading difficulties are in one of three categories (see Figure 5.2):

- Listening difficulties (e.g., ELLs)
- Decoding difficulties (e.g., dyslexia)
- Decoding *and* listening difficulties – the *double whammy*

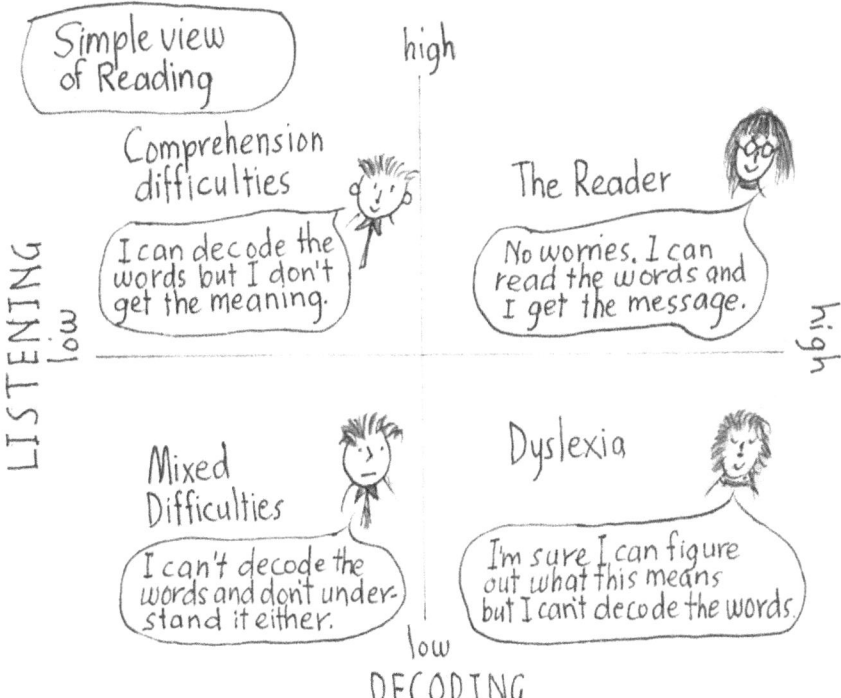

Figure 5.2 Simple View of Reading Difficulties.

Table 5.2 Assessment Data on Reading for Four Students

Class names	Reading comprehension	Language comprehension	Decoding skills	Analysis	Action required
Student A	High	High	High	No issues	Extend, go beyond
Student B	Low	Low	High	Language issues	Focus on language
Student C	Low	High	Low	Decoding issues	Focus on decoding
Student D	Low	Low	Low	Language and decoding issues	Focus on decoding and language

To illustrate, a simulated set of assessment results for reading comprehension, listening, and decoding is presented in Table 5.2.

- Student A ("the reader") had average to high scores for reading comprehension, decoding, and language comprehension. This student was not experiencing comprehension difficulties.
- Student B ("language difficulties only") had average to high scores for decoding but below average listening and reading scores. Comprehension difficulties were due to issues with listening (i.e., grammar and vocabulary).
- Student C ("dyslexia") had average to high scores for listening comprehension but below average decoding and reading scores. Comprehension difficulties were due to issues with decoding.
- Student D ("double whammy") had not reached their potential in either listening or decoding. Comprehension difficulties were due to issues with decoding and listening.

5.6 Conclusion

Assessment of reading comprehension can help teachers make better decisions as to why some students are not reading to their potential and what action to take. Detailed assessment strategies will enable a clear picture of what gaps need to be filled and where to start. For all these readers, the chapters on decoding, vocabulary, and comprehension in this book will help.

6 Teaching reading comprehension

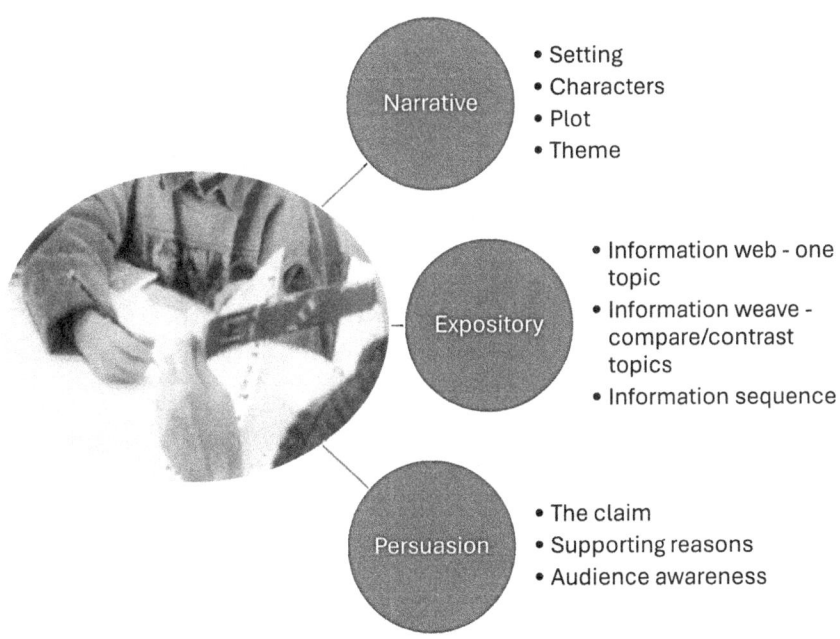

Figure 6.1 Overview of Chapter 6.

6.1 Introduction

> You get to the end of the chapter and then you think back to the beginning, but it's all gone from your mind.

DOI: 10.4324/9781003130789-8

Imagine walking into a school where students' comprehension work was posted on the walls of the classrooms and in school corridors, charts and posters showing the structure of the texts they have read. The topics were different in each poster, but the way the posters were structured was similar. Would you find this interesting?

You would immediately see that this is a school where everyone is working together and using a literacy model that is universally understood. This visual approach to learning literacy is an example of what happens in the text structure approach, an approach that can transform the way students learn, that can move the needle on comprehension.

Students do need to learn text structure. Their school texts require students to learn specific content for tests or exams. There are novels they must read, textbooks they must digest.

Students who want to improve their reading comprehension study skills must examine a text's meaning by recreating and diagramming the structure used by the writer. To find the exact meaning, students must sketch out the structure of a text in the same way as an architect sketches the design of a house.

Every text has structure, whether it is a story, article, speech, advertisement, debate, report, letter, opinion piece, how-to instructions, a to-do list, a movie or book review, biography, recount, diary, biography, etc. Knowing how to *see* the relevant structure is critical for comprehension.

This chapter covers the following topics:

1. Questions and answers
2. Narrative text structure
3. Nonfiction or expository text structure
4. Persuasion/argument text structure

6.2 Questions and answers

Studies of students answering questions indicate that very few students try to answer the questions without looking at the text (Binder et al., 2024). Some do, but only a small number.

In one study, students were better able to answer the questions about the text if they asked themselves, "What do you have to find in the text to answer this question?"

By asking this question to themselves, it focused their attention more on locating the place in the text that had information related to the question. They were better able to answer questions using this strategy than a control group who did not use this strategy (Ayroles et al., 2021).

It seems from the above studies that answering comprehension questions is like this. The student reads the text to find the answer; they do not try to answer questions without reading the text. In addition, if they ask themselves this question – what information in the text will enable me to answer the question – they will get a better test result.

It seems simple enough but in practice, many students go off track and do not answer questions correctly. Looking at student answers to the question about the *Church Story* below, their strategies were -

Strategy A – Used text information and general knowledge
Strategy B – Used text information only
Strategy C – Used only general knowledge

Consider the following text:

Church Story

The minister lit the furnace in his little church so it would be warm for choir practice that evening. Then he went home for dinner. The singers usually arrived promptly, but for one reason or another everyone was late. Just at the time choir practice usually started, the church blew up with a terrible roar. Gas had filtered into the furnace through a broken pipe. As each of the choir members looked at the ruins they wondered, "Was my tardiness tonight an act of God?"

Question: Why did the church blow up?
Student answers to the question

A. Someone blew it up
B. The minister lit the furnace
C. Some gas got into the furnace
D. Choir sang
E. Tardiness

Looking at the answers to the question about the Church Story, it seems that students use three kinds of strategies:

Strategy A – This student combined text information and their personal knowledge, to arrive at the correct **answer C**. The answer required text information and general knowledge that gas and intense heat do not mix well.
Strategy B – The students who gave **answers B, D, and E** used text information, but they are not the best answers, they do not fit with the overall text meaning, e.g., the student who gave answer B did read the text, but general knowledge would tell them that this was not the direct cause of the explosion.

76 *Teaching Literacy Effectively in Modern Classroom for Ages 9–12*

Strategy C – The student who gave **answer A** probably did not read the text at all and instead used only their general knowledge. It is basically a guess.

Practice exercises to improve student test-taking strategies

The passages in Appendix A are an opportunity for students to use Strategy A. Each passage has one comprehension question and five possible answers. The task is to find the best answer and to give reasons as to why this answer is better than the other options. Students need to combine text information with their general knowledge to find the best answer. This is a critical skill for taking tests of comprehension.

The answers to the questions were actual student answers. Questions can elicit answers that are plausible but are not the answer that best fits the text. Students answering questions need to learn how to avoid side-paths that do not match the information in the text.

Answers to the passages in Appendix A: Rubber article – option C, Church story – option C, Scratched foot article – option D, Crows story – option E, Jody article – option B, Rice article - option A.

6.3 Narrative text: fiction

Narrative text has a structure like a spider web, with four anchor points that separate out the main elements of the story: setting, characters, plot, and theme. Setting describes place, time, and mood. Characters divide into major and minor, each with distinctive physical features and personalities. Plot is a series of episodes to solve a problem. The plot can be one episode or more than one. An episode has four parts: problem, reaction, action, and outcome. The plot may have a complication, preventing the characters from taking the actions they want. The theme is the message or moral of the story.

> In this lesson, students read an adapted version of the classic Aesop's fable, "Hare and Tortoise." A fable is a story, except that the characters are animals. A copy of the story is in the chapter's Appendix B, Figure 6.9. Suggestions for the lesson are set out in Table 6.1.

Follow-up practice exercises

Students can practice fiction and nonfiction text structures by studying the passages in Appendices A and B.

In explaining to students how a story works, you might use the following example:

Table 6.1 Narrative Lesson Plan: "Hare and Tortoise"

Lesson sequence	Content – What the teacher might say to students.	Possible student answers to questions asked by the teacher.
Opening	"The purpose of this lesson is to diagram the elements of this story, the Hare and Tortoise." [A copy of the story is shown on the whiteboard] I will read the story to you and then we will construct a web diagram of the story. [see Figure 6.2].	–
Middle	"What is the setting?" "Who are the characters?" "What are the personality features of Hare and Tortoise?" "What is the plot of the story?" [Suggest drawing a graph of the plot – as in Figure 6.3]	"The setting is a school classroom." "The major characters are Hare and Tortoise. The minor character is Hare's Mum." "Hare is over-confident, does not take the writing race seriously. Tortoise does take it seriously." "Problem – The problem is to decide whether Hare or Tortoise is the fastest story writer." "Reaction – Tortoise challenges Hare to a race." "Action - Hare races ahead of Tortoise and has nearly finished the story." "Complication - Hare's mum calls and Hare is distracted." "Outcome - Tortoise wins the race."
Close	A further student task is to complete a story graph of the plot, as in Figure 6.3. Notes - The class might use the web structure to write a summary of the Hare and Tortoise story. Suggest that they use key subheadings in the web diagram to write the summary. The summary must start with a hook to engage the reader, then must explain setting, characters, plot, and theme. The summary must end with a strong conclusion that reaches out to the reader, e.g., " I hope you enjoyed reading this summary of the story of the tortoise and the hare."	

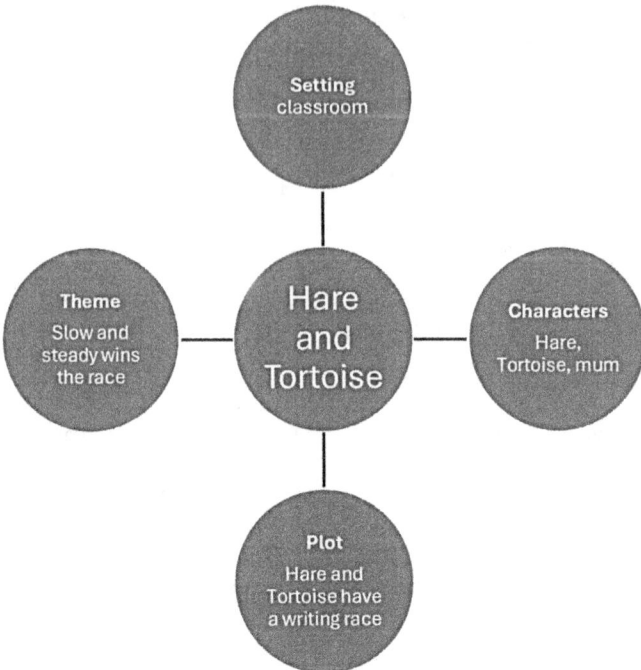

Figure 6.2 Story Web for the "Hare and Tortoise" Story.

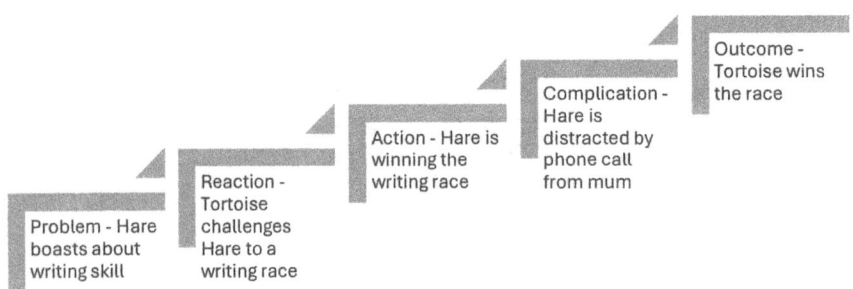

Figure 6.3 Story Graph for the "Hare and Tortoise" Story – Timeline – Action.

6.4 Expository text: nonfiction

Expository or nonfiction texts provide information on a topic. The following nonfiction structures are of two main types: description and sequence.

Description: list, web, weave

List

The list structure is A + B + C + … It is like a shopping list or a to-do list; there is no set order. It could be a list of ingredients or a list of materials.

Teaching reading comprehension 79

(For example, a rescue team might take with them items such as *tents, tools, search dogs, gloves, a tin kettle for hot drinks, a first aid kit, food rations, water, helmet, visor, knee pads, boots, raincoat*, and *waterproof bag*.)

Web

An information web is about *one* thing. It could be about a person, place, animal, or object. The structure has a spider web appearance. There are sub-categories (e.g., features, location, diet). The web structure examples below are about animals.

Weave

This type of text compares two or more things, places, animals, people, or ideas (e.g., famous people, extinct animals, popular activities, well-known cities). It is an extension of the web; instead of describing one topic, it describes two or more topics. It is like weaving a carpet, interlocking strands of information that are similar and different. The lesson example below is a comparison of black, brown, and polar bears.

Sequence: linear, cause–effect, problem–solution, cyclical

Sequential texts present a step-by-step explanation of a situation or phenomenon, from first to last. Time is a key element in this text structure. The sequence could be linear (e.g., a biography), cause–effect (e.g., earthquake leading to destruction of houses), problem–solution (e.g., saving an historic home from redevelopment), or a cycle (e.g., life of a butterfly or the water cycle).

Steps 1, 2, …

Example lessons for web, weave, and sequence structures

Practice passages

Students need to focus on examples of different nonfiction texts. Appendix B has copies of example text passages and empty structure diagrams to use for practice. The notes below explain the example text structures.

Web structure for Snails article

"Have you ever wondered about the life of a snail? There are many unusual things to learn about them. Such as their diet, how they move, where they hide out in the garden, and other things."

"What we will do today is diagram the elements in this short article on Snails."

Note: The text on Snails is in Appendix B, Figure 6.10. Instruction ideas are in Table 6.2 and Figure 6.4 below.

Table 6.2 Lesson Plan: Snails

Lesson sequence	Content – What the teacher might say to students.	Possible student answers to questions asked by the teacher.
Opening	"What are snails? What do you already know about them?"	Snails are ubiquitous. They have a secret life. They live in the garden, have shells, hide under things.
Middle	Now break this text about snails into chunks of information and make a web structure. What categories will there be? (See completed diagram in Figure 6.4.)	What they look like. Where they live. What they eat.
Close	Is there anything else about snails?	They cannot hear. They live for seven years.
Extend	Use the web structure to write a summary of the Snails text. Use information from the web diagram to write the summary. Students write up a summary of the article on snails, to email a friend who does not know very much about snails. Further research: students find out more about snails either at the library or by searching the internet and add this to their summary.	

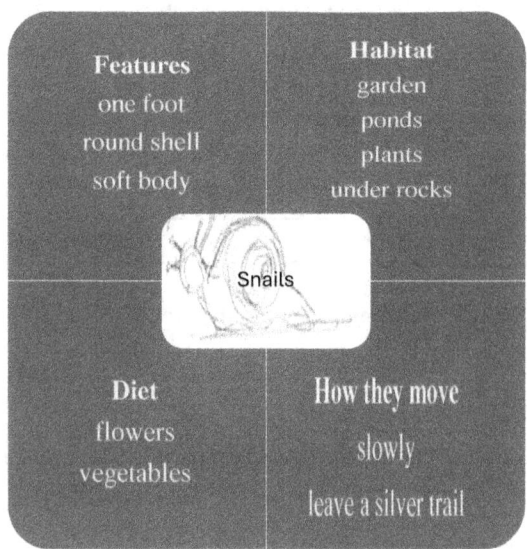

Figure 6.4 Web Structure: Snails.

Web structure for Dogs article

"Have you ever wondered what it would be like to own a dog? There are many things to think about such as their diet, where they are to live, and how to care for them. Dogs are a great friend to have, they are loyal and always are there to greet you, but they need care as well."

Teaching reading comprehension 81

"What we will do today is diagram the elements in this short article on Dogs."

Note: The text on Dogs is in Appendix B, Figure 6.11. Instruction ideas are in Table 6.3 and Figure 6.5 below.

Table 6.3 Leson Plan: Dogs

Lesson sequence	Content – What the teacher might say to students.	Possible student answers to questions asked by the teacher.
Opening	What do you already know about dogs?	Dogs are intelligent, social animals known for loyalty, companionship, playfulness, and their roles as human helpers.
Middle	Now break this text about dogs into chunks of information and make a web structure. the categories are –	Features of dogs – Caring for a dog – Diet – Other things about dogs –
Close/ Extend	Extension question: "Are there any other things about dogs?" Use the web structure to write a summary of the Dogs text. Use information in the web diagram when writing the summary.	"Dogs can only see black and white; some dogs can be vicious."

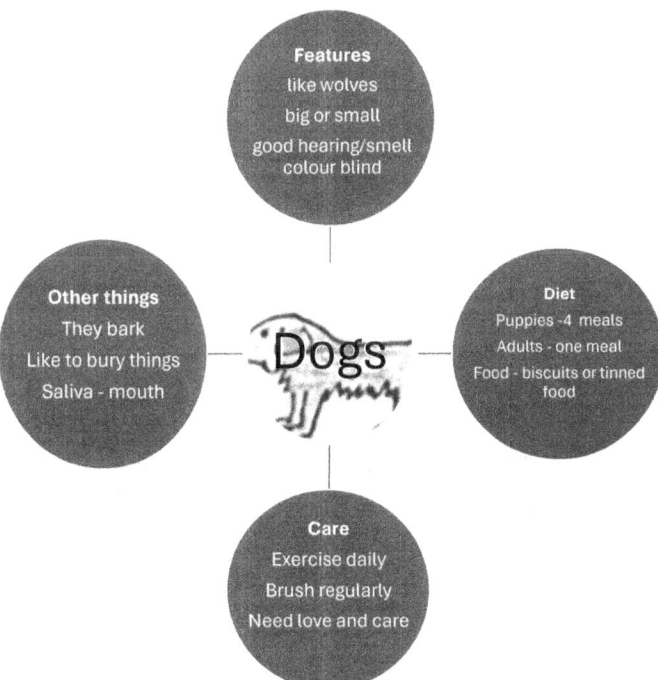

Figure 6.5 Web Structure: Dogs.

Web structure for Cockroaches article

"Have you ever wondered why cockroaches seem to be everywhere and there is no easy way to get rid of them? The answer goes back many millions of years. Cockroaches are *survivors*."

"What we will do today is diagram the elements in this short article on Cockroaches." [We will use a web structure for this. It is the best structure because it is the structure to use when reading and writing about one thing.]

Note: The text on cockroaches is in Appendix B, Figure 6.12. Instruction ideas are below in Table 6.4 and Figure 6.6.

Table 6.4 Lesson Plan: Cockroaches

Lesson sequence	Content – What the teacher might say to students.	Possible student answers to questions asked by the teacher.
Opening	What do you already know about cockroaches?	They are ubiquitous. They have a long history. Can live anywhere.
Middle	Now break this text about cockroaches into chunks of information and make a web structure. What categories are there?	*Features* -*What they look like* *Habitat* - Where they live *Diet* - What they eat *Other things*
Close/ Extend	Is there anything else special about cockroaches? Use the web structure to write a summary of the Cockroaches text. Use information in the web diagram when writing the summary.	They can live without food for several weeks

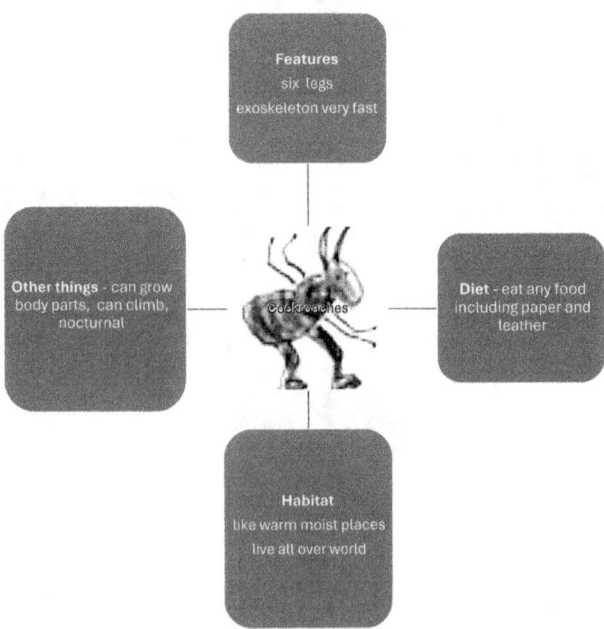

Figure 6.6 Web Structure: Cockroaches.

Teaching reading comprehension 83

The lesson plan in Table 6.4 will take the class through each element in the article's web structure.

Weave/Venn structure for Bears article

"Have you ever wondered how black, brown, and white bears are the same yet different? One difference is where they live, their environment. Animals live in or near places where they can find food."

"What we will do today is diagram the elements in this short article on the Bears."

Note: The text on Bears is in Appendix B, Figure 6.13. Instruction ideas are in Table 6.5 and Figure 6.7.

Table 6.5 Lesson Plan: Bears

Lesson	Content – What the teacher might say to students.	Possible student answers to questions asked by the teacher.
Opening	What do you know about bears?	"There are three kinds of bears: black, brown, and polar bears."
Middle	"Now break this text about black, brown, and white bears into chunks of information using a Venn structure, which weaves the information together."	(See the completed Venn diagram in Figure 6.7.)
Close	Is there anything else about bears? Use the Venn structure to write a summary of the Bears text. Use information from the weave diagram to write the summary.	Black and brown bears both like honey.

Figure 6.7 Weave/Venn Structure: Bears.

Sequence structure for poverty cycle article

"Have you ever wondered why poorer families find it hard to become better off or even rich? There is a word to explain this: the poverty cycle. This phenomenon has a sequence structure."

"What we will do today is diagram the elements in this short article on the Poverty Cycle." The text is in Appendix B, Figure 6.14, and instruction ideas are in Table 6.6 and Figure 6.8.

Table 6.6 Lesson Plan: Poverty Cycle

Lesson	Content – What the teacher might say to students.	Possible student answers to questions asked by the teacher.
Opening	What can you tell me about these poverty cycle? What kind of text is it? How do you know? I will read you a short article on the systemic forces that create the poverty cycle.	It is about how many families find it hard to escape poverty. Sequence. It is step-by-step
Middle Extension	Now we will break the text into chunks of information and make a sequence structure. Write a summary of the article. Use the text structure diagram to sum up the poverty cycle.	[See the diagram in Figure 6.8]

Figure 6.8 Sequence Structure: Poverty Cycle.

6.5 Persuasion text

A persuasion text makes a claim and has arguments to support the claim. An example of this kind of text would be an article on climate change that made the claim that cutting down rainforests endangered the climate. The arguments to support the claim were that loss of rain forest will cause weather patterns to change and there would be global warming, droughts, and loss of unique animals and plants.

A persuasive text can provide information for or against an idea or both. The information in support of the idea may be 100% positive (e.g., a product advertisement). Alternatively, information may be negative (e.g., in a debate where one side opposes an idea or action).

The persuasive text considers the audience, predicts how well the audience will receive the ideas, and understands the need for the audience to be convinced. The persuasive text is aware that the audience might disagree, that opinions will differ, that the audience is open to different ideas, and one needs to present ideas that the audience will accept or at least consider.

An example might be the issue of whether to keep small schools or close them. The persuasive text may say that big schools are impersonal, that closing a small school in a country area will threaten the town, and that workers will have to move away.

6.6 Students with comprehension difficulties

These students may be struggling to understand text that contains unfamiliar vocabulary, ambiguous sentences that need unravelling, sentences that do not link very well to each other, text that requires general or subject knowledge they do not have, and other things. The text may be too difficult to decode accurately and quickly. All these factors will interfere with comprehension.

What not to do

A first impulse may be to put the struggling students into small groups to tackle easier text and do easier questions. It seems an obvious solution, to give them an easier text to read, but this does nothing to help them develop new strengths in reading comprehension.

What to do

A better solution is to include them with the rest of the class during regular instruction on text structure and on test-taking strategies. Even if the text is hard to read by themselves, the class could read it chorally, so no one is embarrassed. This is of more value than being put into a low group.

The opportunity to study the same texts as the rest of the class adds value. It gives these students control, a sense that they are part of the class, not a special case; it does not make them think they are not good enough, that they are dumb.

Deconstructing a text, working out its structure in class, and becoming "savvy" about test-taking skills are important skills for all students to know about, not just the top readers.

Text structure learning gives all students a way to break text information into manageable pieces. It gives them a way to diagram text, to create a product that is their own and that is a summary of the key points of a text.

This is far more helpful than assigning them "easy" books to read. Learning about text structure is necessary for all, not just some.

A lesson for the whole class, regardless of comprehension level, is more equitable. It creates a level playing field. Students who run into difficulty with comprehension should not be segregated into low-ability groups. They do not need "high interest" easy text. This only increases the good–poor reader gap.

Instead, they should cover the same material as the rest of the class and learn the same techniques as the rest of the class. It is better for the whole class to tackle difficult text and for the lesson to encourage all students to face the same challenges.

Some might query this, asking whether the focus should be on giving them tasks they can enjoy, that are within their decoding ability. Yes, decoding is important, but it should not replace comprehension learning. The class can all benefit from decoding instruction, from learning basic rules to more complex rules, but this is a separate literacy topic, to be done at a different time. The literate classroom is not a mirror of society. It does not have the rich and the poor. It does not have big books for some and little books for others. It is a group of critical learners.

This is the focus of the present book, that students need to focus on all key areas, not just some. They need to upskill themselves in decoding, comprehension, vocabulary, writing, and spelling. All these topics need a space in the curriculum and the school day.

6.7 Conclusion

Reading comprehension depends on knowledge. Students who know more will understand more and understand it better.

On the other hand, many students may think the topic is too hard when in fact there is much information in the text that will enable them to answer the test questions. Students often get scared off because they lack text structure strategies for learning. With text structure you have a basic map that demands information from the text. This is critical information for answering test questions in exams. Students need to know that nearly all the information is in the text if they just look for it.

Are the words hard? Then reach for the dictionary and look for context clues in the text. The text will help with vocabulary and ideas. These will enable them to answer the assigned comprehension questions.

Text structure knowledge helps the student to take the key points from a text and create a product, a diagram of the text.

Students can use the diagram to unpack the meaning of new text material. These strategies give them freedom to learn.

Students often give up too easily when they see a hard text. They should not give in. They must persevere. The text is the key. It has all the information they need; they just do not see it. When they learn the structure of texts, and how to diagram the structure, they will be able more easily to reconstruct text meaning.

Every text structure diagram is a product that the student can sell to the examiner or the reader. It is their work, their interpretation of the text. Students can put that product to use, in a writing exercise, giving a presentation. Even if they pin their diagram on the fridge at home, it will show what amazing things text structure strategies can achieve.

Appendix A:

Extension text structure activities

Activity 1: Web structure: Expository text

Rubber

When items made of rubber first came out, they were not well liked. People found that rubber products like toys and shoes turned brittle when it was cold and glue-like when it was hot. The storekeepers who had bought the rubber products had to bury piles of their new goods. Because people lost a lot of money, they became fed up with rubber.	Question: Why did people get fed up with rubber? A. They did not like it. B. They had to bury it. C. They lost a lot of money. D. It turned to glue. E. Stuck on footpath.

Activity 2: Story web: narrative

Church

The minister lit the furnace in his little church so it would be warm for choir practice that evening. Then he went home for dinner. The singers usually arrived promptly, but for one reason or another everyone was late. Just at the time choir practice usually started, the church blew up with a terrible roar. Gas had filtered into the furnace through a broken pipe. As each of the choir members looked at the ruins they wondered, "Was my tardiness tonight an act of God?"	Question: Why did the church blow up? A. Someone blew it up. B. The minister lit the furnace. C. Some gas got into the furnace. D. Choir sang. E. Tardiness.

Activity 3: Sequence structure: Expository text

Scratched knee

Many years ago, a young girl fell and scratched her knee. At first, she paid little attention to the scratch, but after a few days she could no longer ignore it. Her shoe had to be cut away from her foot. Her leg and foot were very swollen. She had such a high fever that her mother called the doctor. "The leg will have to be taken off," said the doctor but the girl and her brother insisted that the leg be saved. Through courage and determination, her leg was saved. Today she can still stand on her own two legs.

Question: Why did the girl's shoe have to be cut away from her foot?
A. Foot was too big for the shoe.
B. Fever.
C. Foot was sore.
D. Leg and foot were very swollen.
E. Doctor said to.

Activity 4: Story web: Narrative text

Two crows

At the local lake, an angler was fishing, using minnows for bait. Two pet crows helped. They pulled on the lines with their beaks. And they put their foot on the line to stop it slipping back into the water. Because the crows were smart, they got a meal. So did the clever angler!

Question: Why did the birds receive a dinner?
A. They were very sneaky.
B. They tricked the angler.
C. They ate the bait.
D. They caught one fish apiece.
E. They were smart.

Activity 5: Sequence structure: Expository

Skin diving

I really think my friend Jody has courage. Yesterday they were having a lesson in skin diving. Because it was Jody's first try, Jody was frightened. Slowly, Jody went into the water. Jody looked worried, with a face that was pale, but Jody followed every order perfectly. The diving coach praised Jody for bravery and skill.

Question: Why was Jody frightened?
A. Fell into the water.
B. Was Jody's first try.
C. Did not know how to swim.
D. The coach praised Jody.
E. Jody has courage.

Activity 6: Sequence structure: Farming rice

Farming rice

A long time ago, many farmers grew their own rice to live on. Most people who bought this rice didn't know how much effort it took to grow and harvest it. The farmers had to start work very early in the morning. They used curved tools called sickles to cut the rice plants. After that, they tied the rice into bundles and left them in the fields to dry for a few days. Then they had to beat the bundles on something hard to shake the grains of rice free. Even though the farmers worked very hard, they didn't earn much money.

Question:
The farmers did not make much money despite what fact?
A. They worked very hard.
B. It was not good rice.
C. There was no one to buy it.
D. Rice is not needed so much.
E. It is too slow.

Appendix B:

Articles and text structure diagrams

"Hare and Tortoise"

Hare was fast at writing stories and could finish a story in class in 2–3 minutes. Everyone was amazed and asked how Hare did it. "It is my genius shining through. I am a phenomenon. My family is talented, but I am the best of them all," boasted Hare. "Look at how fast I write and then look at how slow Tortoise is at writing, always last to finish, plodding along, writing about one word an hour. I am the best writer in this town."

Tortoise did not like the way Hare made fun of slow writers and challenged Hare to a writing competition. "What, sleepy Tortoise beating me at writing, you must be dreaming. It would be embarrassing to compare me with such a slowcoach."

Tortoise stood on tip toe and said, "I can beat you, let's race and see who wins." Hare started writing like a tornado. Just then the phone went, and it was Hare's mum. She asked, "Do you have time to talk?" "Yes, mum, I've got a job on at the moment, but I am way ahead, so I can talk." Meanwhile, Tortoise, letter by letter, word by word, kept writing. By the time Hare finished talking to mum, Tortoise was close to finishing the story. Hare wrote as fast as lightning, but it was too late. Tortoise had won. Everyone in the class cheered. Tortoise grinned with pride. "Slow and steady wins the race," Tortoise beamed.

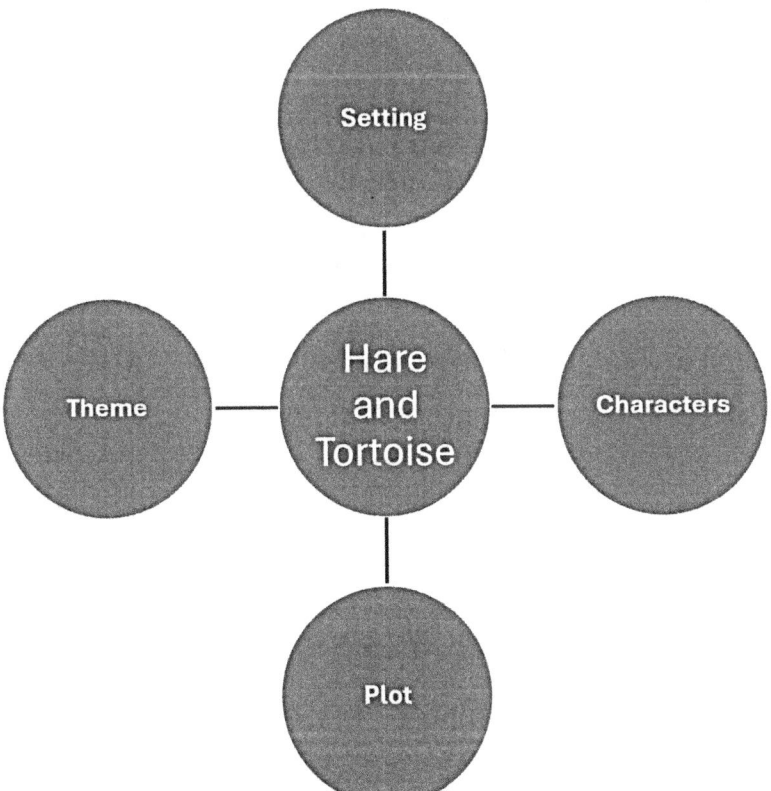

Figure 6.9 Story: "Hare and Tortoise": Blank Copy

Snails
Snails are animals. They live and breathe. They have a soft body and a round shell that covers and protects it. Snails only have one foot. It is a muscle to help them move. Snails can live in the garden or in ponds or on plants. They live under rocks to keep their wetness. They move slowly and leave a silver trail. They eat plants, especially vegetables and flowers. They can see through their antennae. They live for up to seven years.

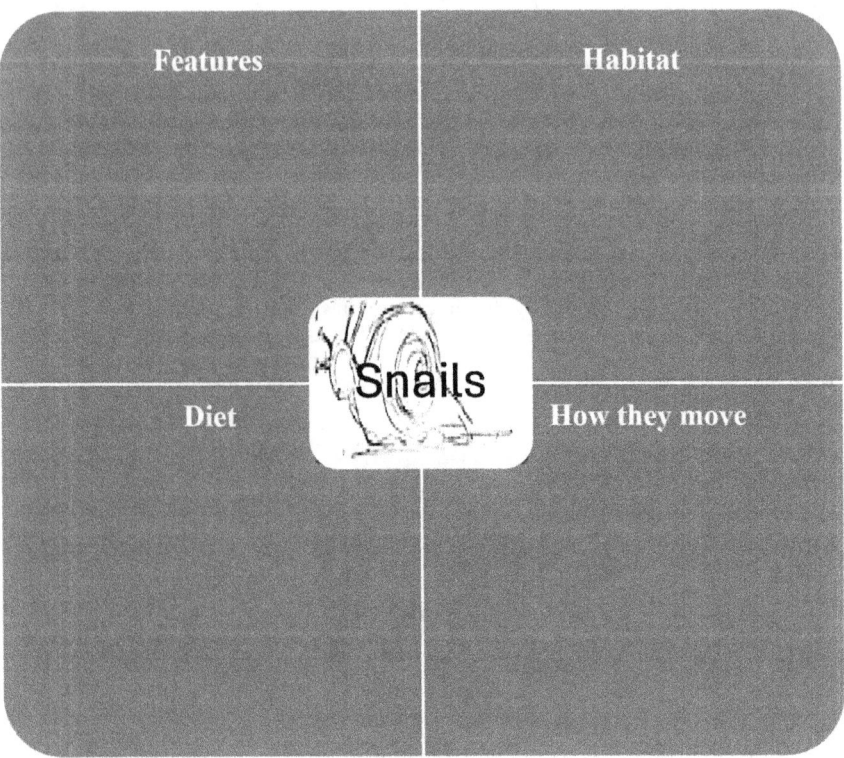

Figure 6.10 Web Structure: Snails Text: Blank Copy.

Dogs
There are different breeds of dogs. There are small dogs like the Pekingese and Chihuahua, and there are big dogs like Great Danes. A dog needs love and care all its life. A puppy needs training to be clean and obedient. We can do this by praising it for doing the right thing at the right time in the right place. Dogs need exercise to stay healthy. Dogs need lots of exercise. You need to keep them on a leash when out walking, in case they fight with other dogs or bite someone. If your dog gets sick you must take it to a vet. Dogs like company. They like to play. Brushing is a good to take away fleas and ticks. A puppy needs four meals a day; an adult dog needs only one meal of dry or canned food a day. Avoid giving too much meat or too many scraps from the table. Give plenty of fresh water. Most dogs like to sleep in a box or basket with paper lining or a blanket. Outdoors, dogs need a doghouse for sleeping. A small dog can live up to 15 years, but a big dog like a St Bernard or Great Dane about 8 or 9 years. When a dog is hot it does not sweat, it pants, saliva comes out of its mouth to cool it down. Dogs like to bury things. They hear and smell better than humans. A dog's eyes see movement but do not see pigmentation. Things look grey or blue to them. They bark if a stranger comes near, but their bark can be friendly. They are related to the wolf family.

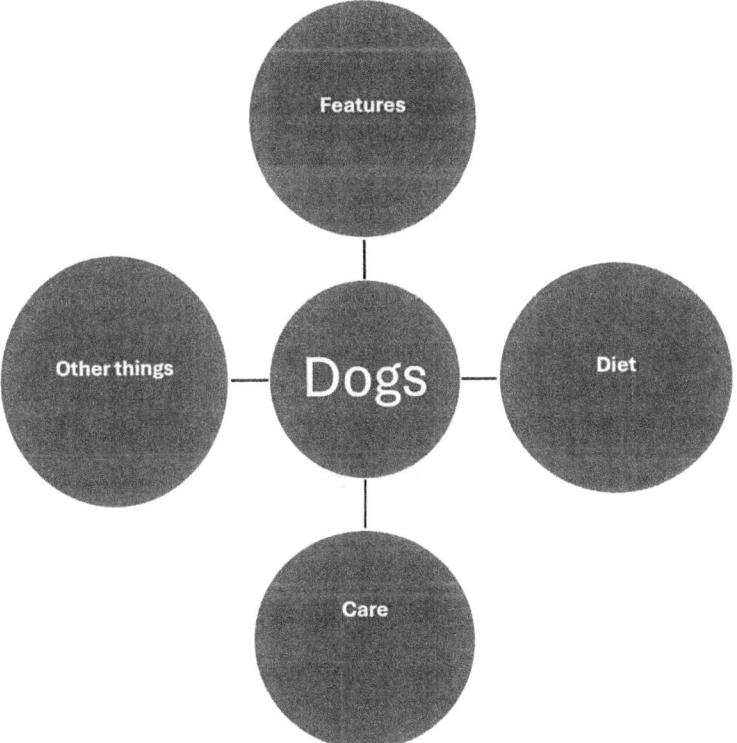

Figure 6.11 Web Structure: Dogs: Blank Copy.

Cockroaches

Where do cockroaches come from? Cockroaches have a long history. They go back millions of years. They vary dramatically in size. The German cockroach is very small about one cm. In contrast, the giant cockroach is nine times that length. Cockroaches have six legs and an exoskeleton for protection. When needed, they grow new body parts. They are nocturnal, which means they come out at night. They are fast and can climb. They can squeeze through the smallest gap. They can go without food for a long time, weeks on end. They will eat anything, even non-foods like paper and leather. Cockroaches like a warm, moist environment. There are thousands of different cockroaches across the world.

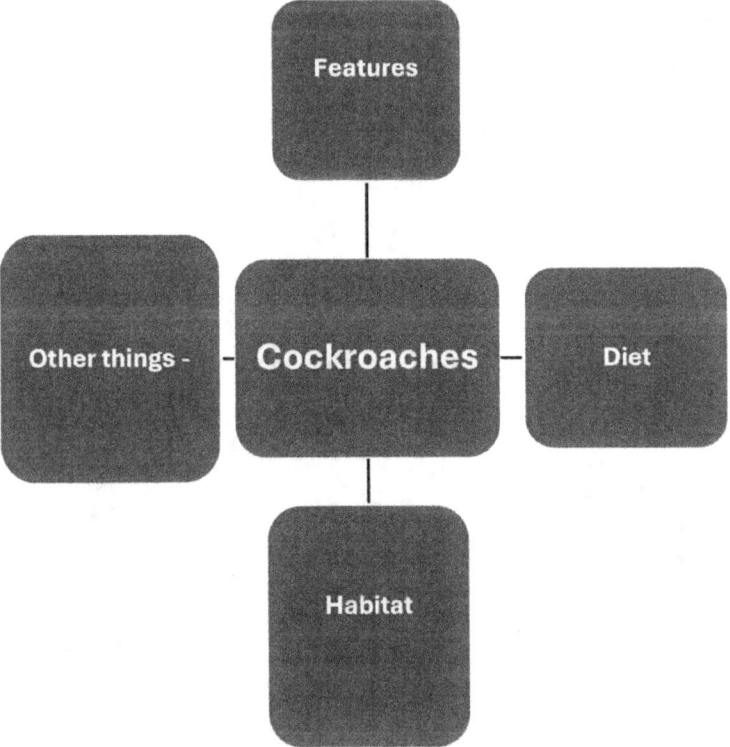

Figure 6.12 Web Structure: Cockroaches: Blank Copy.

Black, brown, and polar bears
Black bears live in plant-rich places, like forests. They live in North American forests. They are small, can climb trees, and they mostly eat berries and fruit.
Brown bears live where they can hunt prey, in forests, mountains, and grasslands. Brown bears, such as grizzlies, live in North America and Eurasia. They are large, eat plants, meat, and salmon.
Polar bears split from brown bears about 500,000 years ago. They adapted to an icy climate. They live in the Arctic. They are the largest bear, have white fur for camouflage, rely on seals for food. They eat meat because that is all that is available.
Black and brown bears hibernate in winter. Polar bears have a year-long source of food but will hibernate if the ice melts. All bears have one thing in common: they have adapted to their environment.

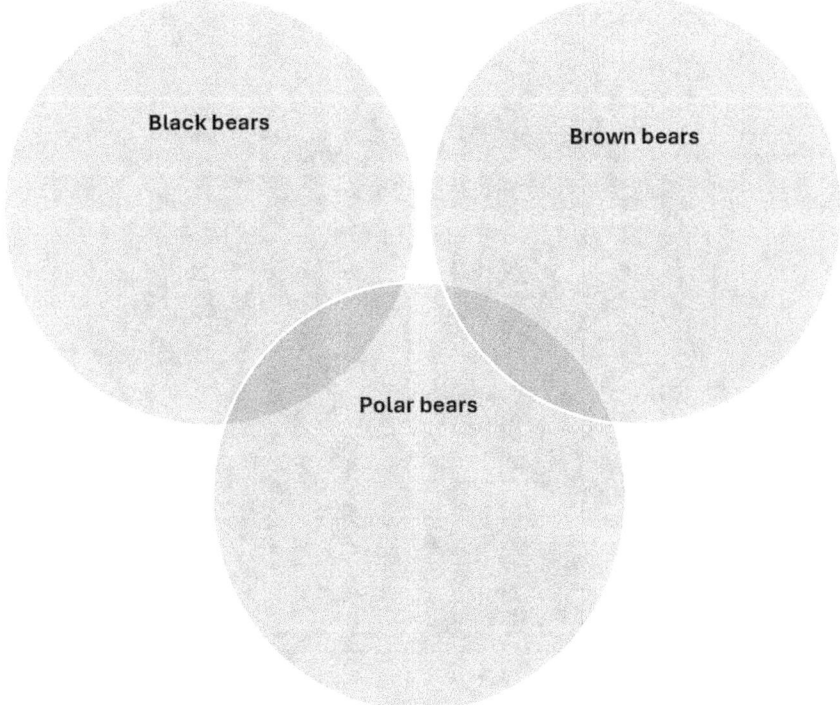

Figure 6.13 Venn Weave Structure: Bears: Blank Copy.

94 *Teaching Literacy Effectively in Modern Classroom for Ages 9–12*

Poverty cycle

The poverty cycle refers to the systemic barriers that can make it difficult for families to escape poverty across generations. While families face limited access to quality education, healthcare, and safe housing due to low income, people often show remarkable resilience and determination. With the right support and opportunities, it is possible to break the cycle and create pathways to upward mobility. Oprah Winfrey grew up in poverty and, through a combination of education, persistence, and unique opportunities, became a media star. Her story is inspiring, but it is important to recognize that people face systemic barriers that make escaping poverty challenging, even with hard work and determination. Oprah now uses her platform to help others overcome obstacles.

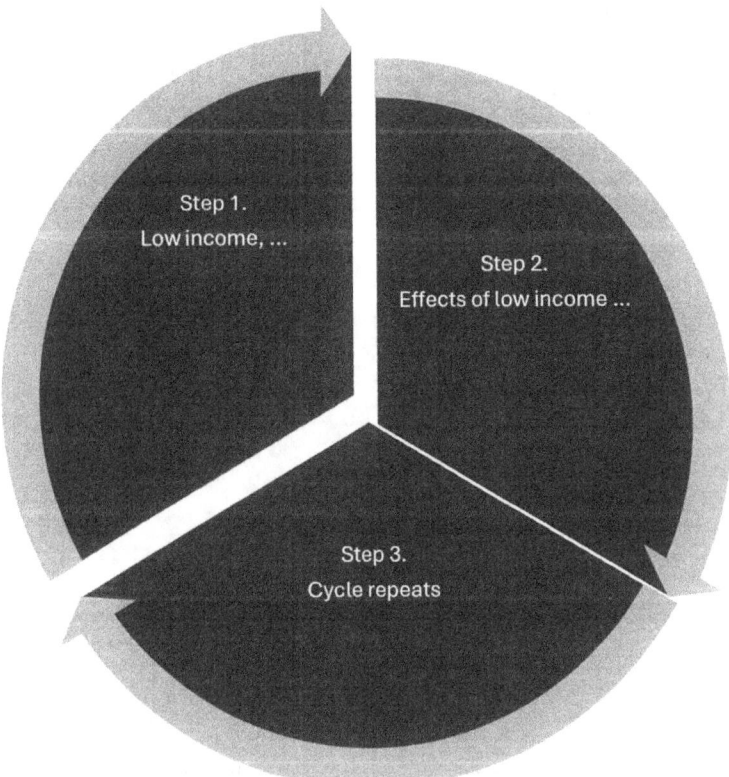

Figure 6.14 Cyclical Text Structure: Poverty Cycle: Blank Copy.

Part 3
Reading vocabulary

Chapter 7, *Vocabulary: What is it?*, explains the science of vocabulary, whether goldfish can sing, wide versus deep vocabulary, and why English never said "no" to a word.

Chater 8, *Assessing vocabulary*, discusses why students' vocabulary may be in decline, explains norm referenced tests, cautions not to label students, and gives examples of 20 literal, figurative, and multi-meaning terms students need to know.

Chapter 9, *Teaching vocabulary*, covers the Big 7 of concept mapping (web, weave, sequence, thermometer), context clues, dictionary/thesaurus, structural analysis, keyword method, detective bookmarks, and word hunting.

7 Vocabulary
What is it?

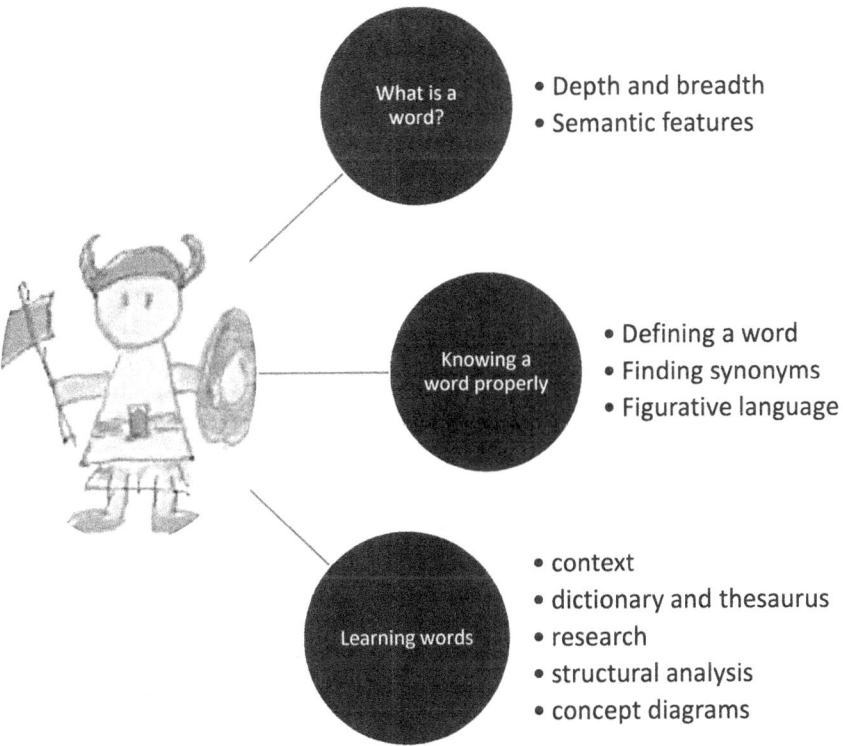

Figure 7.1 Overview of Chapter 7.

7.1 Introduction

> If we're serious about our marks, we have to go and find a better textbook ourselves.

Students in every classroom struggle with textbooks that to them are as clear as mud. Many seek out better books, to step out of the seemingly byzantine texts they are reading, that seem to them overloaded with arcane but necessary vocabulary, that seem a major hurdle for them to overcome. Students are constantly asked to learn new words and they often do learn them but how well do they understand the nature of words, how they work, how the mind stores them in memory?

Words have two dimensions: breadth and depth. Breadth is knowing one aspect of a word; depth is knowing its many aspects, the subtleties of its meaning, and how to use it in writing. Vocabulary is important for reading and writing.

When words in text are unfamiliar to the student, they become a bottleneck to comprehension. Students need a depth and breadth of vocabulary.

Many students are unaware of the structure of words. They have interesting, but technically inaccurate understandings of new words that come up in their studies. How can we teach them effective vocabulary learning strategies that will be more productive? This chapter explains the nature of words, how they work, and how best to store their meanings in memory.

The topics for this chapter are

- Words can have many faces
- Theory – what is a word?
- Knowing a word properly
- Are some words more precise than others?
- Can students significantly increase vocabulary?

7.2 Words can have many faces

In *Hard Times*, the school principal Gradgrind famously said, "Now, what I want is, Facts ... Facts alone are wanted in life. Plant nothing else and root out everything else." And "You can only form the mind of reasoning animals upon Facts: nothing else will ever be of any service to them."

Well, facts are important, especially for detectives solving cases, but facts are not all there is to knowing the meanings of words. Words have other aspects as well. Words have a literal definition, but words are more than this. Words can be metaphors and idioms; they can have multiple meanings.

Words do mean something. When Alice asked Humpty Dumpy, "Must a name mean something?" Humpty Dumpty answered, "When I use a word... it means just what I choose it to mean – neither more nor less." There is some truth in Humpty Dumpty's way of thinking about words, words mean something, but they can mean several things.

The dictionary and the thesaurus give facts about words (i.e., concise definitions of words), but they tell us other things as well, including synonyms for words and figurative aspects; for example, an in-depth meaning for *dog* might include

- a factual definition (e.g., *a dog is a member of the wolf family, carnivorous, barks, often kept as a pet*)
- synonyms (e.g., *canine, puppy, hound*)
- idioms or slang (e.g., *dog's breakfast*: untidy, a mess)
- metaphors (e.g., *thrown to the dogs*: abandoned, left exposed to harm, letting someone else take the blame; *treated like a dog*: treated badly; *turn dog*: turn traitor)
- proverbs (e.g., *let sleeping dogs lie*: avoid interfering; *every dog has its day*: everyone has luck at certain times)
- personal knowledge about dogs (e.g., *We have a dog and he is a beshonfrez, his name is Pucy, he is very friendly and playful. I love my Dog Puce.*)

By incrementally building meanings for words, especially in-depth meanings, the student creates a detailed and nuanced personal vocabulary.

7.3 Theory

Semantic features are a well-known way to differentiate the literal meanings of words. Studies have identified distinctive features. The features use plus/minus signs, called markers. The markers can distinguish between words. Not all words have the same features.

A plus/minus feature might be animateness (i.e., + alive, – not alive). A *fish* is alive, so it would have a plus marker for animateness, but a *rock* is inanimate, so it would have a minus marker. Other distinctive features include, is it human (yes, no), does it move (yes, no), is it sentient (yes, no), is it solid (yes, no) (see Table 7.1)? These features can distinguish between a fish and a rock.

Using this coding, a student could say *the fish died*, because a fish is animate +, but if they said *the rock died*, it sounds unusual, because a rock is inanimate. They could say that their computer *died* but that is more a metaphor.

If we say *the goldfish is a rock star*, it is unusual because *goldfish* has a negative marker for the semantic feature *human*. Goldfish are animate + but they are not human.

Some argue that these features can tell the speaker when to use a word and in what context. Humpty Dumpty might not agree with the idea of distinctive features telling us what words mean and when we can use them in sentences, and that is fair enough. To specify the meanings of all words is complex, and there is still much to learn about how to define words (Harley, 2017). Semantic

Table 7.1 A Semantic Feature Comparison of Goldfish and Rock

	Human	Animate	Moves	Sentient	Solid
Goldfish	–	+	+	+	–
Rock	–	–	–	–	+

feature theory does show, though, that there may be core features that distinguish words in terms of meaning.

7.4 Can students learn enough words to do well in exams and norm-referenced tests?

There are so many words in English. Learning new vocabulary, even if done every day, may not be enough to make a measurable difference to overall vocabulary knowledge. This is not being negative but realistic. There are so many words to learn. Estimates vary but some estimates are that students need to know at least 6,000 word-families, or 36,000 words, to understand their texts (Nation, 2020). Other estimates are that students may need to know more than 80,000 different words (Juel & Minden-Cupp, 1999).

Effects of vocabulary lessons

Reviews of studies on the effectiveness of vocabulary lessons show that they are not very effective. Students do learn the words in the lesson, but this does not transfer to learning new words or to results on norm-referenced tests and exams (Elleman et al., 2009).

Even with dedicated instruction, students can learn only 300–400 new words during the school year (Cervetti et al., 2023). With so few words learned during the school year, it is not enough to be effective on norm-referenced tests and exams.

Effects of extensive reading

Can students build their personal vocabulary through extensive reading? Some believe that extensive reading is important for gaining new vocabulary because surveys show the best readers read many more books than other readers and have a much larger vocabulary. This suggests that extensive reading builds vocabulary.

Is this true? Not everyone agrees (Chetail, 2024). The research on links between extensive reading and vocabulary are all correlational, and a correlation of X and Y does not necessarily mean that X causes Y.

It is a conundrum that students find it hard to learn new vocabulary. Studies show that most readers learn only about five to 10 out of every 100 new words they come across in reading. Poor readers learn even fewer. One reason to explain this may be cognitive; it is cognitively hard to learn new words. A second reason may be that, when reading, students focus more on overall comprehension, not on learning unfamiliar words.

Learning new words is hard for students to do, but does this mean it is better for students, especially those not reading to their potential, to read easy books? Maybe. If the goal is to improve their decoding skills, then, yes, read decodable books about *Roy in Troy*.

But it is not a good idea for the lowest group of readers to learn new vocabulary this way, because easy books consist of easy words students already know; there are no unfamiliar words in those books. The poor readers in the class need a huge vocabulary, too. Giving them easy books is not a solution. It will make things worse.

The solution is to give these students hard books but read the words to them. Read the book to the whole class. When a hard term or expression pops up, the class works out the meaning. Everyone gets the same lesson. Everyone learns new words. It is a win-win for all students, not just some.

7.5 Where words come from

The vocabulary of English is huge, with more than half a million words. It is important to think about where words came from because if students understand the Story of English (as already discussed in Chapter 1), they can understand words better. They will understand why there are so many words and why it is a big job to learn them. It is not something that happens overnight. It takes persistent work, thinking about words and what they mean.

English vocabulary comes from not just one language but many. The British Isles were subject to numerous invasions, the invaders each time bringing with them new languages. English has been called the language of invasion.

Another factor explaining the growth of English is that it was allowed to grow freely. English never said 'no' to a word. This extensive borrowing explains how English has so many words.

English has borrowed many words from Latin (e.g., *obloquy, alibi, agenda*), Greek (e.g., *chameleon*), French (e.g., *emotion*), Inuit (e.g., *igloo*), Italian (e.g., *volcano, rocket*), Arabic (e.g., *alcohol, magazine*), Dutch (e.g., *golf*), Spanish (e.g., *vanilla, mosquito*), American Indian (e.g., *potato, chocolate*), and Hawaiian (e.g., *ukulele*).

7.6 Conclusion

Students need a breadth and depth of vocabulary. The books they read at ages 9–12 have many unfamiliar and technical words. Students need to know what these words mean and be able to define them well.

All students have their own voice and their own ideas, but they need a depth of vocabulary to understand the meaning of what they read. They need a rich vocabulary to express their ideas in a precise way in writing.

Students, when they write, need to ask themselves, "Is this the right word?" In reading, they need to ask, "Why is the author using this word? What are the implications?" Students must have a way with words, to understand fully what the author of a text means and, in writing, to use vocabulary in a precise and imaginative way to communicate their thoughts.

8 Assessing vocabulary

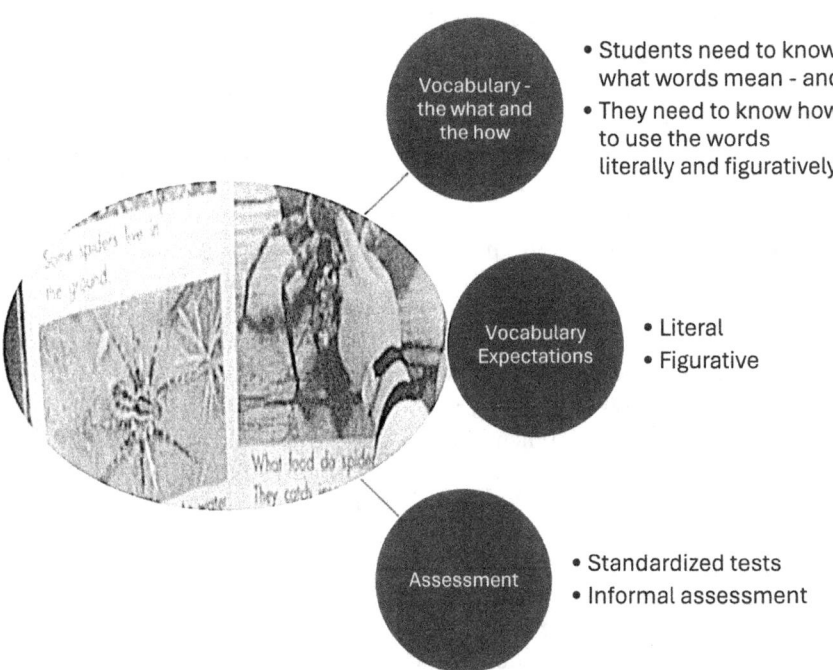

Figure 8.1 Overview of Chapter 8.

8.1 Introduction

> If the teacher's speaking to me and using hard words ... I just don't know what they're saying, what they're talking about, but just listen and pretend that I know what they're saying and all that ...

There is more to vocabulary assessment than testing. Most vocabulary tests check breadth of vocabulary. On the other hand, depth of understanding is

DOI: 10.4324/9781003130789-11

also important, including student knowledge of literal and figurative aspects of words.

We should assess vocabulary. It is important to know what the statistics say. We need to know the range of vocabulary in the classroom because we can plan better lessons. It is just that we must be careful about data interpretation, to avoid putting students into boxes.

A news report said that students in a low-income part of town, had been tested and found to have a developmental language age of three. Were these children deficient in language? Of course not. Some may read the news report and think that poor children have "lesser" language, but this is not the case. In all communities, students learn language in a way that suits that community. It is a working language. It works for them. It may not work for a norm-referenced test, but it is a functional language. Their language is not "lesser".

Data from tests say what is but such data do not say anything about potential to learn. It is the interpretation of the scores that matters.

The chapter will cover the following topics:

- Curriculum expectations
- Norm-referenced assessment
- Informal assessment

8.2   Curriculum expectations

Some national survey statistics suggest that student vocabulary knowledge is declining (Harris, 2024). It is not clear why this is so. Is it that students spend too much time on social media? There may be reasons other than social media, but statistics suggest some cause for concern.

If this is the case, then assessing vocabulary is important. It is helpful to know where each student is at. It gives direction as to lessons needed.

What are reasonable expectations of students in terms of vocabulary knowledge? National curriculum documents (e.g., *Literacy Progressions*) give some direction as to what students need to know. Looking at the documents, the benchmarks seem to be that students must have a *breadth* of vocabulary (i.e., know a lot of words) and a *depth* of vocabulary (i.e., know the words in depth). This includes knowledge of literal meanings, figurative meanings, and multiple meanings. In the *Progressions* for vocabulary, the following receive a mention:

Literal meaning
- Morphology: prefixes and suffixes (e.g., *help* [base word] + *less* [suffix])
- Word origins: etymology
- Synonyms, or nuanced vocabulary (e.g., *discouraged, downcast, let down, deflated*)
- Antonyms, or opposites of words (e.g., *sad* is opposite of *happy*)

Figurative language
- Metaphor
- Simile
- Onomatopoeia
- Hyperbole
- Pun
- Idiom
- Euphemism
- Allusion

Multiple meaning
- Homonyms (e.g., *right, bat, mean*)
- Homophones (e.g., *there/their, know/no*)
- Homographs (e.g., *bass*)

8.3 Norm-referenced assessment

Norm-referenced vocabulary tests offer a snapshot of a student's language at a particular moment.

Labels like *above average* or *below average* can have unintended consequences, influencing how students see themselves and how others see them. After all, a student's language is tied to their personal identity and culture (Cushing, 2023, 2024). Interpreting test scores demands sensitivity.

In the *PAT Vocabulary* Test, the student reads a target word in sentence context and selects the correct meaning from several options. This test requires decoding skill to read the words in the test.

Some students are not fluent in decoding, e.g., dyslexia. This will affect their ability to take a regular vocabulary test.

An alternative is *PAT: Listening Comprehension*. In this test, the student listens to the text and the questions read aloud. The items include short stories and extracts from novels, poetry, and nonfiction. The test is more general than vocabulary, but vocabulary knowledge is an important part.

Another test to consider is *The British Picture Vocabulary Scale* or *BPVS* which is a test of receptive vocabulary. It does not require the student to decode the test words. The examiner asks the student to point to a picture that has the same meaning as the test word.

8.4 Informal assessment

Informal assessment of vocabulary examines student understanding of literal meanings of words, figurative meanings, and multiple meanings.

Literal or denotative meaning

Literal meanings of words are like dictionary definitions. Literal meaning is the generally understood meaning of a word. It does not involve any extra interpretation or inference. Literal meaning is useful for precision and clarity.

Dictionary definition

The dictionary is a main source for finding the literal meanings of words. Another source is the thesaurus, which can give synonyms/antonyms for words (e.g., *new, novel, original, fresh, modern, recent*). The internet can also quickly access literal meanings for words.

The literal meaning of a word in memory is like a dictionary definition. A dictionary definition usually has a consistent pattern; that is, a thing *is* something *for* doing something.

If you apply the pattern to a word, you get a definition. For example:

- A *hammer* is a *tool* for *pounding* nails.
- A *foramen magnum* is the *opening in the skull* through which the *lower brain exits to become the spine*.

Synonyms/Antonyms

Words can also have synonyms with the same or similar meanings. Synonyms of a word are different in nuance but have the same core meaning; for example, *walk* has a core meaning of movement and so do its synonyms like *saunter, trudge, stroll, wobble, teeter, stride*, and *ambulate*.

In certain contexts, synonyms may have a figurative aspect, but generally they are considered literal meanings. They can be defined in the dictionary. The synonym *saunter* for *walk* has a dictionary meaning the same as *walk* except that in addition it means a confident, casual, carefree way of walking.

Antonyms are words that have opposite meanings. Antonyms are not figurative language because they have a literal meaning. An antonym is a word that means the opposite of another word (e.g., the opposite of *discouraged* is *encouraged* or *heartened*).

Morphology

Morphology is the study of morphemes. A morpheme is a minimal unit of meaning in a word. English has many words with more than one morpheme. To work out their meanings, the student must engage in morphological analysis (i.e., unpack the meaning units).

There are two kinds of morphemes:

- A **free** morpheme is a word that can stand alone and has meaning. Words of Anglo-Saxon origin are usually free morphemes: they are real words (e.g., *tree* and *sheep* are free morphemes; they stand on their own as meaningful units.
- A **bound** morpheme is not a word on its own. It needs to be attached to other morphemes. In words of Latin origin, a root word can be bound (e.g., *-rupt*). Prefixes and suffixes are bound. They are not real words. They are added to root words. This is the structure of many words with Latin and Greek origins; they have a two- or three-part structure of

- prefix, which adds meaning (e.g., *pre-* means before, *dis-* means opposite or negative).
- root word (e.g., *rupt* or *scrib*), which is the core meaning of the word
- suffix, which changes word class, such as a verb to a noun or adjective. A suffix can add meaning. For example, *-ian*, *-or*, and *-ist* indicate that the word is not just a noun but a person who does something, as in *magician, physician, actor, inventor, dentist, activist, scientist,* or *artist*.

Figurative language

Figurative language is not meant to be taken literally. Instead of taking words at their exact, literal meaning, figurative language uses words to create a different interpretation, a new idea. It is using words in a non-literal way to create a certain effect or a deeper meaning. Examples of figurative language are metaphors, similes, personification, hyperbole, and idioms. They deviate from literal meaning to give a more nuanced or unexpected meaning.

An informal way to assess figurative knowledge is to go through examples and discuss them with students, what the different terms mean.

Similes

A simile compares one thing with another using *like* or *as*. Some everyday similes are

- *white as snow*
- *good as gold*
- *neat as a pin*
- *smooth as silk*
- *dry as a bone*
- *clear as mud*
- *blind as a brickbat*
- *cold as charity*
- *eat like a bird*
- *sing like an angel*

Similes can add nuances of meaning, comparing something with something else, using *like* or *as* (e.g., *the coat button shines like gold; the river is as dry as a bone*).

Metaphors

A metaphor is a figure of speech where the meaning is not literal. It compares two unlike things. For example, *fledgling writer* compares a young writer to a fledgling bird; *thundercloud eyebrows* suggests that the person is about to explode with anger; a *blanket of cloud* suggests a heavy covering of the sky with cloud, with limited visibility. It is not meant to be literal. It is a way to create a vivid or unusual image in the mind.

Sometimes a metaphor is not a metaphor; for example, *phosphorescent sea* is not strictly a metaphor because sometimes the sea does have a phosphorescent glow, due to certain marine organisms in it.

Examples of literary metaphors are

- *winter of our discontent* – from Shakespeare's *King Lear*
- *my salad days when I was green in judgement* – from Shakespeare's *Antony and Cleopatra*

Personification

Personification is giving human qualities to something not human (e.g., *the room was lonely, our bank account died*). These expressions are not meant to be taken literally. The expression *vengeful sea* is personification: it gives human qualities to the sea, depicting the sea as taking revenge on those who disrespect it.

Oxymoron

Joining together pairs of words that have opposite meanings, to create a striking or thought-provoking effect (e.g., *bittersweet, make haste slowly, cruel to be kind, jumbo shrimp, deafening silence*).

Hyperbole

Hyperbole is an intentional overstatement used for emphasis or effect (e.g., *slow as a snail, sugar kills, a film not to be missed, a must-read book*). Hyperbole is not meant to be taken literally.

Onomatopoeia

This is when words imitate the natural sound (e.g., *buzz, woof, meow, crunch, slurp*). Onomatopoeia is figurative because it adds to the literal meaning. It is not literal because it is not the real sound. It is figurative because it adds meaning; it creates a sound effect that increases the impact of the writing.

Idioms

Idioms are common expressions that do not have their literal meaning. Idioms do not mean what they literally say. They have a meaning different from the literal meaning. Idioms are often culturally specific. They are figurative expressions because they add vividness, emotion, and nuance.

Some examples
- *down in the dumps*: sad
- *cry wolf*: give a false warning of danger
- *drop in the bucket*: very small amount

- *not out of the woods yet*: still obstacles to overcome
- *blow the whistle*: tell on someone
- *given the cold shoulder*: not wanted
- *turn over a new leaf*: make a fresh start
- *storm in a teacup*: big fuss on a small matter
- *in a pickle*: in trouble
- *cat's paw*: used by another for their own ends
- *over the moon*: very happy
- *walk on eggshells*: try not to upset someone
- *read the riot act*: give a severe warning

Connotation

Connotation refers to emotion beyond the literal. It can be figurative language in certain contexts if it adds emotional meaning beyond the literal meaning; for example, *home* in a certain context has connotations of security and warmth that *house* does not.

Connotation can be very useful to convey additional meaning in certain contexts (e.g., *dry – parched; perspiring – sweltering; hungry – ravenous; eat – din; walk – trudge*).

Pun

A pun is a play on words, using the meaning of a word in an unusual way, often to make a joke (e.g., *born and bread in a bakery* plays on the double meaning of *bread/bred*).

Cliché

A cliché is an overused expression, not original. It has been used so many times it has lost its original impact. It is figurative language because it goes beyond the literal meaning (e.g., *as easy as pie; a walk in the park; beauty is skin deep*).

Paradox

A paradox is a statement that seems contradictory but reveals a deeper truth (e.g., *less is more, the only constant is change*). It is figurative language because it goes beyond the literal meaning.

Euphemism

Euphemisms are indirect, softer, more palatable ways of saying things rather than all-or-nothing, harsh, impolite expressions. They are to make the meaning more polite, less offensive, less controversial. It is figurative language because euphemisms are not the literal meanings (e.g., *needs improvement* instead of *fail*; *super energetic* instead of *hyper*; *passed away* instead of *died*; *pre-owned* for *second-hand*; *alternative facts* for *lies*; *financially disadvantaged* for *poor*).

Allusion

An allusion is indirectly referring to something that the audience will likely know about and will understand its implied meaning, such as *a Tik Tok moment* (fleeting, not a serious moment), or *a Taylor Swift writer* (creative, inventive, massively popular).

Rhetorical question

A rhetorical question is a figure of speech where you are not expecting an answer. It does not rely on the literal meaning of the words. Instead, the goal of the question is to create a dramatic effect or a deeper meaning. For example,

- *Who would have thought?*
- *How do you hold a moonbeam in your hand?*
- *What have the Romans ever done for us?*
- *Do you always watch for the longest day in the year and then miss it?*

Multiple meanings

Homonyms

Homonyms are spelled the same and sound the same and can have different meanings (e.g., *bank* to store money, *bank* of a river). Other examples: *can, ring, post, bark, club, top, mine, bar, green, note, sink, fly, train, watch, spring*.

Homographs

Homographs are spelled the same but do not sound the same and can have different meanings (e.g., *bass* – fish and *bass* – musical instrument).

Other examples: *wind-wind, sow-sow, bow-bow, tear-tear, lead-lead, present-present, row-row, contract-contract*.

Usually, sentence context will indicate which meaning to take as correct, as in the following examples:

Sentence context	Meaning
I *object* to taking a bus, it takes too long.	opposed to
The *object* is to win this game.	the aim
The photo was of an angler catching a *bass*.	fish
She plays the *bass* at music practice.	instrument

Homophones

Homophones sound the same but are not spelled the same and have different meanings (e.g., *no-know, eight-ate, aloud-allowed, meet-meat, acquiesce-aqueous, passed-past*).

Usually, sentence context indicates which meaning is correct, as in the following (correct meaning in italics):

Sentence context	Homophones
grown in the garden	carats *carrots*
sea food	muscle *mussel*
eats grass and has long ears	hair *hare*
needed to bake a cake	flower *flour*

8.5 Conclusion

This chapter started with a summary of vocabulary expectations at each age level. Norm-referenced tests do not usually indicate what students know and do not know. This is why informal assessments can reveal exactly what specific aspects of vocabulary students need to know.

This can be achieved gradually by covering curriculum expectations at each age level and checking whether students understand these requirements.

Assessing vocabulary, formally and informally, will indicate the range of vocabulary knowledge among students in the classroom. It gives a foundation to design lessons to extend current vocabulary knowledge.

When students have a grasp of *what* they are supposed to know in terms of vocabulary, and *how* to learn it, they are in a better position to use their vocabulary knowledge for reading and writing.

9 Teaching vocabulary

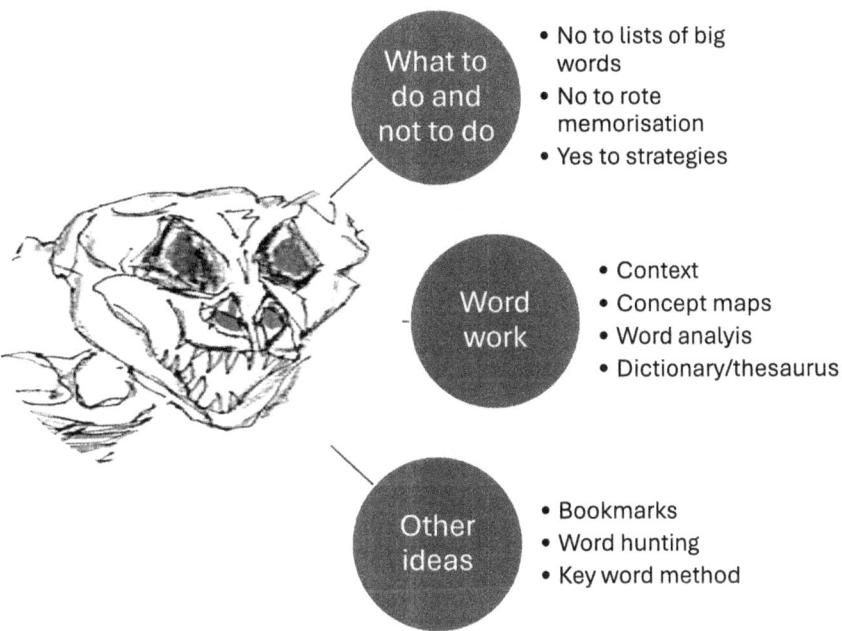

Figure 9.1 Overview of Chapter 9.

9.1 Introduction

> I would like to know how to teach one student in the classroom.

Raise your hand if this has happened to you. You've gone over the same vocabulary with students again and again… and yet they still forget it! Why does the instruction not stick? The answer is that students need a structured way of learning words. This means learning key strategies so students can build their

DOI: 10.4324/9781003130789-12

own vocabulary. It is not about learning words, there are too many words to learn in school. It is about learning *how* to learn words.

This chapter will cover the following topics

- Word work
- Keyword
- Method
- Bookmarks
- Word hunting

9.2 Word work

Strategy 1: Context clues

Text examples

The student comes across a new word in the text (e.g., *The Smith family are **peripatetic**. They travel a lot.*). The sentence context helps to clarify the meaning of *peripatetic*, which is moving from place to place, usually for short periods of time.

In the well-known novel, *Charlotte's Web*, the author used dialogue to clarify word meaning:

> "I was just thinking," said Charlotte, "that people are very **gullible**."
> "What does gullible mean?"
> "Easy to fool," said the spider.

Sometimes, it is better not to reach immediately for the dictionary but to see if context can help. Context can give clues to meaning, and if necessary, the dictionary can confirm the meaning.

Exam example

Comprehension tests in exams will give a passage to read and the student must work out the meaning of a specific word in the text. In one exam, the text read: *The quads handle almost everything but, like all machines, they have their **limitations**. With very low tyre pressure they can handle mushy snow but in soft powdery snow they can become bogged.*

The exam task was to decide which of the four options below was the best synonym for **limitations**:

expectations	purposes	specifications	shortcomings

The text information mentioned that the quad bike worked in certain conditions of mushy snow but not in others, like powdery snow. The student can use information in the text to determine that the correct synonym is *shortcomings*.

Strategy 2: Dictionary and thesaurus

Dictionary

In the example of *gullible*, the student could check the dictionary. The dictionary definition is "easily persuaded to believe something." It turns out that *gullible* is from French origins *guille* but the French word originally was from Latin, *gula*, meaning throat or gullet. In the 1500s, it gained the meaning of *deceive*.

Thesaurus

The thesaurus is a resource for finding synonyms of unfamiliar words. Possible synonyms for **gullible** are *over-trusting*, *easily deceived*, *naïve*, and *credulous*.

Synonyms from a thesaurus can help to reveal the meaning of a word (e.g., **conflagration**: blaze, fire, inferno; **condemnation**: disapproval, censure, reproach, castigation; **obloquy**: shame, humiliation, ignominy, stigma, vilification).

Strategy 3: Concept maps

Concept maps are ways to connect an unknown word to related words to glue the meaning of the unknown word into memory. Three concept map designs can help with this: the web, the weave/matrix, and the spectrum/thermometer.

Web - focus on one concept

The web (or concept wheel) is a summary of information about one vocabulary concept. It uses sub-categories: attributes, synonyms, and so on.

In Figures 9.2–9.5, there are web diagrams for the following focus words: *tiger, the state of California, fish,* and *chameleon*. In the cartoon classroom scene shown in Figure 9.2, the teacher links the word *tiger* to related words that could be linked to *tiger* in memory: superordinate (tiger is an animal), coordinate (it is a member of cat family), features (meat eater, has fur, and so on), and example (the Siberian tiger).

The class could do research to find other information about tigers to add to the web, e.g., tigers do not usually eat every day, they are an endangered species, their main enemies are illegal hunters and habitat destruction, they have soft toepads to walk silently, their nearest relative is the lion, the Siberian tiger's stripes are for camouflage.

Weave/Matrix: comparing more than one concept

This method of comparing items shows similarities and differences (e.g., fruit bats versus long-tailed bats, oranges versus lemons, and different varieties of apple).

Figure 9.2 Cartoon Showing Students Learning a Web Structure for *Tiger*.

The weave is an effective and cognitively efficient way to compare different animals (e.g., the alligator, lion, and bear) (see Figure 9.6).

A clever example of a weave/matrix structure occurred in *The First Case* (Nilsson, 2015), where Detective Gordon used this structure to discover who in the forest was stealing acorns (see Table 9.1). The culprit, to steal the acorns, had to be able to climb, leave footprints in the snow, and be able to climb trees. Using the weave diagram and comparing different suspects in the forest, the detective concluded that the culprit or culprits must be either squirrels or mice.

Sequence – where there is a step-by-step process

A sequence structure can be a linear sequence where there are several steps in the sequence, or a cause-effect, as in an earthquake and its effects.

The vocabulary word might be *amphibians*. The dictionary definition is that *amphibians* are creatures that live in water or on land. The word itself comes from Greek *amphibios*, where *bio* means *life*, and *amphi* means *both*.

To go further than the definition, the student could show the steps in the transition from water to land. The steps must be in order; one step must come after the other, as shown below:

Teaching vocabulary 115

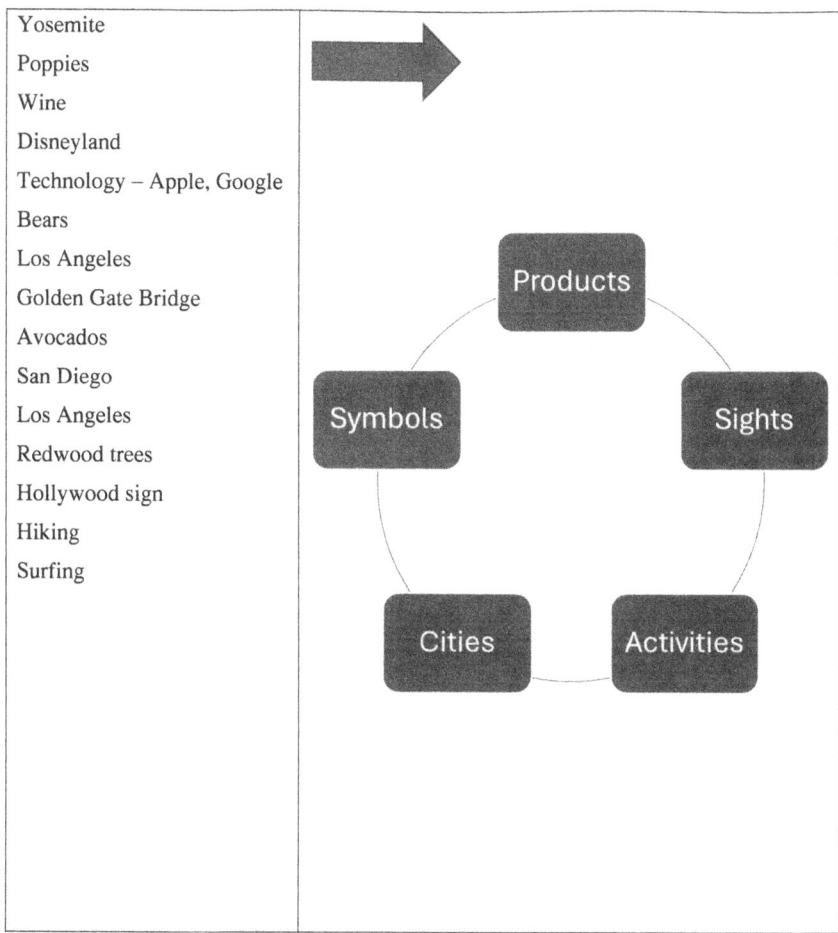

| Yosemite |
| Poppies |
| Wine |
| Disneyland |
| Technology – Apple, Google |
| Bears |
| Los Angeles |
| Golden Gate Bridge |
| Avocados |
| San Diego |
| Los Angeles |
| Redwood trees |
| Hollywood sign |
| Hiking |
| Surfing |

Figure 9.3 Web Diagram for *California*.

1. Amphibians hatch from eggs.
2. When they are little, they live in the water because they have gills.
3. They grow lungs and go out of the water. They also grow legs.
4. Frogs and salamanders are amphibians because they go from water to land.

Thermometer – using precise language

Choosing the right word for the right situation, it is important to consider what word fits best. If students think about nuances of meaning as something like a thermometer, they are better able to see the range of words available to them. The core meaning might be the same for a word (e.g., *fear*, but there may be a range of synonyms that express fear, from a mild sense of fear such as *anxious* to a major sense of fear such as *terrified*: *anxious, worried, alarmed,*

116 *Teaching Literacy Effectively in Modern Classroom for Ages 9–12*

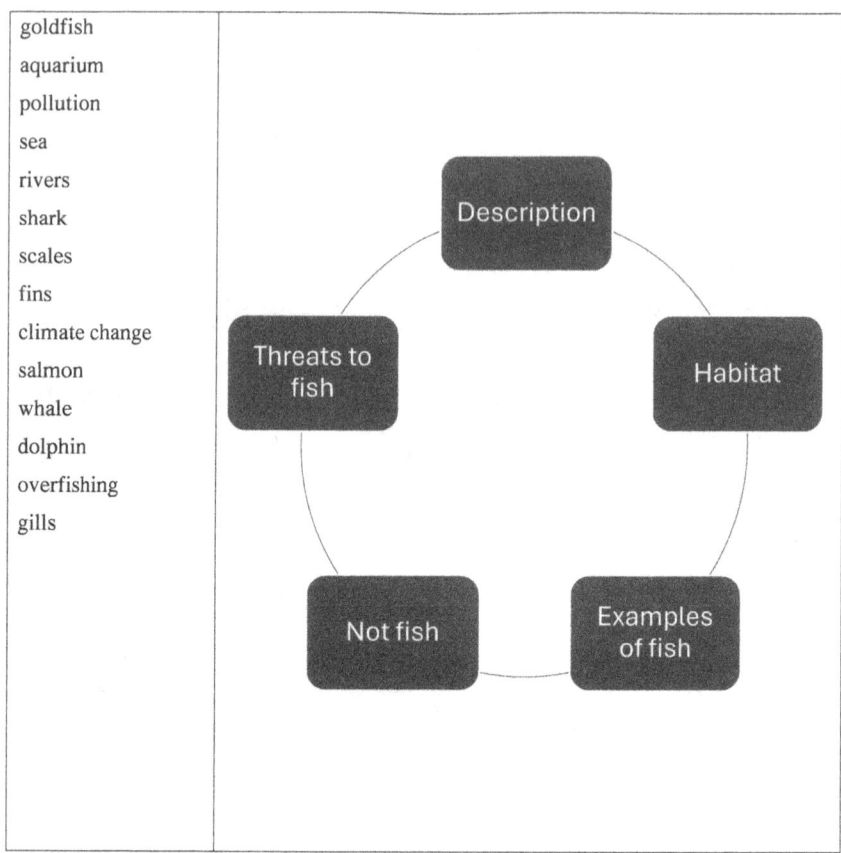

Figure 9.4 Web Diagram for *Fish*.

apprehensive, uneasy, frightened, scared, aghast, shaking like a leaf, petrified, panic-stricken, terrified). (See the thermometer diagram in Figure 9.7.)

Strategy 4: Structural analysis

Structural analysis is a way of working out the meanings of words by breaking them into morphemes (i.e., the minimal units of meaning in words). Morphemes are the building blocks of words. Every word is made of one or more morphemes (e.g., *cat* is one morpheme, *cats* is two morphemes: *cat* + *s*).

Many words of Latin/French and Greek origin have a three-part, *prefix–root word–suffix* structure. These components are all morphemes and have meaning.

Morpheme analysis is an effective way to work out meanings of words; for example, *improvisation*, from the Latin root *provisus*, means *foreseen*; in context, it often refers to spontaneous creation of something, without using a

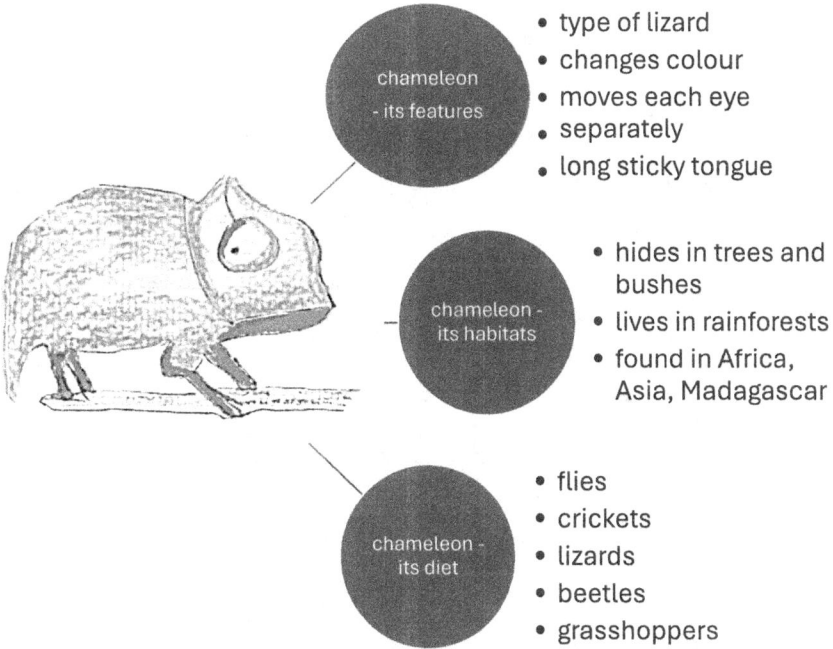

Figure 9.5 Web Diagram for *Chameleon*.

script, as in musical performance or a speech. A performer making up music or a speech on the spot, without a script, is doing something they did not foresee.

To work out the meaning of *improvisation*, the student must identify that the prefix *im-* means *not*. So, im- + provisus means *unforeseen*. The suffix -ation means that the word is a noun. This way of breaking longer words into meaningful units is morpheme analysis. It takes advantage of the fact that morphemes are the smallest units of meaning in words. By doing exercises like that in Table 9.2, students can study how structural analysis works.

9.3 Keyword method

The keyword method is a mnemonic, a memory strategy. It is a way to remember that hard-to-recall, tip-of-the-tongue word (Levin, 1993; Shaughnessy, 2003). The researchers who made up the strategy did several studies and found that the keyword method improved memory for the names of cities, states, people, and uncommon words. The strategy is to create an image in the mind that is of a different thing but has a similar sound to the word you want to remember.

The technique is not for every word, just words that students find hard to remember. In learning a foreign language, it can be useful. In Spanish, the

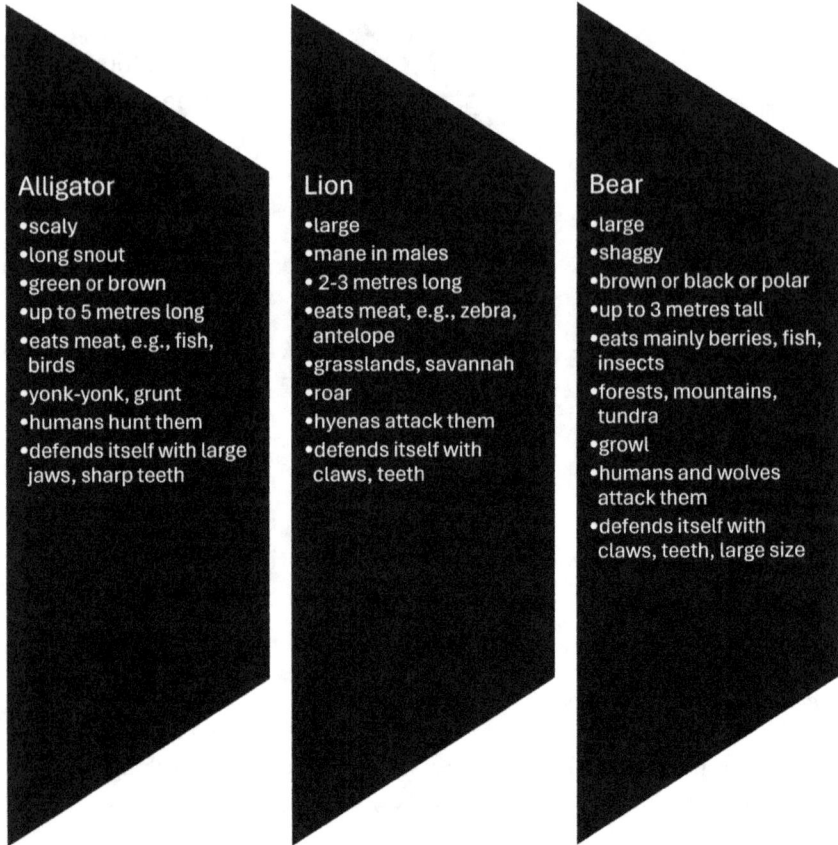

Figure 9.6 Weave/Matrix Diagram to Compare Alligator, Lion, and Bear.

Table 9.1 Detective Gordon's Weave Diagram to Compare Suspects

List of suspects	Can climb trees	Leaves footprints in the snow	Eats acorns
Birds	✗	✔	✗
Foxes	✗	✔	✗
Hedgehogs	✗	✔	✗
Mice	✔	✔	✔
Squirrels	✔	✔	✔
Rabbits	✗	✔	✗

word for *cat* is *gata*. Using the keyword method, you can relate *gata* to an image of a cat walking across a gate. The association of *cat* and *gate* in a mental image makes the Spanish word easier to remember (see Figure 9.8).

A word this writer found hard to recall was *obsequious*. It means fawning or servile, following someone, being attentive to an excessive degree. The root

Figure 9.7 Thermometer Diagram: Synonyms for *Fear*.

word is *sequ*, so *obsequious* means to follow, as in *sequence*. What the student must do is imagine an *oboe* (ob) on a *seat* (*sequious*). This image of an *oboe* on a *seat* can help to recall the word, *obsequious*. The student can design their own image if it fits the criterion: must sound like the word and indicate its meaning.

Another example of a word that is hard to remember is *lachrymose*, which means crying or tearful. The keywords *laundromat* and *lacquered moose* both sound like *lachrymose*, so the student creates an image of someone at the laundromat crying because they have so much washing to do. Or they create an image in their mind of a "lacquered moose" with a tear in its eye (see Figure 9.9).

In one study, the keyword method was used to remember phobia words (Carney & Levin, 2008). You could argue that the method worked well because these are Greek words and each keyword focused on a prefix (e.g., *harp* matches the prefix *harpaxo* in harpaxophobia).

Table 9.2 Prefixes and Suffixes

Question: What is the difference between the structure of words in each column below?

1	2	3	4
redo	hopeless	conductor	dictate
return	joyless	inventor	dictator
review	sleepless	creator	predict
reform	harmless	refrigerator	contradict
react	sightless	director	edict
reprint	luckless	donor	addict
replace	soundless	debtor	dictatorial
replant	groundless	collector	verdict

Answer

1	2	3	4
Same prefix: *re-*, means again	Same suffix: *-less*, means without	Same suffix: *-or*, means a person	Same root word: *dict*, means to speak

Question: What is the difference between the structure of words in each column below?

1	2	3	4
hopeful	hopeless	biceps	triceps
joyful	joyless	bicycle	tricycle
mindful	mindless	biped	tripod
careful	careless	biennial	triennial
harmful	harmless	bifocal	trifocal
doubtful	doubtless	bisect	trisect
fearful	fearless	biathlon	triathlon
restful	restless		

Answer

1	2	3	4
Suffixes: *-ful*, means full of	Same suffix: *-less*, means without	Same prefix: *bi-*, means two	Same prefix: *tri-*, means three

Question: What is the difference between the structure of words in each column below?

1	2	3	4
visible	audible	interstate	intrastate
invisible	inaudible	international	intranational
vision	audition	intercontinental	intracontinental
visor	auditor		
evidence	audience		
		benevolent	malevolent
		benefactor	malefactor
		benediction	malediction

(Continued)

Teaching vocabulary 121

Table 9.2 (Continued)

Answer

1	2	3	4
Same root word: *vis/vid*, means see	Same root word: *aud*, means hear	Same prefix: *inter-*, means between; *bene-*, means good	Same prefix: *intra-*, means within; *mal-*, means bad

Figure 9.8 Keyword Image for Spanish Word *Gata*.

Figure 9.9 Keyword Method to Recall "Lachrymose".

This was a positive learning activity for vocabulary because it was about remembering Greek words, and students do need to learn such words for specialist subjects.

- Harpaxophobia: fear of being robbed. Imagine a harp being stolen by robbers.
- Doraphobia: fear of fur. Imagine a door covered in fur.
- Pnigophobia: fear of choking or smothering. Imagine a pig choking slightly on its food.
- Dendrophobia: fear of trees. Imagine a dentist drilling into a tree.
- Katagelophobia: fear of being laughed at or embarrassed. Imagine a cat looking at someone with ridicule.
- Ophidiophobia: fear of snakes. Imagine orchids with snakes slithering around them.
- Antlophobia: fear of floods. Imagine an ant floating along in a flood.
- Chionophobia: fear of snow. Imagine being hit on the chin with a snowball.

9.4 Bookmarks

In *A Complicated Case* (Nilsson, 2016), there were several unfamiliar words that students could check out with an online or hard copy dictionary making sure that the located meaning fits with the story context (see Figure 9.10).

He had once been such a <u>distinguished</u> young toad.

It was a nasty, <u>obnoxious scoundrel</u>, said the detective <u>vehemently</u>."

"There there," said Buffy, <u>stroking</u> the big crow <u>cautiously</u> on her head.

She sang about how good she was at <u>investigating</u> things. I investi-ga-ga-gate!"

Figure 9.10 Bookmarking Unfamiliar Words Spoken by Detective Gordon and Buffy in *A Complicated Case*.

Teaching vocabulary 123

Figure 9.11 Blank Copy of Word Detective Bookmark.

Students can keep a word detective bookmark (see Figure 9.11) on a piece of paper to write down any new words. Using context clues and a dictionary, write a definition of each new word.

9.5 Word hunting exercises

- As an extension exercise, at home, students could hunt for unfamiliar words in books, articles, and the internet, and report back to the class (e.g., *daunted, pedigree, podium, conflagration*).
- In class, students develop concept maps for the words they have found (e.g., *conflagration*). They decide on a vocabulary structure (e.g., concept wheel) and brainstorm related meanings, using categories.

9.6 Conclusion

Words are a core part of language knowledge. The richer a person's vocabulary, the smarter they are.

Vocabulary is important. A visitor to another country knows that vocabulary is more useful than grammar.

Knowing a word is not just a dictionary exercise. Students need a breadth and depth of vocabulary. They need to be able to use words precisely and figuratively. Students must learn how to use words effectively.

Fast mapping of words is something students do naturally, to gain a basic meaning for a concept (e.g., *dogs have four legs and bark*), but students also need to add to this, to give breadth and depth to their vocabulary knowledge.

Vocabulary depth is about digging deep into the meanings of words, taking control, knowing how to use words precisely, and knowing their literal and figurative meanings and multiple meanings. Using different study techniques will help students do this.

Part 4
Writing

Chapter 10, *Writing: What is it?*, explains the "simple view" of writing, why students have difficulty, why teaching is not improving exam results, and why we must teach text structure.

Chapter 11, *Assessing writing*, explains curriculum expectations for ages 9–12, norm-referenced tests, discusses examiner comments on student work, and gives three writing checklists for students to use.

Chapter 12, *Teaching writing*, provides the teacher with 10 writing prompts, eight different writing planners (two fiction, five nonfiction, and one debate), sentence diagramming and combining activities, and 12 sentence starters for students to use.

10 Writing

What is it?

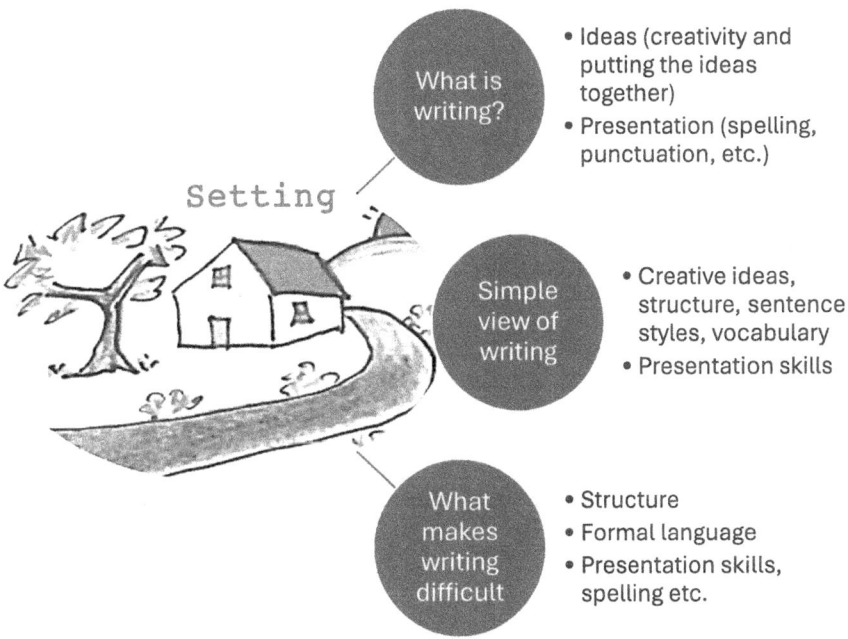

Figure 10.1 Overview of Chapter 10.

10.1 Introduction

> I wish I was doing a lot better than I am.

When you read about writers and the way they write, the message is that good writing is about getting words on the page, perseverance, and daily practice. It is 90% perspiration and 10% inspiration. This is a positive message for aspiring writers. It is saying that effort will have rewards.

DOI: 10.4324/9781003130789-14

A sizeable minority of students do not do well in national writing tests. For many, writing is a struggle. Why is this? It may be that, despite years of writing activities at school, they do not yet understand what writing is. They do not understand how writers structure their work. Without this understanding, the student lacks a writing GPS to tell them what to do and where to go.

Students write hundreds of stories or essays during their time in school yet often do not understand what they are doing or why.

Writing depends on ideas, i.e., interesting and creative things to write about, and presentation - grammar, spelling, punctuation, handwriting. Writing at school is different to everyday, informal writing such as a letter/email to a friend where you use colloquial expressions, sometimes with incorrect grammar and spelling errors. Friends do not usually care about such things, but schools do. Writing in school is much more formal, with benchmarks and expectations to meet.

The present chapter covers the following topics:

- Why write?
- Defining writing
- Simple view of writing
- Good writers and poor writers
- Can students learn to write well?

10.2 Why write?

It does matter for the student to know *why* they are writing. There are three reasons for gaining skill in writing:

1. Writing helps to remember facts and ideas and the links between them.
2. Writing encourages critical thinking, it involves coming to grips with complicated ideas, to think about the implications, the main ideas, and the evidence underpinning them.
3. Writing builds new knowledge; the student must connect with the topic, make connections, and pick out the key concepts.

10.3 Defining writing

What is writing?

- It involves the basic skills of spelling, punctuation, and grammar.
- It involves expression of thoughts and ideas in print.
- It involves planning and structuring what to write.
- It involves tailoring the content to the audience.
- It involves purpose, a reason for writing.
- It involves knowing about text structure (e.g., stories, essays, and reports).
- It involves arguing in a convincing way.

10.4 Simple view of writing

There are two faces to writing. The first is having something to write about, some ideas. This is the content side of writing.

The second is presentation skill, to write with style and to have control of writing conventions (i.e., spelling, punctuation, and grammar).

The *simple view of writing* is based on these two elements: writing conventions (especially spelling/punctuation/handwriting) and ideas. Each is necessary but neither is sufficient. To have one without the other is not enough. Students need skill in ideas and writing conventions (see Figure 10.2).

A meta-analysis of 30 studies (Graham & Eslami, 2020) found that for English language learners (ELLs), *ideas* predicted 41% of their writing scores, and *spelling* predicted 31%. These two elements made up most of the variance in student writing. The message from these studies is that both elements are part of writing well.

The best writers are good at ideas - quality of writing and spelling - presentation skills. In the scatterplot (Dymock & Nicholson, 2016) the top writers had higher scores in writing quality and presentation skills – see Figure 10.3. These are correlational data, but they strongly suggest the two factors go together. A good writer has good ideas and is a good speller.

10.5 Students with writing difficulties

The simple view of writing predicts writing difficulties. It predicts that writing difficulties will be due to problems with spelling/punctuation/handwriting or generating ideas, or both (see Figure 10.4) and that the interaction of these two things explains four different kinds of writer:

Figure 10.2 Simple View of Writing.

130 *Teaching Literacy Effectively in Modern Classroom for Ages 9–12*

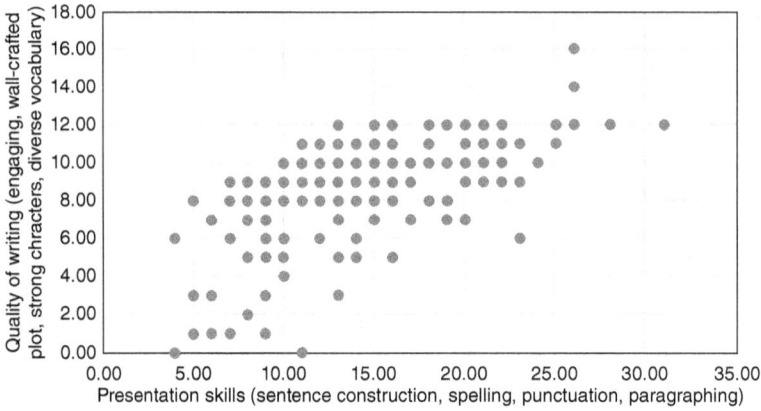

Figure 10.3 Scatterplot of Scores for Story Quality and Presentation.

Figure 10.4 Students with Writing Difficulties.

In the simple view of writing, students who do not write well have:

- good ideas and spelling– the writer.
- good ideas but spelling not so good, e.g., dyslexia - spelling is what is holding them back.
- good spelling but ideas not so good, e.g., English Language Learner – ELL. Grammar and vocabulary are holding them back in writing.
- ideas and spelling both not so good – double whammy. It is a double whammy for them. Difficulty with spelling and ideas is holding them back.

10.6 Can students learn to write well?

Yes, they can. This is the finding of many studies on the effects of writing lessons (Graham et al., 2023). Students can learn to write better. The amount of writing is not a factor. It is more about learning study strategies for writing.

Lessons work but they only work for the material they cover. There does not seem to be much transfer. To check for transfer, there needs to be regular assessment, using norm-referenced tests and external exams. This will indicate whether lessons are making a difference.

It is interesting that doing lots of writing is not enough to improve general writing ability. It may be a case of repeating the same mistakes over and over, this does not move the student forward.

It is the same issue in other areas, such as sport, it is no use running around on the training field unless it makes a difference in the big game.

Some evidence-based recommendations are (Graham et al., 2024) –

- Be strategic (e.g., plan, set goals, get feedback).
- Be creative and think critically.
- Know how to write a good summary (i.e., the key points).
- Use the right structure for the topic (e.g., web, weave, sequence, and argument).
- Write across different content areas and learn new things (e.g., social studies).
- Read, read, read.
- Motivate yourself (e.g., show others your writing, pin up your writing, and be proud of it).
- Learn the conventions (spelling, punctuation, grammar, etc.).

The cautionary note is that despite efforts to implement the above recommendations, school curricula designed to help students to write better have limited effects. Teaching of writing is effective for the writing done in class, but the results of the teaching do not transfer as well to new writing tasks on norm-referenced tests (Graham et al., 2023). Why is this? It may be that writing done in class lacks focus, lacks structure. Students listen but they do not change their approach. It is hard to change students' ways of writing. They must think differently. In the next chapters, we explain how to achieve this.

10.7 Conclusion

Students write but do they know how to write? Many students learn to write but do not learn to compose. They can write but do not know how to write well.

Without structure, a student's work does not stand up; it lacks coherence and does not convince or satisfy the reader. Writing must resonate, be well argued, and convince the reader (i.e., make the reader think differently about a topic).

Writing is a balancing act for students. They need to be creative. They need to have something to write about. On the other hand, they need to make sure that they write with style, few or no errors, and no loose ends in their work.

The key messages about writing are that students must be able to

- Compose fiction and non-fiction
- Write with their own voice, not copy
- Engage with the audience
- Structure and plan their writing
- Draw on vocabulary that is broad and deep
- Use correct spelling, punctuation, grammar
- Use legible handwriting

Effective writing is 90% perspiration and 10% inspiration. That is the challenge but also the excitement of writing.

11 Assessing writing

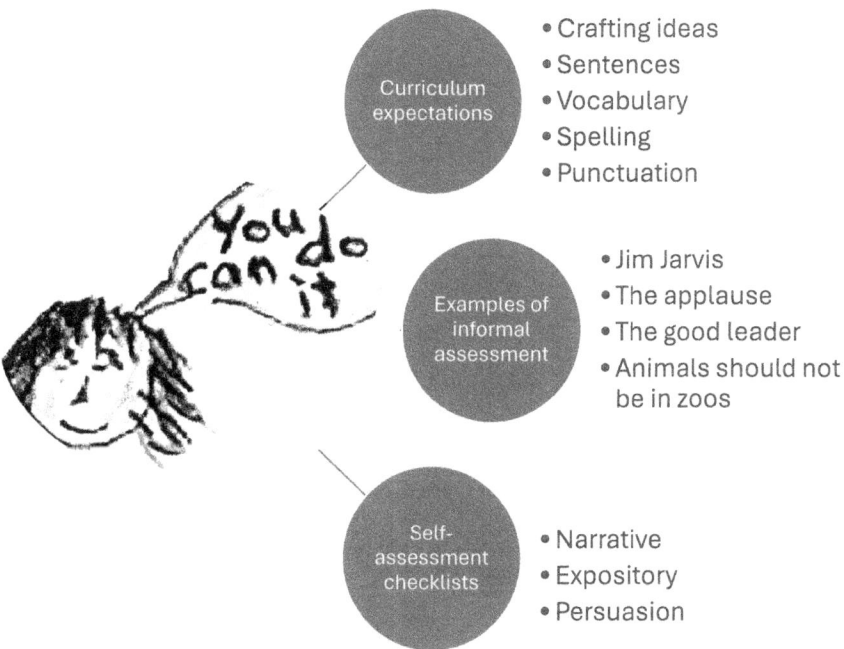

Figure 11.1 Overview of Chapter 11: Assessing Writing.

11.1 Introduction

> Picking out the main points, writing a summary, ... most just copy the text and usually copy the wrong bit.

Studies show that writing lessons enable students to write specific things better, but the key question is, will the learning transfer to other writing tasks?

DOI: 10.4324/9781003130789-15

National assessments show that many students do not write well enough to meet basic expectations. Why not?

Their class workbooks may be full of their writing, but where is it going? What have they gained from the lessons? Did they learn skills that will transfer to new writing tasks, that will have positive outcomes in exams? Many students know how to write, but they do not know how to compose. They have not learned how to structure their work. They need to think like a writer and use the structures that effective writers use.

Exams and tests are not everything in writing, but for the typical student they make the difference between academic success and non-success. Students need to be able to write well enough to achieve their potential in test situations. This is why it is so important to assess writing, to assess whether what they are learning is making any substantive difference when it comes to tests that matter.

The present chapter covers the following topics:

- Curriculum expectations
- Formal assessment
- Informal assessment
- Writing checklists

11.2 Curriculum expectations

Writing expectations vary across jurisdictions, but when reading these documents, we see common threads and goals across ages 9–12. The points listed below in Table 11.1 are not a complete summary of curriculum documents, which tend to be much more of a long list, but it does list points that make sense in terms of students improving their writing skills.

Standards and expectations are important because they give information on what is valued by education authorities and what things exams and national tests are likely to assess and what examiners will give credit for. The expectations are a window on what writing standards are required of students.

11.3 Norm-referenced assessment

Norm-referenced tests of writing are the best way to measure whether the student is writing at their age level.

The WIAT-3 (Wechsler Individual Achievement Test-Third Edition) assesses ability to write an essay. It is suitable for ages 9 to 12. There is a set time period to complete the essay. Scoring is on organization, coherence, ideas, vocabulary, and mechanics such as grammar, spelling, punctuation. It also counts number of words written.

The Test of Written Language-Fourth Edition (TOWL-4) (Hammill & Larsen, 2009) is suitable for ages 9 to 12. It assesses writing of a fictional story. There is a set period to write, 10 minutes. The prompt is an illustrated drawing.

Table 11.1 Some General Writing Expectations at Ages 9–12

Age	Crafting ideas	Grammar and vocabulary	Spelling and presentation
9–10	Ability to write fiction and non-fiction: Fiction or Narrative: setting, characters and plot, must convey feeling, emotion, atmosphere Nonfiction Descriptive: introduction, key points, conclusion Persuasive: claim, supporting details	Varied sentence structure Varied sentence length Breadth and depth of vocabulary	Correct spelling, legible handwriting, advanced punctuation (e.g., semi-colons)
11–12	Ability to write a wide range of fiction and non-fiction: Fiction: stories, poems, prequels, situations and scenes, flashbacks, monologues Nonfiction: character portraits, biography, diary, epistolary (e.g., letters/emails, feature articles, book/film reviews, research reports, reviews of literature, short answer essays) Persuasive text: opinion pieces, argument, debate Qualities needed: coherence, cohesion, must answer the question, well argued, engages with audience, relevant tone and voice	Broad, nuanced, and deep vocabulary. Range and variety of sentence structure. Transition markers (e.g., *furthermore, although*) Figurative language (e.g., metaphors, rhetorical questions). Nounification, namely making a verb into a noun (e.g., *reducing the traffic* becomes *reduction of traffic*).	Correct spelling, legible/fast handwriting, advanced punctuation (e.g., parentheses, ellipsis) Acknowledge information sources

Scoring for content is on style, plot, characters, and vocabulary. Scoring for mechanics is on spelling, punctuation, paragraphing, and grammar.

11.4 Informal assessment of writing

When assessing writing, markers look for well-crafted ideas, a compelling structure that carries the reader along, and language that has pace, rhythm, excitement, imagery, and variety. Markers value presentation, including spelling, punctuation, and paragraphing.

If the key to a good grade is knowing what the marker wants, it is important to find out what markers say about student writing.

Marker comments on student writing are a window on the criteria that students need to meet to write effectively. Here are some examples of marker comments.

Student writing sample 1: "What will happen to Jim Jarvis?"

This sample is from material published online by the Standards and Testing Agency (2018) in the UK for national curriculum assessments under Open Government Licence v3.0.

The student writing was based on a story called *Street Child* by Berlie Doherty. The student had to write a prediction about what would happen to Jim Jarvis, one of the characters. Overall, the scoring described below for this writing indicated that it was moving toward examiner expectations (see Figure 11.2).

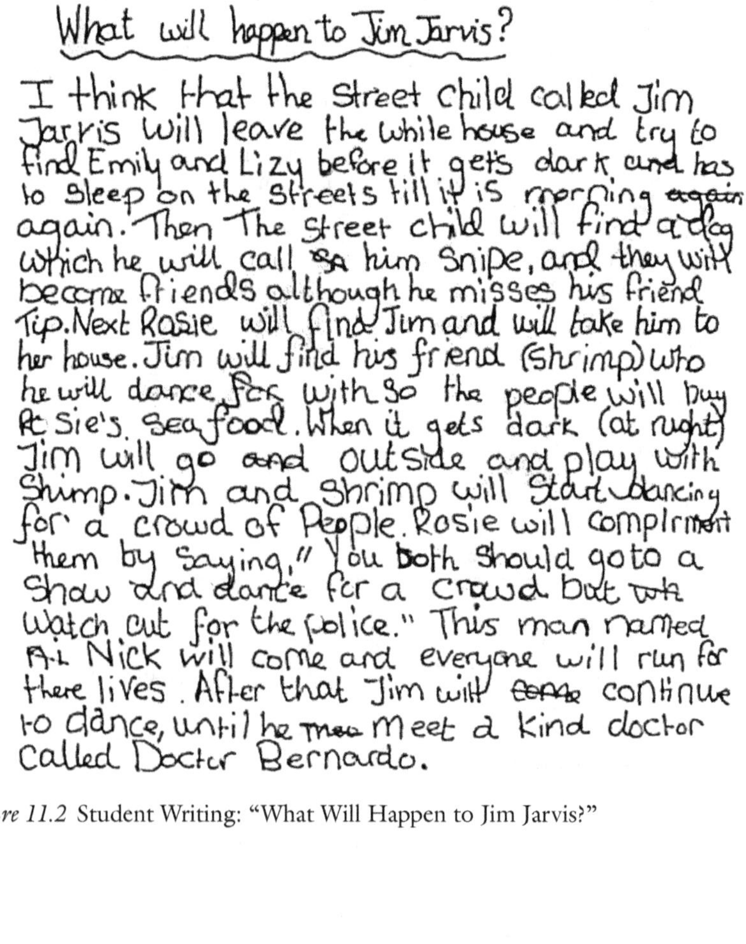

> What will happen to Jim Jarvis?
>
> I think that the Street Child called Jim Jarvis will leave the while house and try to find Emily and Lizy before it gets dark, and has to sleep on the streets till it is morning again. Then The street child will find a dog which he will call him Snipe, and they will become friends although he misses his friend Tip. Next Rosie will find Jim and will take him to her house. Jim will find his friend (Shrimp) who he will dance with so the people will buy Rosie's seafood. When it gets dark (at night) Jim will go outside and play with Shrimp. Jim and Shrimp will start dancing for a crowd of People. Rosie will compliment them by saying, "You both should go to a Show and dance for a crowd but watch out for the police." This man named P.L Nick will come and everyone will run for there lives. After that Jim will continue to dance, until he meet a Kind doctor called Doctor Bernardo.

Figure 11.2 Student Writing: "What Will Happen to Jim Jarvis?"

Here is a transcript of the essay (170 words):

What will happen to Jim Jarvis?

I think that the street child call Jim Jarvis will leave the white house and try to find Emily and Lizy before it gets dark and has to sleep on the streets till it is morning again. Then the street child will find a dog which he will call Snipe, and they will become friends although he misses his friend Tip. Next Rosie will find Jim and will take him to her house. Jim will find his friend Shrimp who he will dance with so the people will buy Rosie's seafood. When it gets dark at night Jim will go and outside and play with Shrimp. Jim and Shrimp will start dancing for a crowd of People. Rosie will compliment them by saying, "You both should go to a show and dance for a crowd but watch out for the police." This man named Nick will come and everyone will run for there lives. After that Jim will continue to dance, until he meet a kind doctor, called Doctor Bernardo.

Scoring

1. Ideas: Positive aspects mentioned were that the student made detailed predictions. Was able to answer the question.
2. Grammar and vocabulary: Positives were sentences grammatically correct. Used adverbials to give cohesion (e.g., *then, next*). Used subordinating conjunctions (e.g., *until he meets a kind doctor called Doctor Bernardo*). Used time connectives for cohesion (e.g., *after that, next*). Used dialogue.
3. Spelling/Punctuation/Handwriting: Positives were that most words were spelled correctly, even tricky words like *friends, compliment*. Handwriting was legible but not joined. There was advanced punctuation (e.g., use of an apostrophe for possession). Essay lacked paragraphing.

Student writing sample 2: "Applause" (241 words)

This writing sample is another exemplar published online by the Standards and Testing Agency (2018) in the UK for national curriculum assessments under Open Government Licence v3.0.

For this writing task, the student researched key moments in the lives of performers, such as Olympic athletes and musicians, and then described in detail the opening moments of a performance or competition. For the writing sample shown below, examiner marks suggested that the script was above examiner expectations (see Figure 11.3).

The Applause

I am in the dressing room with the music ringing in my ears; the small room is bustling with tall skinny girls chattering and giggling, But - but all I can think of is the stage and the applause. My racing heart thuds underneath my silky tutu. Thud. Thud. Thud.

Then suddenly the stage director is at the door, calling my name. My name. My stomach gives an unexpected flutter and I take a deep breath. As the stage door swings open, I tell myself everything will be okay - nothing could possibly go wrong. I have been training for this since the age of three. Tall Bulky men with headsets and clipboards keep ushering me in the right direction. Half of me wants to run onto stage and dance my heart out but there is also a part of me that wants to go and hide away. Adreneline ~~was~~ is circling its way around my body and rushing into my fingertips.

Walking into the wings is like waiting for your death. Although I was extremely excited, I was even more nervous. I stopped a few centimetres from the stage entrance with the whole quer de ballet behind me and slowly took a shaky, deep breath. The stage was ~~like~~ a lit up arena waiting to be danced on. The crowd, which seemed to consist of about a million people, erupted as I walked on to stage. I gave a little smile, and began to dance.

Figure 11.3 Student Writing: "Applause".

Here is a transcript of the Applause essay (241 words):

Applause

> I am in the dressing room with the music ringing in my ears; the small room is bustling with tall skinny girls chattering and giggling but all I can think of is the stage and the applause. My racing heart thuds underneath my silky tutu. Thud. Thud. Thud. Then suddenly the stage director is at the door, calling my name. My name. My stomach gives an unexpected flutter and I take a deep breath. As the stage door swings open, I tell myself everything will be ok – nothing could possible go wrong – I have been training for this since the age of three. Tall Bulky men with headsets and clipboards keep ushering me into the right direction. Half of me wants to run onto stage and dance my heart out but there is also apart of me that wants to go and hide away. Adreneline is circling its way around my body and rushing into my fingertips. Walking into the wings is like waiting for your death. Although I was extremely excited, I was even more nervous. I stopped a few centimetres from the stage entrance with the whole quer de ballet behind me and slowly took a shaky, deep breath. The stage was like a lit up arena waiting to be danced on. The crowd, which seemed to consist of about a million people, erupted as I walked on to stage. I gave a little smile, and began to dance.

Scoring

1. Ideas/Composition: Positive aspects: Strong opening, drew in the audience straight away. Used first person to add drama and tension. Effective use of repetition.
2. Grammar/Vocabulary: Positives are the variation in sentence length and structure (e.g., multi-clause sentences). Used metaphor. Single-word sentences added tension (e.g., *Thud. Thud*). Used expanded noun phrases (e.g., *bulky men with headsets and clipboards*). Positives for vocabulary were interesting word choices (e.g., *ushering, arena*). Used imagery (e.g., *an unexpected flutter*).
3. Spelling/Punctuation/Handwriting: Positives for spelling were that almost all words were correct; some were tricky words: *adreneline* for *adrenaline* and *quer de ballet* for *corps de ballet*. Joined handwriting was legible. Used advanced punctuation (e.g., dashes, semi-colon).

Student writing sample 3: "What are the qualities of a good leader?"
(254 words)

This writing sample is from exemplars published online by the New Zealand Qualifications Authority (NZQA, 2024). The task was to write an article for a school or community website on the qualities of a good leader and to write 250–350 words.

Overall, the scoring shown below for the writing was that it met examiner expectations.

> *What are the qualities of a good leader?*
>
> *What makes a good leader is someone who is caring and willing to lisson to people around them. Another thing that makes a good leader is someone that is always reliable, also on time. Wants to help when they can and even when they can't they will still be helpful and will always do their best to help you. Leaders often are knowledgeable on quite a lot of things and are always happy to chat with you. Leaders at school want to build a better community. Leaders of today build leaders of tomorrow. Leaders are always there when you need them. Someone who will always build you up and make you feel better when you are sad. Someone who will shoe leadership by getting everyone involved. Most leaders want to make a change for good. A leader won't say I because all good leaders know that we all together make the change. And a good leader would lisson to everyone's advice. They would want you to become a leader in your own way too. Leadership is shown though everything you do. Also it can be about the way you act. It takes someone to be kind to everyone and always to be a true leader. A good leader also has to help people learn. A leader should always be equal when giving out jobs. A great leader gives credit when credit is due. A leader helps us by showing us the way. A leader won't show off. A great leader empowers everyone around them.*

Scoring

1. Ideas/Composition: Positive aspects: The essay was on topic, answered the question. The tone of the article was appropriate. Relevant ideas given to answer the question. There were details about goals of a leader (e.g., to build a better community) and the qualities of a leader (e.g., to listen). Areas to improve: less repetition of ideas (e.g., *willing to listen, listen to advice*). Too much repetition of ideas.
2. Structure: Positives were the structure in the essay. Areas to improve: ideas were jumbled, lacking coherence. Some awareness of sequence but many of the ideas read like a list.
3. Grammar/Vocabulary: Positives: Correct construction of sentences. Tenses, vocabulary correct. Areas to improve: Too many simple, short sentences, needed more variety. Too much repetition (e.g., *leaders are, leader is*). Confusion of pronoun reference (e.g., *you*). Some words were well chosen (e.g., *empowers*) but too much repetition.
4. Text conventions and spelling: Positives were accurate punctuation (e.g., full stops, capital letters correct). Few spelling errors.

Student writing sample 4: "It is cruel to keep animals in cages and zoos"
(258 words)

This writing sample and examiner comments are from a NAPLAN (National Assessment Program – Literacy and Numeracy) marking guide published online by the Australian Curriculum Assessment Authority (ACARA, 2013).

The task was to write a persuasive essay on the topic: *It is cruel to keep animals in cages and zoos*. The examiner's comments on the essay covered 10 different aspects of writing, as shown below.

The scoring did not indicate an overall level of writing skill. The reader could infer that it was at or above expectation, since nearly all sub-scores were at or near the maximum score.

> *It is cruel to keep animals in cages and zoos*
>
> So you think that you wouldn't mind having bars surrounding you, faces peering in any minute of the day, and kept away from your natural habitat? If humans can have a voice why can't animals? The statement suggesting that it is cruel to keep animals in cages and zoos is, I think, accurate. Animals have romed this land before the destructive race of humans and we should not have the right to take control of their lives.
>
> If animals are kept in zoos or cages all of their life they have no chance if or when they are let out into the wild. Although some zoos make claim that they have technology to provide the prisoner with products to make their enclosures seem natural, it will never be the same. In the wild animals grow up learning to be predators to catch their own food, to know which animals are of danger to them, and develop skills such as fastness and attacking methods. What skills are they going to learn in a small enclosure?
>
> Zookeepers may argue that being kept in a cage increases the chance of survival and allows reproduction to continue. Even though this is true, rather than locking them away, humans could help by protecting their natural environment, preventing the amount of deaths by human progress. I hope that it would be agreed that blaming the animals, by locking them up, for our mistakes is certainly cruel. Like all living things, animals have personalities too which furthermore conveys why zoos and caging animals is cruel.

Scoring

1. Audience – score 6/6 – Strongly argued. An engaging opening that uses emotive language (e.g., *bars surrounding you*).
2. Text structure – score 4/4 – Strong introduction, body, and conclusion.
3. Ideas – score 5/5 – Advocates for animal rights and freedom in the wild. Elaborated ideas. Uses refutation. Gives a recommendation to the reader: *humans could help by …*

4. Persuasive devices – score 4/4 – Emotive devices such as appeal to the reader. Modality, *we should not have the right ...*, conditional mood, *if animals are kept ...*, rhetorical question, *if humans can have a voice, why can't they?*
5. Vocabulary – score 4/5 – Precise words used but some inaccuracy (e.g., *skills of fastness.*
6. Cohesion – score 4/4 – Used connectives (e.g., *if or when, even though ...*), word associations, *bars/enclosures/prisoners.*
7. Paragraphing – score 3/3 – Structured paragraphs, directed reader's attention.
8. Sentence structure – score 4/6 – Sophisticated sentences, but a few errors.
9. Punctuation – score 4/5 – Used commas for listing, apostrophe for possessions – one missing question mark.
10. Spelling – score 5/6 – All simple, common, and difficult words spelled correctly (e.g., *surrounding, technology, destructive*). Challenging words spelled correctly – *environment.* Some spelling errors with difficult words – *predetors, inclusure, firthermore.*

11.5 Differences in student writing

Studies show that skilled and less skilled writers differ significantly in the quality of their writing and in their understanding of conventions of writing (Graham et al., 2017). What specifically is the difference?

In one report by markers for a national writing assessment (NCEA Interim Assessment Report, 2024), several practical things were mentioned that a student could do to meet standards, such as answering the question set. Other points that separated skilled and less skilled writers were

Students at or above the standard
- Understood test instructions
- Followed directions
- Understood the purpose of the writing
- Understood the audience for the writing
- Planned their answers and structured their writing
- Wrote relevant and believable supporting points
- Clear writing
- Precise vocabulary
- Tone was right for the audience
- Varied sentence structure
- Used correct conventions (e.g., spelling, punctuation, handwriting)

Students at borderline or below the standard
- Did not understand test instructions
- Did not follow directions, such as length

- Did not understand the audience or purpose
- Did not write relevant ideas
- Did not plan answers and structure their writing
- Writing not structured, not logical, was hard to follow
- Tone was not right for the audience
- Vocabulary was not precise
- Sentences were not varied
- Did not use conventions correctly (e.g., spelling, punctuation, handwriting)

11.6 Informal student self-monitoring

The following checklists are suggestions for students to check off that they have met the brief for the writing task they are doing.

Student checklist for fiction writing

The checklist below is for writing a fictional story (see Table 11.2).

Table 11.2 Student Checklist for Fiction Writing

Story checklist: does the story have	Sample of student writing	Check if done
A title	The big shake	✔
Hook: does the opening sentence grab the reader's attention?	I woke up in the night. The door was swinging. It was an earthquake.	✔
Setting: when does the story take place, where is it set, what is the atmosphere – bright, cloudy, ominous?	The door swung faster. The clouds cleared and all I could see was the moon.	✔
Characters: do they come alive, have distinctive features, have personalities, show emotion?	I was scared. I hopped back into bed and said to myself, "Deep breaths, deep breaths!"	✔
Plot: What is the problem facing the characters, what do they feel, what action will they take to solve the problem, what is the outcome?	I locked the door and turned the light on, but it started flickering… Outside the window, the elicktrisatey lines were wobbling. I was OK after that. My mum invited me to sleep with her.	✔
Theme or message: what are the lessons learned in the story?	I learned that if you are in danger, stay calm.	✔

Student checklist for nonfiction writing

The checklist below is for nonfiction writing (see Table 11.3).

Table 11.3 Student Checklist for Nonfiction Writing

Checklist: does the writing have	Sample of student writing	Check if done
A title	*Dogs*	✓
Hook: is there an opening sentence to grab the reader's attention?	*Can I tell you something about dogs? Dogs are kind, gentle animals who are great if you are willing for a responsibility.*	✓
Middle: is the essay divided into categories, small chunks of information on each sub-topic?	Origins: *Dogs are part of the Canidae family. They are related to foxes and wolves.* Features: *Dogs are mammals. Some dogs are big, some are small. There are different breeds of dog like Chihuahua, Dalmatian, and Great Dane. Chihuahuas are the smallest breed.* Diet: *Adult dogs eat two meals a day.*	✓
Final sentence: strong ending, takes a position	*Dogs are friendly and playful creatures known as "man's best friend."*	✓

Student checklist for argument/persuasion writing

The checklist below is for persuasive writing (see Table 11.4).

Table 11.4 Student Checklist for Nonfiction Writing

Checklist: does the writing have	Sample of student writing	Check if done ✓
A title	*Should students have homework?*	✓
Opening sentence: a hook to grab the reader's attention	*This is a question that has been bugging everyone for centuries… Do students need homework?*	✓
Reason 1 for	*It makes learning easier*	✓
Reason 2 for	*It gives time to catch up with schoolwork*	✓
Reason 1 against	*More work after school is boring*	✓
Reason 2 against	*More work after school takes up family time*	✓
Conclusion	*There will never be an agreed answer to this question but personally, I hate homework!*	✓

11.7 Conclusion

When assessing writing, certain elements need to be in place. Student writing must have structure, and different kinds of writing need different structures. For a narrative, the plot must be engaging. For descriptive writing, the information needs to be well assembled, detailed, and well researched. For persuasive writing, the arguments need to be tight, so that the reader is convinced.

A window into how well students write is their performance on external tests. The results of these tests show that many students do not meet curriculum expectations. They are writing, but it is not working for them. The teacher can gain insights by reading examiner comments on student essays. Examiner comments will reveal the qualities of writing valued by them. The teacher can use the comments as a basis to design successful teaching of writing.

This is why assessment matters. It can show where students are at in their writing, their status, and can give insight into what students need to do to improve.

12 Teaching writing

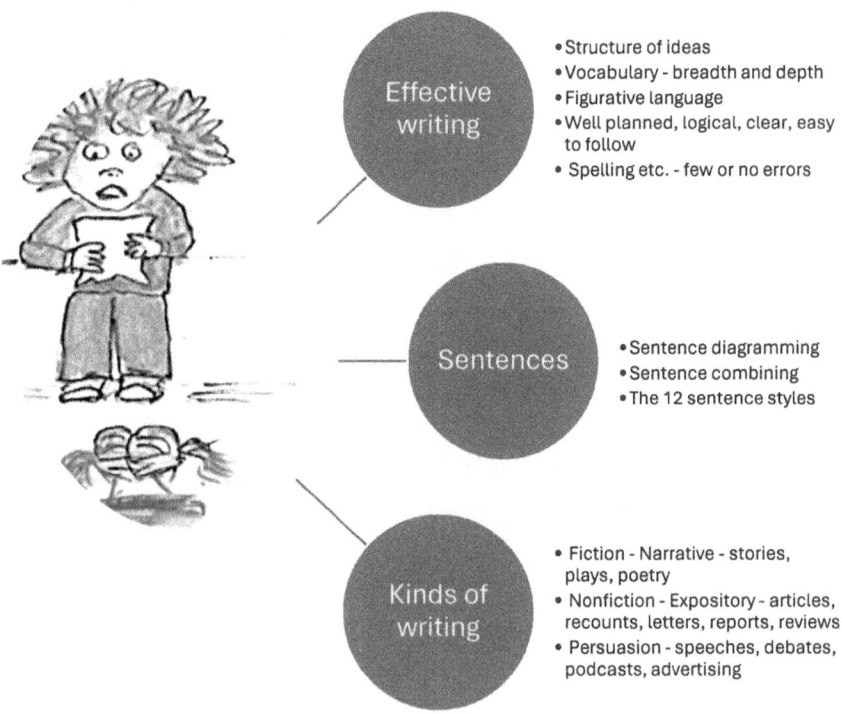

Figure 12.1 Overview of Chapter 12: Teaching Writing.

12.1 Introduction

> Oh, I copy the hard bits out of my book, and the easy bits I just write down in my own words.

DOI: 10.4324/9781003130789-16

In a national writing exam, students had 30 minutes to write an essay. The person monitoring the exam wrote:

I watched five students write their names on the paper, and then promptly stopped writing.
Another student spent so long trying to decide what to write, that all he wrote was a heading.

It will help students if they plan and assemble their ideas and get words on paper as quickly as possible. Too often in exams and tests, students go blank, do not know how to crank themselves into action. Using a writing planner can be an effective bridge that enables the student to write and get the task done well.

Students can develop knowledge of how to write. Practice in using text structure and thinking in a structured way of what to write, and how to write it, will build writing skills. Knowledge of how to compose is the key.

This chapter will cover the following topics:

- Fiction writing
- Nonfiction writing
- Persuasion writing

12.2 Fiction: Narrative writing

Narrative writing, or story writing, is imaginary; it is made up. A story has invented characters, settings, and events. A story happens in the imagination and is not real; it never actually happened.

A student might ask themselves, what about historical fiction? Is it fiction? Yes, it is fiction because, although based on actual events, the story is made up.

Would a diary or recount or biography be fiction? These texts have characters and events. The answer is no, none of these is fiction; they are factual, about real people and events that happened. In contrast, fiction must be made up, not real.

Every fictional story is about someone or something not real. Even if the story is based on something real, it is still a story because it turns the facts into something that did not happen. A story is not real.

Students are often required to write stories for assignments, tests, and exams. The test asks them to write a made-up story, focusing on setting/characters, a problem to solve, a complication, and an ending.

Narrative writing prompts
Writing prompts given in exams and tests show the kinds of topics that students might be required to write on. For example:

1. You have found something. A box. What is inside? How did the box get there? What happens when you open the box?

2. Make up a story where someone says, "What a mess." It might be a messy person, a tricky situation, an untidy place, a mix-up between two people, or a plan that has gone wrong.
3. Write a story about a character who found an object that did amazing things, like Aladdin's lamp. Alternatively, make up your own imaginary object.
4. Write a story about what happened to a character or characters after they read one of these signs – *Marvel Park - Enjoy yourself; Wanted: Brave employee; You should not be reading this; Last fuel for next five hours of driving* – or make up your own sign.

Planning the story

> ☺**Hot tip**: Give students a story planner to use before they start writing (see chapter Appendix, Figures 12.3 and 12.4).

It is important for students to have a plan for the story, to give it structure and direction. The story must have four elements: setting, characters, plot, and theme. See the proficient and advanced story planners in the chapter Appendix.

Points to consider are

- Setting: must mention place, time, and mood
- Characters: must include major and minor characters - appearance, personality
- Dialogue: must make characters come alive. Let their emotions show.
- Vocabulary: must use descriptive and vivid vocabulary (e.g., *rough, tall, dull, nice, noisy, greedy, funny, formal, brainy, angry, lonely, obsessive, peculiar, mischievous, inscrutable, unfathomable, effervescent, blasé, brilliant, courageous, changeable*).
- Plot: must have at least one episode with four parts: problem, reaction to the problem, action to solve the problem, and an outcome. Every story starts with a problem that needs attention, with action to resolve it, and an outcome. The plot usually moves quickly and has a complication of some kind. There is a high point of action, usually in the middle of the story. An effective plot needs to be exciting, gripping, puzzling, and mysterious, whatever makes the audience want to keep reading. It must have flow, including change of pace, sometimes fast, sometimes slow.
- Theme or message: there should be an implied or explicit message, about lessons learned.

An example of how to open a story – setting and characters

The First Case (Nilsson, 2015) has a suspenseful opening to this detective story. The setting is the forest, in winter, covered in snow. A squirrel, following a path in the snow late in the night, is crying out, "wretched thieves, thieving wretches." Thieves have stolen the squirrel's acorns. The squirrel approaches the police station, a little house at the end of the pathway, with a light shining in the window. As the squirrel enters the station, the squirrel notices a locked glass cabinet, and inside the cabinet are a baton and a pistol. To the squirrel, the house is quite strange. In the squirrel's house, there are no chairs or tables, just nuts.

The story opening is an example of describing the setting and introducing one of the characters. In this story, there are two major characters, the police chief, Detective Gordon, who is a toad, and a detective in training, a mouse called Buffy. The plot of the story is how the two detectives managed to solve the crime of the stolen nuts.

12.3 Nonfiction writing

Nonfiction writing is descriptive, informative, and factual. It is not a narrative; it is not fiction. It is about reality, real things that currently exist or have existed.

A description of something like the history of rubber is nonfiction because it is about real people, ideas, things, and events that happened in the history of rubber (e.g., rubber's discovery, production, and uses).

Nonfiction writing is about real facts that happened, whereas in fiction writing, the story is imaginary; it is about things that never really happened, except in the mind of the writer. A fiction story may be based on reality (e.g., an historical novel), but it is not reality.

There are several types of descriptive writing.

List

☺**Hot tip**: Give students a list planner to plan their writing (see chapter Appendix, Figure 12.5).

A list structure is when the writer describes a series of items, one item after the other, using commas, until the final item. Alternatively, the writer might use a list that is numbered or bullet-pointed (see list diagram in Figure 12.2).

The writer may give a random list, such as shopping list, goods produced in Bolivia, items found in a sparrow's nest, or list of ingredients in a recipe.

The writer may write a listicle. This is an article that includes lists (e.g., list of places to visit, 10 best movies, five ways to lose weight, 50 best cafes, a list of results of a study).

Connective words in a list text might include *and, additionally, also,* or *finally.*

The student can use the list structure to write an amusing and unexpected piece, like

Jobs to Do

1. Bank
2. Dry cleaner
3. Forge in the smithy of my soul the uncreated conscience of my race
4. Ring mum

Web

> ☺**Hot tip**: Give students a web planner to plan their writing (see chapter Appendix, Figure 12.6).

In a web structure, the information is about *one* thing (e.g., a biography of a famous person like Marie Curie). A web-like piece of writing will have sub-topics (e.g., Marie Curie's upbringing, beliefs, research, discoveries, other things) (see web diagram in Figure 12.2).

It has categories to describe that one thing (e.g., a text about Tasmanian tigers might include habitat, diet, descriptive features, and enemies). Writing tip: Give students a web planner (see chapter Appendix).

A web structure focuses on one topic. It is more complex than the list structure. It is called a web as it resembles a spiderweb. In a web structure, the attributes of a person, place, or thing are discussed. The attributes have a common link.

An article with a web structure might be about pine trees or cockroaches – but must be about *one* topic.

Connective words in a web text might include *attributes of, characteristics are,* or *for example.*

Weave/Matrix structure

> ☺**Hot tip**: Give students a weave planner to plan their writing (see chapter Appendix, Figure 12.7).

In a matrix structure, the writer compares two or more concepts (see weave diagram in Figure 12.2). The student might be writing about two or more persons, animals, ideas, things, or topics (e.g., comparing seagulls, sparrows, and magpies in terms of features, habitat, and diet).

Teaching writing 151

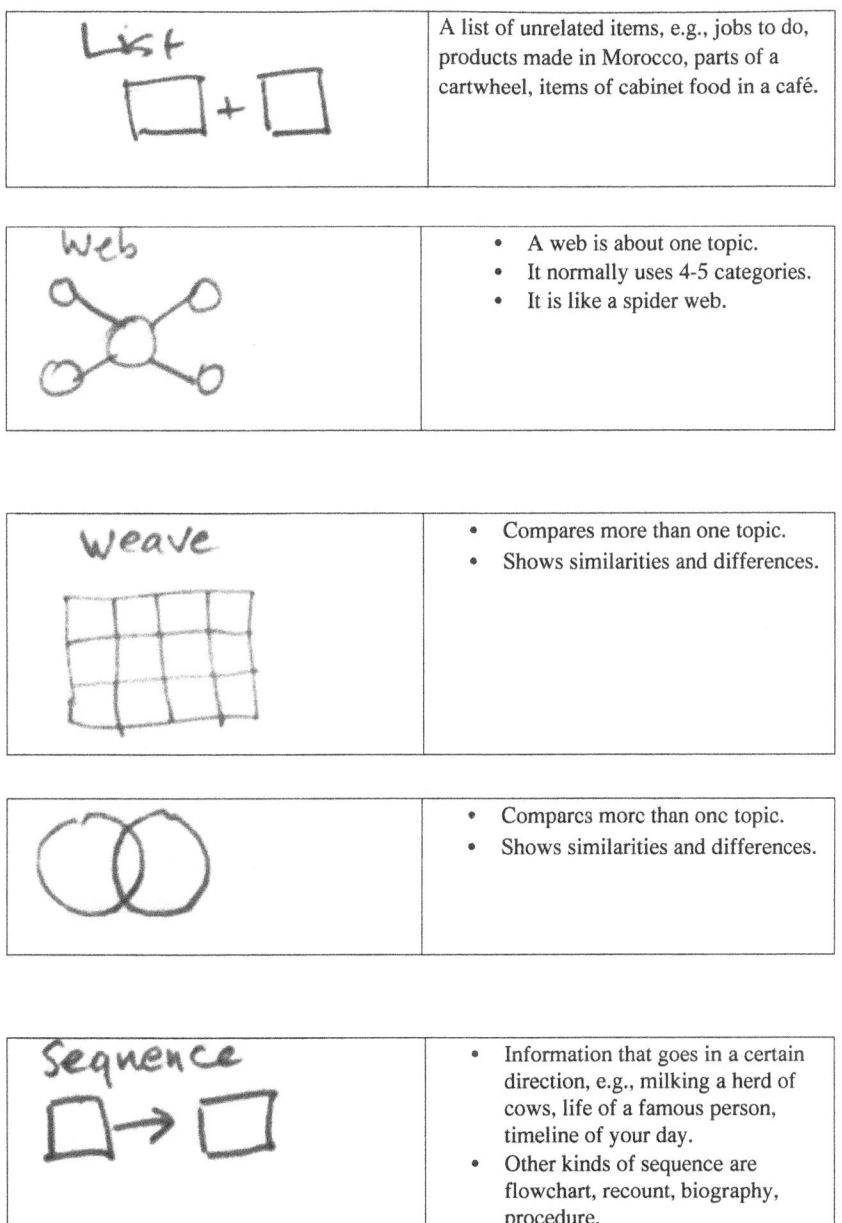

Figure 12.2 Nonfiction Text Structures: List, Web, Weave/Venn, Sequence.

If the writer wants to compare two topics with overlapping features, they will use a Venn structure (see Venn diagram in Figure 12.2).

An example of a Venn structure is when there are overlapping similarities and differences (e.g., Martin Luther King and William Wilberforce). They were both activists for freedom but lived in different time periods.

There are certain signal words that the student could use in a weave text, such as *on the other hand, unlike, share, same as, different, but,* or *in contrast*.

Venn structure

Connective words in a Venn text might include *overlapping, intersection, one is this and the other is that, share,* and *both*.

Sequence

> ☺**Hot tip**: Give students a sequence planner to plan their writing (see chapter Appendix, Figures 12.8 and 12.9).

For the student writing about information that has a sequence structure, there are several kinds to use (see Figure 12.2).

- When writing a **linear string** text, use a step-by-step structure, one step must follow the other (e.g., cake recipe with steps 1, 2, 3, 4, and so on), or a history of Uzbekistan from time A to time D. There are certain connective words to use in linear sequence texts (e.g., *and then, later, finally, to begin with, after, before, now*).

The writer can use the linear string structure to write fun pieces like the following report by a pupil about their school trip to the museum (based on Townsend, 1983):

> *7 a.m. Boarded coach*
> *Ate packed lunch, drank low-calorie drink*
> *7.10 Coach stopped for a pupil to be sick*
> *7.20 Coach stopped for another pupil to go to the toilet*
> *7.30 Coach left school drive*
> *7.35 Coach returned to school to collect the teacher's bag*
> *7.40 Driver appeared to be behaving oddly*
> *…*

A History of Words for Students (Richards, 2022) is a descriptive text with a linear sequence structure. The book shows how writing started with clay tablets, followed by paper made from papyrus, then quill pens, fountain pens, ballpoint pens, and finally writing on computers, smart phones, and other technology.

- When writing a **cause–effect** text, make sure one event causes other events to happen (e.g., an earthquake). There are certain connective words to use in a cause–effect text (e.g., *as a result, led to, consequence*).
- When writing a **cyclical** text, describe a cycle that repeats itself (e.g., the life cycle, rain cycle, poverty cycle, negative thinking cycle). There are certain connective words in a cyclical text (e.g., *stage, phase, process, progression*).
- When writing a **continuum** text (e.g., biography, describe a pattern of events over time). A biography will use connective words like *born in, went to school at, worked in, believed, suddenly, unexpectedly, meanwhile*, and *finally*.
- When writing a **problem–solution** text, a problem leads to a solution (e.g., bridge collapses, solution is to build a ferry). There are certain connective words used in sequence text (e.g., *to begin with, to start with, in the first place, next, and then, and finally*). An example of a problem–solution text was an article about the problem of dead cars:

Problem: There's one big problem in our area: dead cars. For years people have been dumping rusty old cars in the bush and on the side of the road. On one road there are nearly 60 dead cars.

Solution: The Air Force offered their help as a community project. Together with the local Council, they decided to collect all the dumped cars into one place. Then the cars would be crushed, loaded onto a large truck and trailer, and taken away for recycling.

12.4 Persuasion writing

☺**Hot tip**: Give students a persuasion planner to plan their writing (see chapter Appendix, Figure 12.10).

Persuasion writing is an important skill. Examiners look for succinct arguments, convincing points, and supporting information. Examiners value correct spelling and punctuation, sophisticated grammar, engaging vocabulary, and paragraphing.

Writers who can persuade are able to consider the audience, predict how well the audience will receive their ideas, assess how strong their arguments are, understand the importance of negotiation, and understand the need for the audience to be convinced before agreeing. These are the skills of persuasion.

The persuasive writer is aware that the audience might disagree, aware that opinions will differ, aware of what the audience are likely to accept, and aware of how to be reasonable so that the audience will accept or at least consider their viewpoint.

Persuasion writing is about arguments. Arguments make a claim and then back it up with data or examples in support. The claim may be that it is wrong to destroy rainforests. Reasons would be that (a) loss of forests is causing global warming (e.g., icebergs are melting and droughts are more common) and (b) if forests are gone, unique animals living in those forests will become extinct and the world will lose unique plants that can cure disease.

A persuasive essay states the claim or position up front, presents their arguments in the middle, and ends with a personal plea or a prediction or a summary.

The most effective persuasive writing looks for compromise. Novice writers do not usually seek compromise. They will insist on saving the rainforests at all costs!

With more advanced persuasive writing, there is more of a sense of obligation (e.g., "Humans should save the rain forests because it will help the planet to survive").

There are more indicators of uncertainty (e.g., *maybe, surely*). There is more of a sense of personal accountability (e.g., *My feeling is that* …).

To sum up, a persuasion text can be for an idea, against an idea, or both. The default persuasive essay is a list of arguments for and against, with rebuttals.

Imagine writing on the topic of whether to ban zoos. The student starts by examining both sides of the question. On the plus side, zoos can be useful for research and for protecting animals. Breeding programs can enable the breed to survive. In zoos, their medical needs are met and they are well fed. These are arguments for having zoos. An opposing argument is that it is cruel to keep animals in cages to entertain humans and that this is mistreatment. A conclusion for the writing may be a middle path: to care for animals but do this in their natural habitat.

Writing prompts

Persuasion writing is important not just in itself but for examinations and tests.

National tests often assess persuasive writing using prompts.

Prompts in previous tests have included

1. Choose a hero that you think deserves a "hero award" and convince the reader why this person deserves the award.
2. Do students spend too much money on toys and games? Work out your own position on this topic. Convince the reader of your opinions.
3. Should everyone learn to cook? Write to convince the reader of your opinion.
4. Write to convince the reader to change a certain rule or law (e.g., to change the rule against using mobile phones in school hours).
5. Choose a hobby or sport and convince the reader why they should try this.
6. Choose the best movie or television show or book that you have ever read or seen and persuade the reader why they should see or read this.

Teaching writing 155

12.5 Grammar – sentences

Students talk in sentences but may still not understand that a sentence has a formal structure of subject, verb, and object. It is important to have this understanding because writing requires the student to use formal grammar for writing tasks.

Writing can contain a range of grammatical devices. There are prepositional phrases (e.g., *the cat was sleeping on the sill of the window*), relative clauses (e.g., *the laptop you gave me is very easy to use*), and the passive voice (e.g., *the cat was chased by the dog*).

One approach to learning sentence structure is sentence diagramming. Another is sentence combining.

Sentence diagramming

Sentence diagramming is a way to explain sentence structure. The student must show visually each part of the sentence, its skeleton.

Step 1: Draw a horizontal line and then a small vertical line through the middle. On the left of the line, write the *subject*, and to the right of the line, the *verb*. This is a basic sentence (e.g., "The cat / drank").

Step 2: Draw another vertical line if there is a direct object (e.g., "The cat / drank / the milk").

Step 3: Put adjectives and adverbs on diagonal lines below the words they modify (e.g., "The \Burmese cat/ \quickly drank/ the \warm milk").

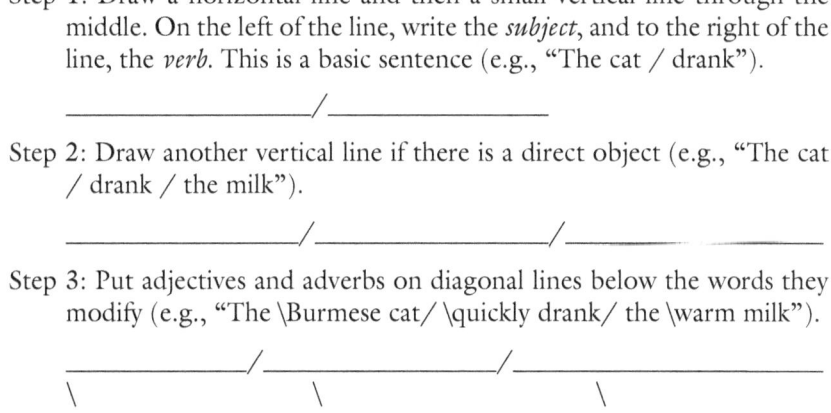

Sentence combining

Sentence combining is a way to learn about different sentence structures. The student must combine information *across* sentences so as to compose more complex sentences and in that way improve the quality of writing. For example,

- Elfin is a mouse.
- Elfin is grey.
- Elfin has brothers.
- Elfin has sisters.

Answer: Elfin is a grey mouse with brothers and sisters.

An activity for students is to create their own sentence exercises from books, articles, and other text material (see Table 12.1).

Table 12.1 Sentence Combining Examples

Sentences	Combined
It was Monday. It was in the morning. It was sunny.	It was a sunny Monday morning.
Mrs Smith came back. She had a fishing net. Mrs Smith had a tin of tuna.	Mrs Smith came back with a fishing net and a tin of tuna.
The tree branches bend. They are low. They have snow on them.	The tree branches bend low with snow.
The cat did not come here yesterday. No one saw the cat at breakfast today.	The cat did not come yesterday, and no one saw the cat at breakfast today.
They loaded the container onto a truck. The truck carried the container to the port. They then put the container on a ship.	They loaded the container onto a truck, carried it to the port, and put it on a ship.

The 12 kinds of sentences

When students use different sentence styles, it gives variety to their writing. Students can use these styles when writing and revising their work, to make their work more convincing (Hunter, 2008).

It is important for the writer to vary not just the sentence style but its length. Most sentences are too long. Some say that sentences should never be more than 20 words. Sometimes it is better to have a few words. Students will write more effectively if they vary sentence length.

The 12 kinds of sentences are

1. A very short sentence, used for immediate impact, to gain attention, five or six words (e.g., *be in the present, less is more, parting is such sweet sorrow*).
2. A repeating pattern (e.g., from a famous sentence: *fight on the beaches, fight on the landing grounds, fight in the fields*).
3. Adverb at the front, called a fronted adverbial (e.g., *Suddenly, the lights went out*). Use it sparingly to create surprise or drama. Some adverbs to use are *subsequently, shortly, previously, thoughtfully, probably, surprisingly, remarkably, foolishly,* and *erratically*.
4. The em dash, which is slightly longer than a hyphen, is a punctuation mark used instead of a parenthesis or comma and is used to add information that is not essential. It can add variety to the sentence, but use it sparingly (e.g., *Their sister – the one who lives in London – has won Lotto!*).
5. The W start is where the writer uses one of the 5Ws – who, what, where, when, why – at the start of a sentence (e.g., *When the orchestra began to play, the audience came alive*). The TH in *though* can be effective as a starter (e.g., *Though many have tried to recreate the sound of Tweety Bird, few have succeeded*).
6. The paired double is where you have two clauses, and you want to join them without having to use *and*, so you pair them up using a semi-colon (e.g., *I wanted to go to New York; I had saved enough money*) or a comma (e.g., *Hi there, how are you?*).

7. Prepositional phrase at the start of the sentence. Some prepositions to use for this include *in, on top of, by, with, from, over, behind, near, prior, after,* and *upon* (e.g., *In a hole in the ground, there lived a hobbit*). A more modern use of a prepositional phrase would be *On top of spaghetti, all covered in cheese …*
8. A verb at the start of the sentence, using an -ed or -ing verb, attracts the attention of the reader (e.g., *Recalled to life, the sparrow raised its little head …; startled by the quiet of the traffic jam …; Sailing into the darkness …; Haunted by the memory of the whale …*).
9. Alliteration, which repeating words that start with the same sound (e.g., *sprawled in sleep, suspecting nothing …; deep into the darkness; a big brown bear boldly bounds by*).
10. Metaphor and simile. This can create a vivid picture in the mind. A metaphor is when you write that one thing is a totally different thing. A well-known metaphor is Shakespeare's *All the world's a stage and all the men and women merely players*. In contrast, a simile is when you write that something is *like* something else. A well-known simile is from the *Forrest Gump* movie: "Life is like a box of chocolates, you never know what you're gonna get."
11. Colon: the colon is a punctuation mark that enables the writer to spell out several pieces of information in one sentence or to focus on a single point. It is a good way to add drama or to focus on an important point. In that famous line by Christopher Robin, it may have been better to use a colon: "Remember: you are braver than you believe, stronger than you seem, and smarter than you think."
12. The Oxford comma is the comma placed before the final "and" or "or" in a sentence when you have three ideas, and you need to separate them with three commas. Using it can help to avoid sentence ambiguity (e.g., "I love my parents, Lady Gaga and Humpty Dumpty" implies, without a second comma, that your parents are Lady Gaga and Humpty Dumpty. If you use the Oxford comma to separate the three elements, "I love my parents, Lady Gaga, and Humpty Dumpty", the true meaning is clear.

Conclusion

To write effectively, students must understand how an experienced writer writes and the structures they use to communicate their ideas.

Students must use the same structures in their own writing. Every writer knows that feeling of going blank under the pressure of writing. The bell goes and you must write. The prompt is *the wind hissed*, you stare at the empty page, what can you possible write about that? Students must learn how to cope with such pressure. When the prompt comes, they must act quickly, use their writing planner, jot down ideas, and then start. It is as easy as that and as hard as that. If there is time to write, the writer can do research, choose words carefully, revise and revise. Students need to learn this discipline as well. Writing is a craft. A writer is like a carpenter; they know how to make things and know how to fix them when they go wrong. This is the art.

158 *Teaching Literacy Effectively in Modern Classroom for Ages 9–12*

In addition to knowing how to generate ideas, students need knowledge to make them glow and flow. They must learn how to write sentences that have structure, know how to combine sentences, vary them in length, and use them to write more effectively. All these factors are critical for making an impact in the game of writing.

Appendix: Writing planners (Figures 12.3–12.10)

Figure 12.3 Story Planner – Proficient.

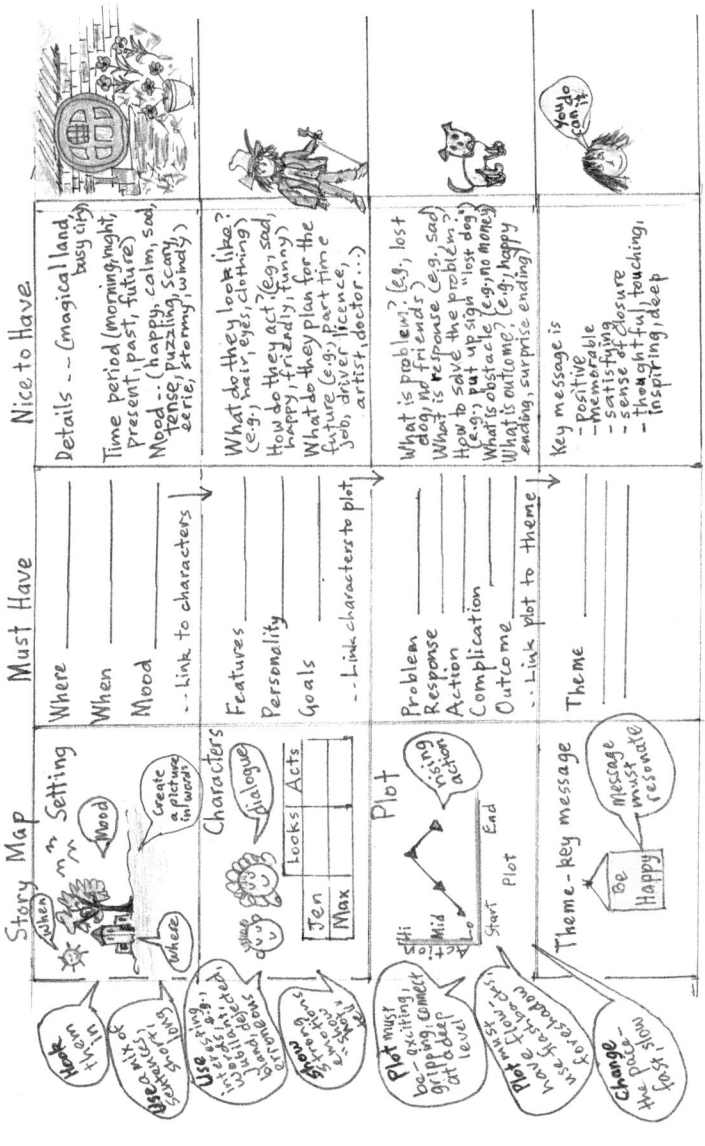

Figure 12.4 Story Planner – Advanced.

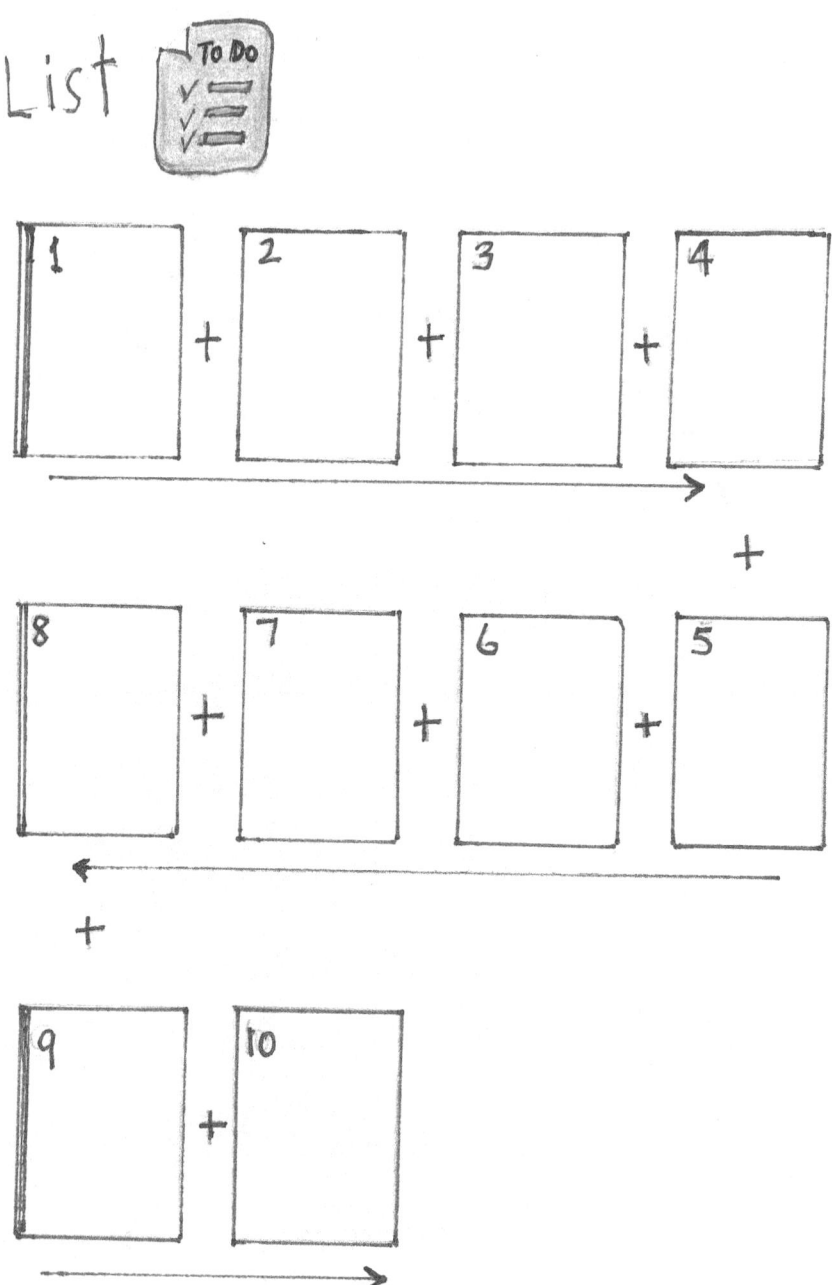

Figure 12.5 List Planner.

Teaching writing 161

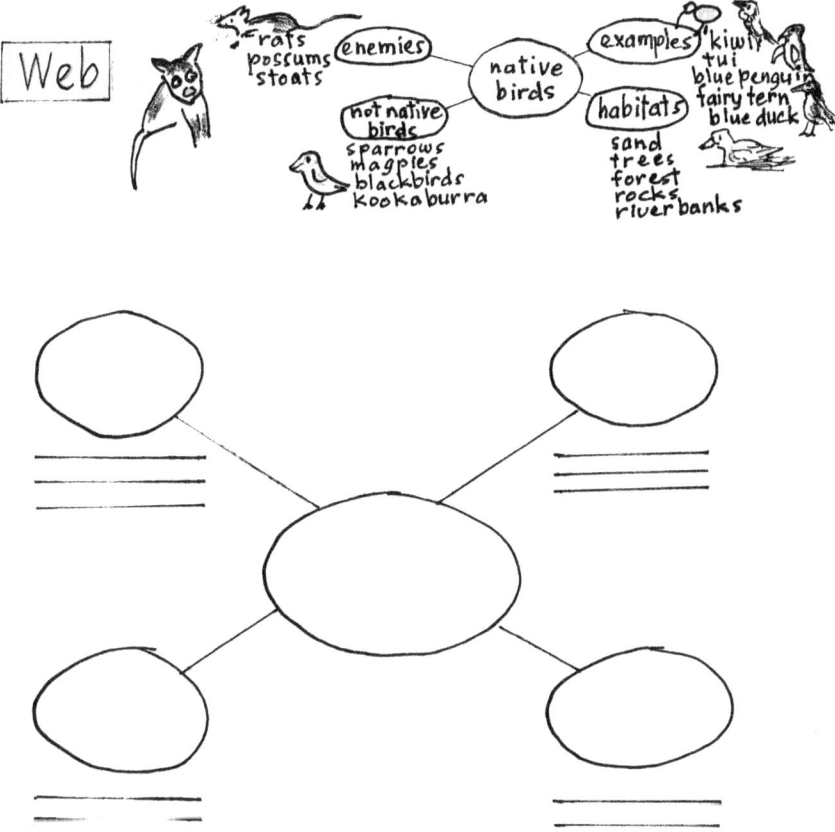

Figure 12.6 Web Planner.

Figure 12.7 Weave Planner.

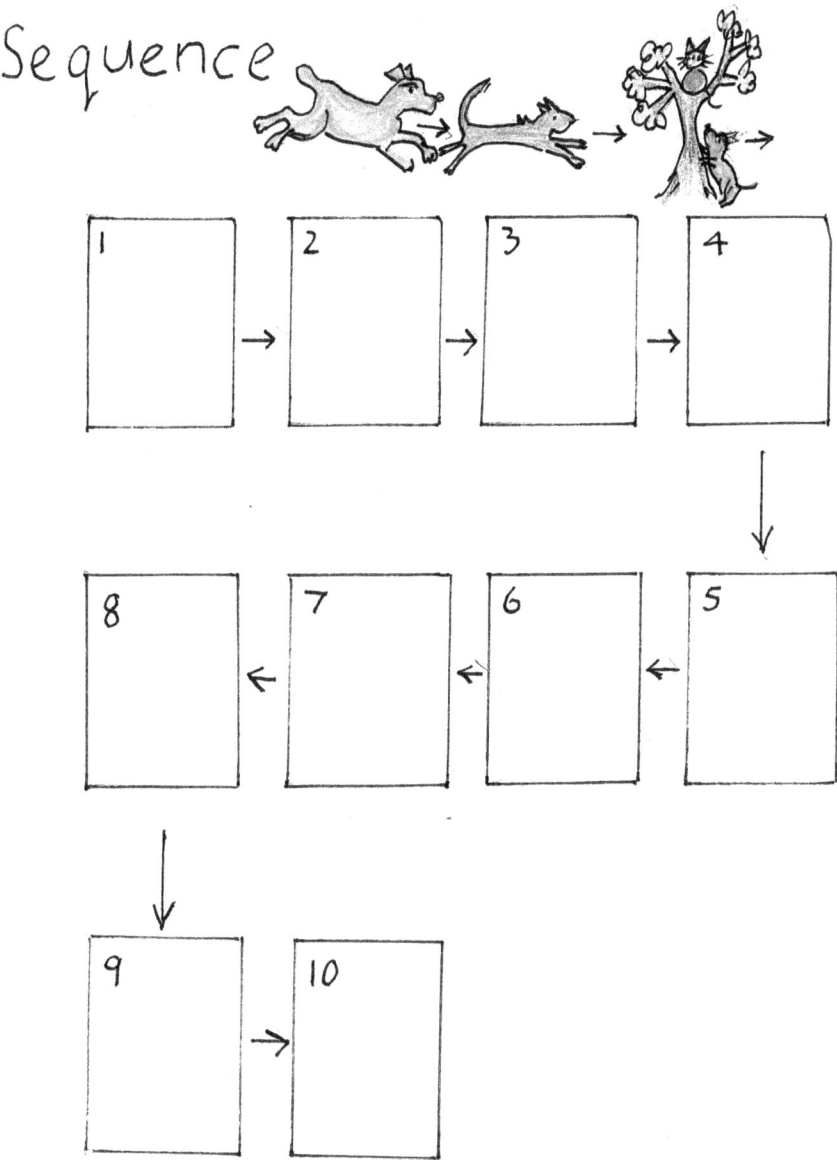

Figure 12.8 Linear String Planner.

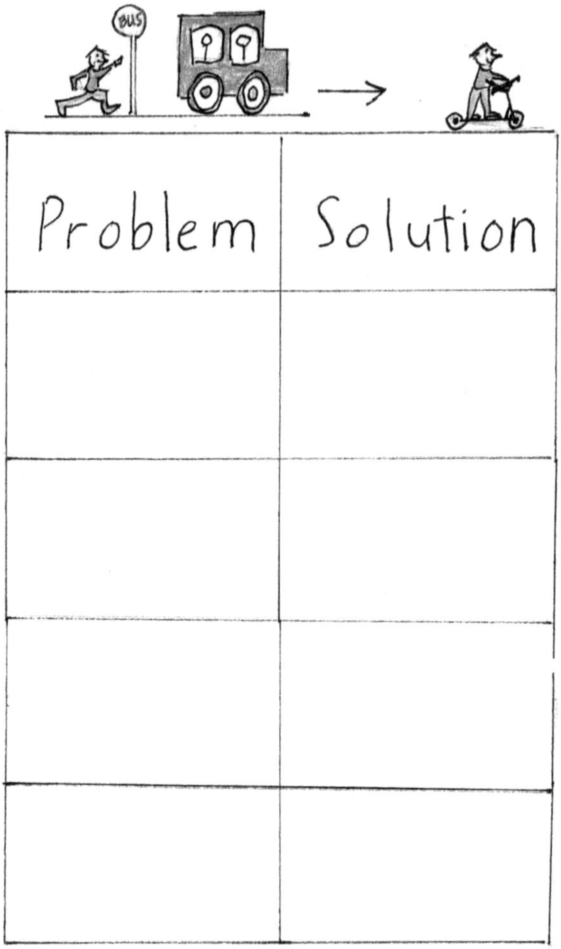

Problem	Solution

Figure 12.9 Problem–Solution Planner.

Teaching writing 165

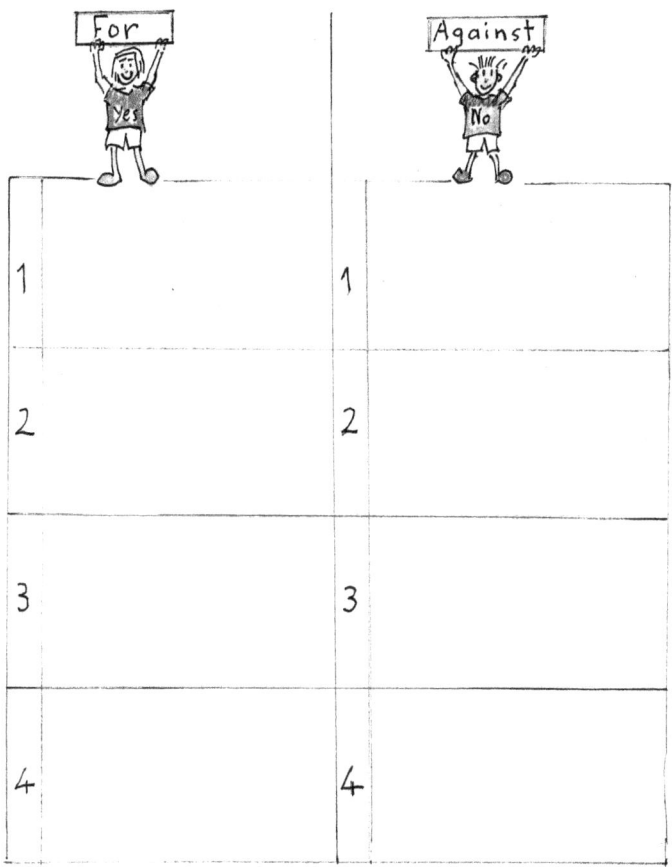

Figure 12.10 Persuasion Planner.

Part 5
Spelling

Chapter 13, *Spelling: What is it?*, covers spelling rules, types of errors, the statistical speller, painting imaginary billboards, quirky spelling, Latin and Greek spelling, and "Bee" spellers obsessed about spelling in a good way.

Chapter 14, *Assessing spelling*, covers norm-referenced tests, case studies of what examiners say about student spelling, a scope and sequence spelling chart with 27 steps to follow, the Big 8 spelling rules, eight spelling charts for student practice, eight spelling quizzes, and 14 punctuation tips.

Chapter 15, *Teaching spelling*, covers "morphological" spelling of words with a prefix–root word–suffix structure, and for struggling students, there are 18 mini quizzes that test consonant and vowel phonics patterns, homophones, plural and past tense endings, and Latin suffixes.

DOI: 10.4324/9781003130789-17

13 Spelling

What is it?

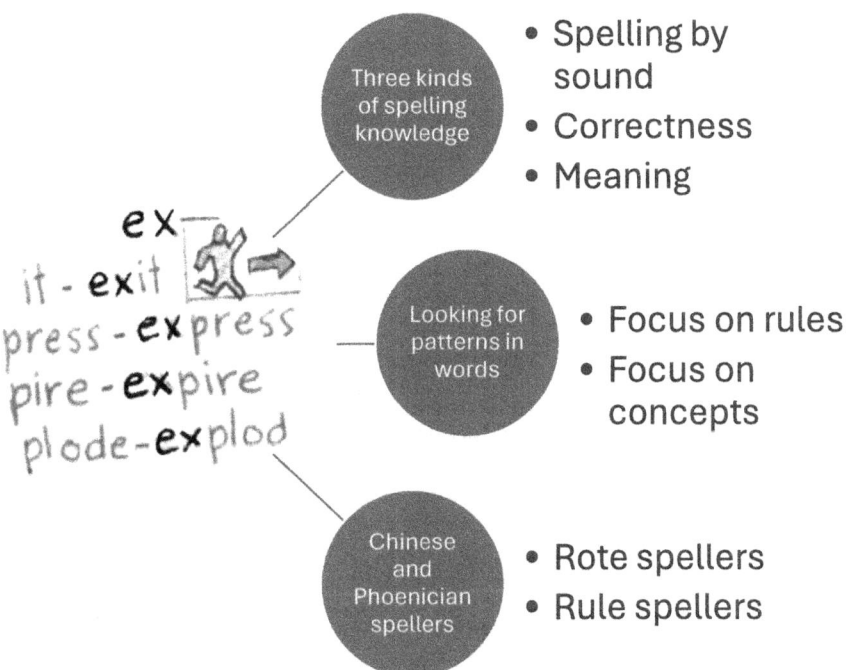

Figure 13.1 Overview of Chapter 13: Spelling: What Is It?.

13.1 Introduction

> "I'm just like anybody else in the school ... everybody says hi to me, but the trouble is, when they scream out, "How do you spell *Freddo*?" I can't do anything like that."

Many students spell the way they talk, but when they talk, they say the sounds differently - "What are you doing?" sounds like "Wotcha doon?"

The student who is an effective speller does not spell the way they talk. The student must stand back from informal talk and think about the rules that underpin spelling. Students must teach themselves more effective ways to spell words.

What is spelling? It is writing alphabetic characters in a sequence that corresponds to the sounds/phonemes in the word, but using conventional spelling as revealed in a dictionary.

Spelling skill requires knowledge of letter-sound rules and exceptions to the rules. The student must store in memory regular spellings like *jump*, ambivalent spellings like *green*, which could be spelled *grean*, and exception spellings, like *come* and *laugh*

Spelling is a challenge for many students. National tests show that nearly 30% of students are moving toward the basic standard required for success in school but are not there yet. They have not reached their potential in spelling.

Spelling is linked to privilege, class, culture, and language. It is an important skill, yet under-researched. Studies are still ongoing to find the best pathway to learn to spell well.

The chapter will cover topics such as:

- The mind of the speller
- Word analysis
- Three faces of spelling
- Statistical spelling
- Imagery and spelling
- Quirks of spelling
- Classifying spelling patterns for learning
- What makes a top speller?

13.2 The mind of the speller

The successful speller is always searching for method, regularity, history, structure, and coherence. When students understand this way of thinking about spelling, it gives them a new direction in learning to spell well. Spelling is no longer about rote memory.

English has become a mix of words from many languages – which adds complexity but richness as well; that is what makes spelling so awesome. English consists of a massive number of words, some say more than a million words, and the number keeps growing.

The main building blocks of English spelling are words with Anglo-Saxon, Latin, and Greek origins which have their own spelling patterns. Spelling has changed over hundreds of years, as scribes and printers worked out new spelling rules (see Figure 13.2), but they did it to add method to English spelling.

Spelling – what is it? 171

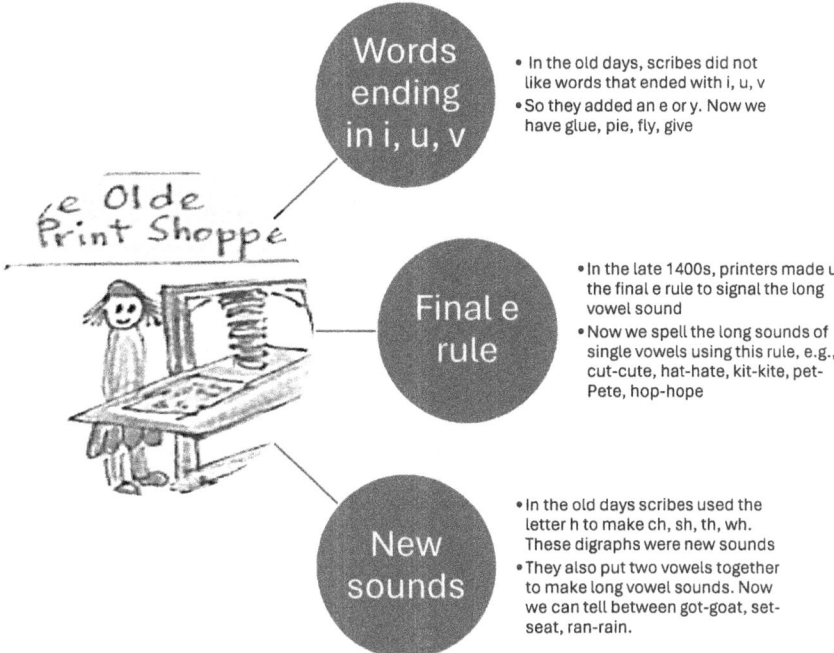

Figure 13.2 How Printers Changed the Rules.

When you look at the big picture, there are several sides to spelling: there are regular sound–letter patterns, such as consonant and vowel digraphs, and regular meaning patterns, such as suffixes and prefixes. The regular patterns enable the student to spell many words correctly (e.g., *brand*, *setting*). Spelling in English is about sound and meaning. Sometimes the meaning patterns override the sound patterns in a trade-off that pushes out sound to preserve meaning (e.g., the c sound in *medicine* is different from the *c* sound in *medical*, which is a good thing because it tells the reader that the two words share *medic*, so they are linked in meaning).

To spell accurately, students must acquire knowledge of the letter–sound rules and the meaning structure of words. Both are necessary. When you look at spelling this way, it is not about rote memory. There are many cognitive aspects to it.

13.3 Spelling archaeology – digging into morphemes

In the higher levels of schools, most text material is littered with technical, unfamiliar words with Latin/French and Greek origins. When digging out the bones of these words, students uncover structures that are not just sound-based but meaning-based. They are looking into old words, from the ancient past, with different spelling structures.

To spell them, the student must unpack these borrowed words as clusters of morphemes or meaning units.

So, what are morphemes? Below is a short description of morphemes and what they are like:

Morphemes are minimal units of meaning in words. A morpheme can be long or multisyllabic (e.g., a *salamander*, an amphibian, is one morpheme but four syllables in length). In contrast, the suffix *-s* at the end of a word is also one morpheme, but it is only one letter in length and indicates plurality (e.g., *dogs*).

Free morphemes

A free morpheme is a meaning unit, like *road*, that can stand on its own. It has its own independent meaning. A compound word has two free morphemes (e.g., *railroad*).

Bound morphemes

Root words

The Latin root word *spond* is a *bound* morpheme, meaning to *pledge* or *promise*. A *bound* morpheme is not a real word. To form a real word, a root word needs a prefix or suffix or both. It needs something added to it.

Prefixes

A prefix is a bound morpheme; it is not a real word. A prefix is added to the front of the root word (e.g., *re-spond*). The prefix *re-* means *again*. The meaning of *respond* is to *answer*, or *pledge again*. The new word *respond* is a verb.

Suffixes

A suffix is a bound morpheme. It is not a real word. It comes at the end of the word and changes the form class (e.g., *respondent* with the suffix *-ent* is a noun).

Student activity

Wong (1986) taught students at ages 11–12 how to dig out and spell morphemes in Latin-based words.

In the lessons, students used a spelling grid like that shown in Table 13.1. They had a copy of the grid. They discussed the first two words and broke

Table 13.1 Student Copy of Spelling Grid

Word	Number of syllables	Syllables in word	Base word	Add suffix	Change in spelling
information	4	in-for-ma-tion	inform	+a + tion	
education	4	e-du-ca-tion			drop e
vacation		va-ca-tion			
action					
station					
inflation					
election					
formation					
relation					
correction					

Note: (1) A base word is a real word. In this exercise, some base words have a prefix in front of the root word (e.g., in + flate + ion, where the root word *flate* means to "blow into"). (2) Answers to the grid are at end of this chapter.

them into parts to spell them. Then they did the rest of the words on their own. What students did was

- read the word in the grid aloud
- count the number of syllables and write the number in the grid
- spell the base word and write it in the grid
- add the suffix *-ion* and write it into the grid
- write onto the grid any change to the spelling (e.g., drop *e*, add *a*)

In the study, students did one spelling grid a week for several weeks. Each week, the grid had a set of new Latin words to spell. Learning time each week was 20 minutes.

The study found that, when students were tested on their ability to spell the grid words, their scores went from 27% correct before the lessons started to 78% correct a week after the lessons finished, and two weeks later it was still high, at 79%. They had remembered how to spell nearly all the Latin words correctly.

13.4 The three faces of spelling

There are three important spelling skills (Apel et al., 2012):

1. Spelling by sound/phonemes. Students spell the sounds they hear in the word. This is spelling by sound, and it may not always be correct (e.g., *rane* for *rain*).
2. Orthographic spelling, namely conventional or correct spelling (e.g., *shirt*, not *shert*).
3. Morphemic spelling (e.g., past tense *-ed* is a suffix morpheme, such as *faked*, not *fakt*).

Should students learn spelling skills in that order: by sound, then by correct spelling, then by morpheme structure? That would mean the first stage in learning to spell is spelling by sound. The second stage is to make sure the sounds are spelled correctly – this is orthographic knowledge. The third stage is to focus on morpheme knowledge for spelling. Some studies, however, have found that it is better to engage in all three ways of spelling at the same time (Joye et al., 2022).

13.5 Statistical learning of spelling rules

An important way that students can and do learn spelling rules is via *graphotactic* or statistical learning. This learning happens when students work out spelling rules on their own, without instruction (Treiman, 2018; Treiman & Altmiller, 2021, 2025).

Students are sensitive to variance in spelling patterns. They notice recurring spelling patterns when they are reading and writing. They notice spelling patterns such as

- short *o* sound spelled *a* when it comes after *w* (e.g., *was*).
- short *e* spelled *ea* before the letter *d* (e.g., *bread, spread, head, dead, instead*).
- *ch* sound spelled *-tch* at the end of a word after a short vowel (e.g., *ditch, fetch, catch*).
- *th* letters together occur frequently, so *th* must be one sound, not two different sounds
- in a word like *rubble*, there is a double b – this is the doubling rule
- some words that end with ik sound are spelled *ic* (e.g., *panic*)
- same spelling for past tense *-ed* and plural *-s*, even though the sounds vary.

Such spelling patterns do have some regularity in that they work for many words, such as spelling *a* for *o* sound after w (e.g., *was, wand, wad, squash, watch*), spelling -ck after a short vowel (e.g., duck, brick, wicked), and *-igh* for a small set of words with the long *i* sound (e.g., *knight, sight, fight, night, right*).

13.6 Learn the rules, then learn the exceptions

Exception spellings are in words that have few or no relatives with that spelling (e.g., *they, who, of, laugh*). Regular spellings are words that share with many other words the same letters and sound sequence (e.g., *cat, rat, bat, mat*).

How do students learn to spell exception words? It seems that regular spellings are the foundation. When students know the regular spelling rules, it enables them to learn the exception spellings more easily.

This is because irregular words do have partial regularity, so the student only has to remember the exception to the rule, not the whole word (e.g., *they* – the exception is the spelling of *ey* for the *ay* sound).

The scatterplot in Figure 13.3 below, using test scores from one study (Dymock & Nicholson, 2017), shows that students who can spell regular words well can also spell irregular words.

What does this mean in practical terms? It means students who focus their energies first on learning regular spelling rules will find it easier to learn exception spellings. It will make learning easier.

How do you learn exception spellings? Practice is the key. In one study (Dymock & Nicholson, 2017), students learned to spell words both by practice and by learning spelling rules. Learning rules had more transfer value, but practice was also important for learning words.

In the study, the practice group had a list of 10 words. They read the words aloud, covered the words, spelled them from memory, uncovered the words, and checked their spellings. They also spelled the words in alphabetical order and wrote them in sentences. It was all practice, writing the words again and again. In the study, the rules group learned rules that could transfer to new words. They also engaged in practice, spelling the words several times.

The study showed that students can learn to spell words. Practice is important; so is rule knowledge. Learning rules can help to spell new words. Here are some examples:

- the ai/ay rule helps to spell words like *terrain* and *betray*
- the *-ies* rule for words ending with *y* (e.g., *babies, flies*)
- the apostrophe in "not" words (e.g., *don't*).
- the possessive apostrophe (e.g., *they lost the students' essays*)

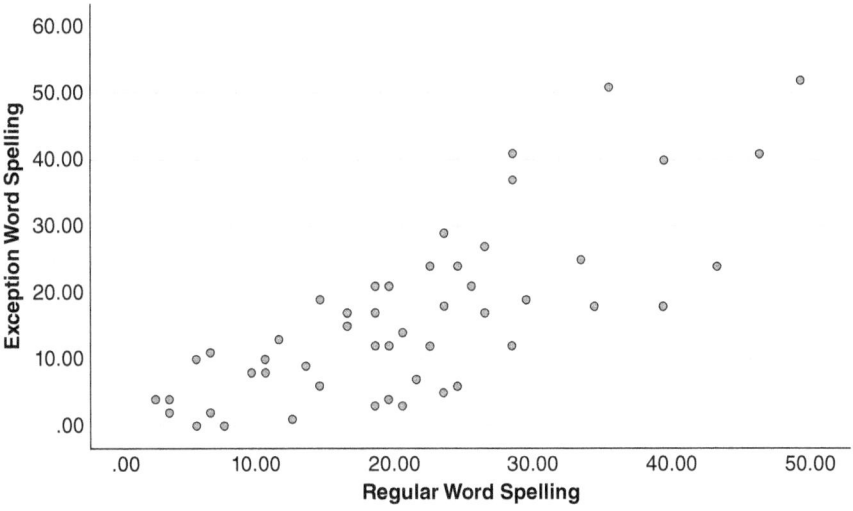

Figure 13.3 Scatterplot of Student Scores for Spelling Regular and Exception Words.

- *ch* as *-tch* at the end of a word (e.g., *ditch, kitchen*)
- Latin words, like *conflagration*
- Greek words, like *claustrophobia*

13.7 Does instruction in spelling make a difference?

Do spelling lessons make a difference? Yes, but it seems that the lessons only work in a significant way for the specific words taught. The lesson learning does not usually transfer to new words (Graham & Santangelo, 2014). Others have found the same pattern of results; that is, words learned in spelling lessons did not transfer to new words or to tests and exams. One study was definite about lack of transfer, "Spelling … approaches … are significantly more effective in increasing performance on taught words than on … words not taught" (Petersen-Brown & Kromminga, 2024, p. 3333).

Do spelling lessons with a focus on morphology (i.e., focusing on root words, suffixes, and prefixes) get better results. They do get good results but, again, only for the words taught. One report concluded, "Morphology instruction is effective … for words that are directly taught" (Colenbrander et al., 2024, p. 119).

The fact that students do learn the words taught to them is a positive because there are many words that students need to learn for their studies at school. If you are writing your ideas about a novel or writing about a scientific concept, you do want to be able to spell the main characters and key concepts. Learning specific words is helpful. It is just that the learning may not transfer to when you must spell a new word that you have not been taught before.

A positive way to think about spelling lessons is that they do help students to spell the words taught in the lesson. This is a good result. If lessons focus on spelling strategies that make it easier to spell the taught words, this is a bonus. Students can get better at spelling. The elusive goal is to help them improve their general spelling ability. Spelling progress will not happen without lessons, so it is important for students to keep going, to persevere.

13.8 Imagery and spelling

Imagery can help to remember spellings of tricky words like *zany tibia gypsy phylum biceps aorta*. In one study (Radaker, 1963), students had to imagine each letter of the word pasted or painted or stapled onto a huge screen or billboard. In their mind, the letters had to be large and in dark print on white background. The findings were that the imagery group improved enough to make gains on a norm-referenced test of spelling, more than did a comparison group that did not get the training.

13.9 Little quirks of spelling

There are many unusual spellings in English, but there are ways to remember them:

Spelling – what is it? 177

- Over-pronounce tricky words (e.g., *fry-end* for *friend*; *choc-oe-late* for *chocolate*).
- Look for relatives, or words with similar core meanings (e.g., *heal-healthy*).
- Final *v* sound is always spelled *ve*: *love, give, active*.
- The *kw* sound is always spelled *qu* (e.g., *quit, queen, quick*).

Note: For more information, see the quirky spellings in Appendix A of this chapter.

13.10 How to classify words for learning

Imagine that a student has this list of eight words to learn: *history, ransack, cattle, ancient, was, fight, medicine, laugh*. Is there a way to group the words in patterns that will make it easier for the student to learn them? The spelling chart in Figure 13.4 shows one way to group the words. It groups the list of words into those with transfer value, so students can use the rules to spell other words, and words with no transfer value, that students will have to learn as exception words.

The reasons for grouping the words this way are

- *medicine, ancient, history*: why do they have transfer value? It can be argued that words with Latin and French origins do have transfer because they have relatives (e.g., *ancient – ancestry*). In Latin words like *ancient*, the *ci* spelling

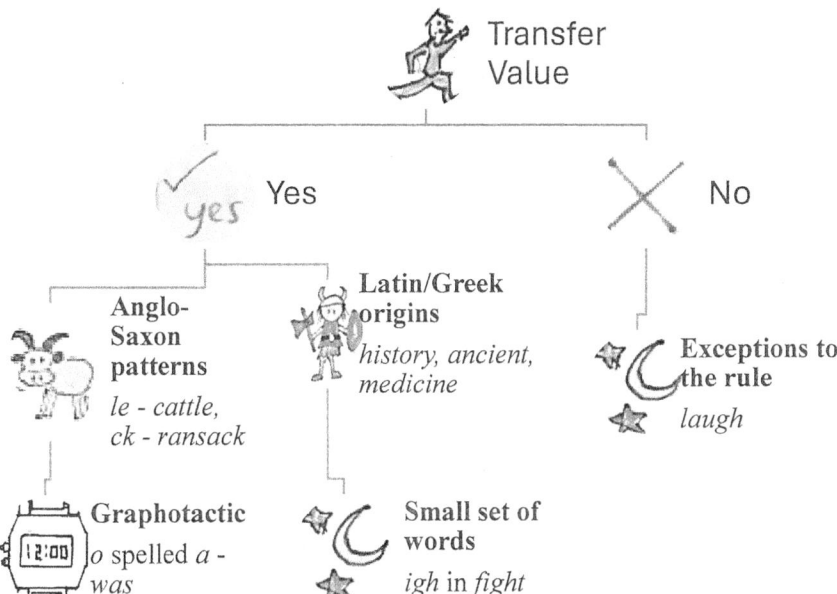

Figure 13.4 Classification of Words for Spelling in Terms of Transfer Value.

has a *sh* sound. If the student knows the *ci* spelling for *sh*, it will help to spell *ancient*. It is the same with *medicine* and *history*; they have relatives (e.g., *medic, medical, medicine, paramedic, history, historian, historical*). If the student thinks of relatives, they will see that the root word stays the same spelling, even though the sounds change, so it will be easier to spell these words.

- *cattle, ransack*: why do they have transfer value? It can be argued that *cattle* is a word that has spelling relatives (e.g., *rattle, battle, kettle*). These words all have the -le syllable pattern. It is the same with *ransack*: this word is of Viking origin and has relatives (e.g., *sack, backpack, attack, shack*).
- *fight*: why does this word have transfer value? The *-igh* spelling has relatives; it matches to a small set of words (e.g., *light, sight, might, tight, right*). A spelling tip is that *-igh* is often followed by the letter *t*.
- *was*: why does this word have transfer value? It is a statistical pattern, where the *o* sound is spelled *a* after the letter *w* (e.g., *was, watch, want, what, wasp*).
- *laugh*: this word does not have transfer value because it has very few relatives. The *au* spelling for ar is rare, with only a couple of relatives: *aunt, draught*. The gh spelling for f is rare, with only a few relatives such as *tough, cough, rough,* and *enough*. Because the spelling au for ar and gh for f are so rare, the spelling chart has *laugh* in the "no transfer" column as an exception word.

Student activity

A possible activity is to give the above words to the class, before showing them the chart, and ask for their thoughts on how they would classify the words. It will generate discussion for sure!

13.11 Do students focus too much on spelling?

Some say that students focus too much on correctness in spelling. The arguments for saying this are that

- Too much attention is paid to spelling correctness.
- Pointing out spelling misses in student writing does not help them to spell better.
- Priority should be given to composition skills, not spelling.
- Technology is making spelling skill redundant (e.g., spell-checks, predictive text).
- Learning vocabulary is more important.
- Spelling is part of writing, not a separate subject.
- Spelling instruction is for individuals who need it, not the whole class.

While these are understandable reasons not to focus on spelling, studies show that spelling skill is important. In one study, when between 3% and 13% of words in essays were misspelled, marker ratings dropped significantly compared with marks given to the same essays, written with correct spellings (Graham et al., 2011).

13.12 What makes a "Bee" speller?

Zaila Avant-garde, at age 14, out-spelled other amazing student spellers to win the *Scripps National Spelling Bee* in the US. To win the competition, Zaila had to spell *murraya*, a type of tropical tree. She asked for the origin of the word, it was from Latin, before attempting to spell it. Other words she spelled correctly were *querimonious* and *solidungulate*.

When she was given a word to spell, she asked for a clear pronunciation of the word, so she heard all the sounds. She asked for the origin of the word. She said she spent seven hours a day improving her spelling. Daily practice was her routine.

What strategies made her so successful? There may be many factors, especially perseverance and the will to win, but successful strategies also include hearing every sound in the word - phonemic awareness, looking for the origin of the word - its etymology, and dedicating serious amounts of study time to learn the spellings of words.

13.13 Conclusion

Lack of spelling skill will have a negative effect on achieving long-term goals like success in exams. Student work does not have to be marred by spelling pings. All students have the potential to spell correctly. Society sees spelling skill as a sign of success. Spelling is not sufficient to succeed in life, but it is essential. The speller needs a range of strategies to grasp the deep structure of spelling. When students come across words with interesting spellings, encourage them to tell you all about it! Give positive feedback, e.g., "Good job, *raucous* is a nice example of a word with Latin origins." There is so much to learn in spelling; it is an exciting journey.

Answers to Spelling Grid (Table 13.2)

Table 13.2 Student Spelling Grid – Answers

Word	Number of syllables	Syllables in word	Root word	Add suffix	Change in spelling
information	4	in-for-ma-tion	inform	+a +t ion	
education	4	e-du-ca-tion	educate	+ tion	drop e
vacation		va-ca-tion	vacate	+ tion	drop e
action	2	ac-tion	act	+ tion	
station	2	sta-tion	state	+ tion	drop e
inflation	3	in-fla-tion	inflate	+ tion	drop e
election	3	e-lec-tion	elect	+ tion	
formation	3	form-a-tion	form	+ a + tion	
relation	3	re-la-tion	relate	+ tion	drop e
correction	3	cor-rec-tion	correct	+ tion	

Appendix A:

Quirky spelling patterns

1. Spelling of consonant sound after short vowel
   -ck (e.g., *duck, sick, wreck, clock, back*)
   -tch (e.g., *catch, kitchen*; exceptions: *such, much, rich*)
   -dge (e.g., *edge, judge, badge, ridge, lodge*)
   -ff, -ll, -ss, -zz (e.g., *tell, bass, buzz*; exceptions: *if, gas, this, us, yes, bus, plus, quiz*)
   -s for z sound at end of word (e.g., *as, is, was, has, his*)

2. Long vowel sound spellings
   ai in the middle – as in *rain, sail, paint, retail* – and *ay* at the end (e.g., *day, play, array*)
   oa in the middle (e.g., *toast, soap, road, coat*)
   -k after a long vowel sound (e.g., *make, like, week, soak*) and after other vowel and consonant combinations (e.g., *book, fork, talk, think*)
   -ge after long vowel sound (e.g., *age, huge, oblige*) and after other consonant and vowel combinations (e.g., *large, plunge, urge, gauge*)

3. Consonants that need special attention
   Final v is always spelled -ve, as in *gave, have, behave, active*.
   Letter q is always followed by u, as in *queen, quit, technique*.

4. Words ending in -y
   Change y to i before adding a suffix (e.g., *carry – carried, happy – happier, try – tried*)
   Exception 1: if y comes after a vowel (e.g., *play – player, enjoy – enjoyed*)
   Exception 2: if y is before -*ing*, -*ish*, -*ist* (e.g., *fly – flying, baby – babyish*)

5. Plurals
   Most nouns change to plural by adding *s* (e.g., *bats, pigs, girls*).
   Nouns ending in *y*, change the *y* to *i* and add -es (e.g., *fly – flies, baby – babies*).
   If y follows a vowel, keep the *y*, add -s, as in *toy-toys, chimney-chimneys*.
   Nouns ending in *f* or *fe* change to -ves (e.g., *elf – elves, leaf – leaves, life – lives*); or if they end in o, they sometimes add -*es* (e.g., *tomato – tomatoes*).
   Some plurals are irregular pattern (e.g., *mouse – mice, foot – feet, woman – women*).

6. Adding suffixes
   If word ends in final e, drop the e before adding a suffix starting with a vowel (e.g., *take – taking, leave – leaving, stone – stony, fine – finer*; exception: *finely*).

7. -ed past tense marker
   Always spell past tense -ed even though it can have three sounds: -ed as in *ragged*, *t* as in *jumped*, or *d* as in *hugged*.

8. Over-pronunciation strategy
   Over-pronounce to make sounds more noticeable (e.g., *choc-o-late, k-now, ni-gh-t*).

9. High-frequency irregular spellings
   Focus on the regular part and separate out the exception (e.g., *they = th + ey*).

10. Latin suffixes ian - ion
    If suffix denotes a person, it is <u>ian</u> (e.g., *tactic<u>ian</u>, magic<u>ian</u>*). If not a person, it is *-ion* (e.g., *stat<u>ion</u>, nat<u>ion</u>*).

11. The two spellings of the s and j sounds
    Spell s sound as s before a, o, u (e.g., *sat, sock, fussy*).
    Spell s sound as c before e, i, y (e.g., *silence*).
    Spell j sound as *j* (e.g., *jingle, jiffy, jelly, jeans, jetty*).
    Spell j sound as g before e, i, y (e.g., *ginger, huge, cage, gentle, revenge, gypsy*).
    Rule: Spell s and j sound with c or g only if they are followed by e, i, y.

12. Small sets of words with same spelling
    Some spellings occur in small sets of words. For example:
    l<u>igh</u>t, sight, right, tight, night
    c<u>ou</u>ld, would, should
    <u>kn</u>ow, knife, knot, knee, knight
    wh<u>ere</u>, there.

13. Doubling rule
    In a two-syllable word, spell one consonant after a long vowel sound (e.g., diner – di<u>nn</u>er, tiny – ti<u>nn</u>y) and two consonants after a short vowel sound, and before *-le* (e.g., rifle – ru<u>ffl</u>e).
    Exceptions: Do not double if the word already has two consonants (e.g., *fitter - fitful, sadder – sadly, redder – redness, shipping – shipment*).

14. Prefixes and suffixes
    As pupils learn the meanings of prefixes and suffixes, this will help with spelling. For example:

    Prefixes
    re- means "again": *report, release, recover, replace, return*
    un- means "not": *unwilling, unbundle, unproven, unveil, unacceptable*
    dis- means "not": *disagree, dislike, disappear, disqualify, discover, disappointment*
    ex- means "out": *explain, expansion, explode, export, express*
    trans- means "across": *transfer, transport, transaction*

intro- means "before": *introduce*
sub- means "under": *submarine, substantial*
pre- means "before": *prevent, predict, preview*

Suffixes

-ity: *security, publicity*
-ive: *inventive, excessive*
-ment: *excitement, statement*
-ible: *invisible, incompatible*
-ate: *concentrate*
-less: *wireless*
-sion, -tion, -cian: *extension, action, magician*

Appendix B

Latin root words, prefixes, and suffixes (Tables 13.3–13.5)

Table 13.3 Common Root Words with Latin Origins

Latin root	Meaning	Examples
form	to shape	deform, misinform
port	to carry	deport, import, export
rupt	to break or burst	disrupt, bankrupt
tract	to draw or pull	attract, extract
scrib, script	to write	prescribe, describe
spec, spect, spic	to see watch, or observe	inspector, disrespect
struct	to build	construct, destruct
dict	to say or tell	dictator, diction, dictionary
flect, flex	to bend or curve	flex, reflect, deflect
mit, miss	to send	admission, admit, dismiss
cred	to believe	credence, credible
duc, duce, duct	to lead	conduct, conductor
pel, puls	to drive or push	compel, expel, propel
pend, pens	to hang or weigh	pendant, pendulum
jac, jec, ject	to throw or lie	interject, deject
ped	foot	centipede, pedal, pedestrian,
vid, vis	to see	vision, invisible
aud	to hear or listen	audio, audience, audition
vit, vita, viv, vivi	to live	revival, vitality
leg, legis	law	illegal, legal, legislature
greg	group crowd; to assemble	congregate, desegregate
capit, capt	head or chief	capitol, captain, chief
spir spire	to breathe	perspire, respirator, expire
mob, mot, mov	to move	automobile, motor, mobility
cide	to kill	homicide, suicide
cise	to cut	excision, scissors,

Table 13.4 Common Prefixes with Latin Origins

pre-	re-	in-, im, ir, il	dis-	en, em	in-, im	mis-
precook	recharge	inconsiderate	disable	enable	incoming	miscalculate
preschool	refresh	intolerable	disagree	endanger	inboard	misbehave
prepay	reconstruct	informal	disrespect	enrich	inbreed	miscount
pre-soak	recapture	inexperienced	disobey	enrage	infield	misdeal
pre-test	research	impartial	distrust	enjoy	imprint	misuse

pre-	inter-	de-	trans-	super-	semi-	anti-	mid-
precook	interchange	debug	transalpine	superglue	semiautomatic	anticlockwise	midcourse
preschool	intercity	debrief	transatlantic	supermarket	semicircle	antisocial	midair
prepay	intercontinental	deactivate	transport	supermodel	semiformal	antislavery	midnight
pre-soak	interconnect	debark	transcribe	superpower	semiskilled	anticlimax	midpoint
pre-test	interact	debar	transmit	superstructure	semidetached	antisubmarine	midship

Spelling – what is it? 183

Table 13.5 Common Suffixes with Latin Origins

Suffix	Meaning	Purpose	Example
-able, -ible	able to be	adjective	capable, horrible
-ion, ation	state, result	noun	decision, action, automation
-ity	quality, state of	noun	sobriety
-ment	state, act, result	noun	impediment
-al, -eal, -ial	has character of	adjective	historical, arboreal, social
-ent, -ant	participle	adjective/noun	resistant, mutant, redolent
-ary, arium	connected with	adjective/noun	literary, library, aquarium
-ure	act of	noun	tenure, scripture
-ous, eous, ious	full of, like	adjective	copious, aqueous
-ence, -ance	state of, quality	noun	audience
-ian, -an	belonging to,	adjective	Italian, librarian,
-ify	to make	verb	mollify
-ate	possessing	adjective	inanimate

14 Assessing spelling

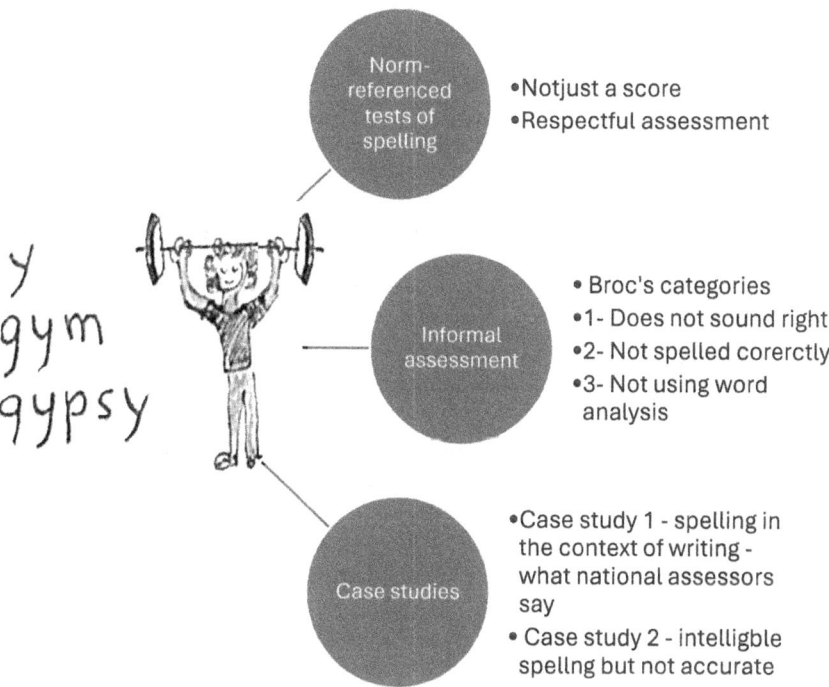

Figure 14.1 Overview of Chapter 14: Assessing Spelling.

14.1 Introduction

> I need help with my spelling and my writing.

Spelling is not about rote memory. It is impossible to remember the spelling of hundreds of thousands of words by their look. Students initially do this but discover it does not pay off. Too many words look the same. Too many sounds

DOI: 10.4324/9781003130789-19

have too many different spellings. Students must be able to spell words according to letter–sound rules, sound by sound, syllable by syllable, morpheme by morpheme.

Assessment of spelling skill gives the teacher insight as to whether students are on the right track or using strategies that will not serve them well.

Spelling skill is not just about whether the student can spell words correctly. It is about a person's identity. It is one thing to test and get a score, another to assure the student that they are not dumb and that they can improve their spelling with some practical but effective strategies.

Spelling is important for school success, but it is also about a student's sense of belonging and wellbeing.

The Appendix to the present chapter offers spelling activities and teaching suggestions to make spelling happen as well as a list of important punctuation marks that students should revise to improve their skills.

This chapter covers the following topics:

- Formal assessment of spelling using norm-referenced tests
- Informal assessment and the three types of spelling error
- Case studies of student spelling
- Spelling activities for the student who struggles with spelling

14.2 Formal assessment

To gain accurate assessment data, it is best to use a published, norm-referenced measure of spelling that can be used to assess an individual student or a whole group of students at one sitting.

The Wide Range Achievement Tests (WRAT5) (Wilkinson & Robertson, 2017) assess math, reading, and spelling. The spelling subtest is a list of 45 words.

The Schonell Spelling Test (Schonell & Schonell, 1960) is still used in some schools and in some research studies. There are about 100 words. It gives a spelling age for students from ages 6 to 12. There may be a copy of the test online.

14.3 Informal assessment: analysis of student spelling attempts

Student spelling attempts can be studied by using three categories. Broc et al. (2021) coded the spelling attempts of students ages 7 to 13 and found three different groupings:

- Did not sound right, some sounds missing (e.g., *hungry – hage*)
- Did not use conventional spelling (e.g., *shirt – shert*)
- Did not use morphemic spelling (e.g., *jumped – jumpt*)

Case study 1

The writing example below – the original copy is in Figure 14.2 – was done for a national test of writing (Australian Curriculum, Assessment and Reporting Authority [ACARA], 2013).

Transcription

> When I was going home and me and my mum saw a dead kangaroo it was sad. Dogs get shot every time. Animals are very important for our earth. Animals get killed for nothing. Animals respect our homes. Why don't we respect their homes.

The student writing received the following scores:

Audience 1/6, structure 1/6, ideas 2/6, persuasive devices 1/4, vocabulary 2/5, cohesion 1/4, paragraphing 0/3, sentence structure 2/6, punctuation 1/5, spelling 1/6.

Notes from examiner comments were that the essay lacked correct spelling, although some simple words were correct (*I, was, going, and, me, my, mum, it, sad, get, are, for, we*), and one common word was correct (*animals*). Missed attempts included *hoem, sor, dedth, cagaro, borg, sot, ever, tim,* and *vare*.

The overall scoring for the "Animals Getting Cewd" essay was very low and was probably partly due to the spelling difficulties of the student.

Analysis of "Animals Getting Cewd"

In the essay, there were 44 words and 23 were missed attempts. Put another way, 52% of words in the story were spelled conventionally, 48% were not.

Using the categories above, some of the missed spellings were

1. Did not sound right, some sounds missing (e.g., *killed – cewd*)
2. Did not use conventional spelling (e.g., *home – hoem*)
3. Did not use morphemic spelling (e.g., *jumped – jumpt*)

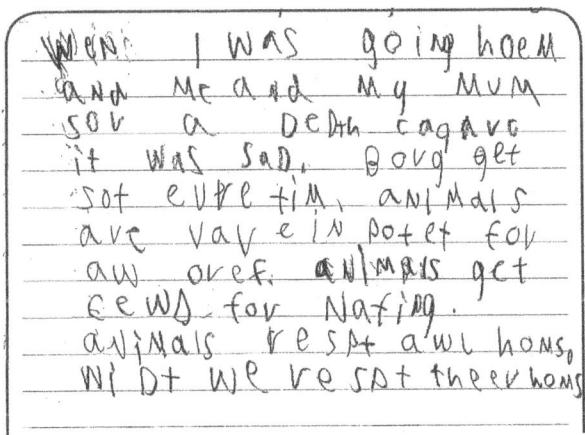

Figure 14.2 "Animals Getting Cewd".

How would you group the spelling attempts in this writing? Many of the missed attempts could be deciphered by sound (e.g., *hom* for *home*), but some words did not have a plausible spelling (e.g., *cewd* for *killed*, *dt* for *don't*). How would you group these attempts? One way is to see what spelling rules would apply to them:

Consonant sounds
b/d consonant confusion: *borg/dog*
c/k confusion: cagaro/kangaroo, cewd/killed
wh: wen/when, wi/why
consonant digraphs *sh, ng*: sot/shot, cagaro/kangaroo

r- and l-affected vowel sounds
r-affected vowels: *impotent/important*, orfe – earth, our – awl, theer – their
l-affected vowel sound *ill*: cewd/killed

Vowel sounds
short vowel sound *o: borg/dog*
split digraph: *homs – homes, tim – time*
vowel digraphs *aw, ea, oo: sor/saw, dedth/dead, cagaro/kangaroo*
final *y: vare/very, wi/why, evre – every*
other vowel sounds: *awl/our, oref/earth, nafing/nothing*

Morpheme endings and root words
-ed past tense: *cewd/killed*
root word: *respt/respect, einpotet – important*

Punctuation
Abbreviated words: *dt/don't*

The spelling was intelligible but at a high cost of accuracy and was not enough to meet standards at this level. What does the student need to do to improve? To this writer, the student would benefit from going back to basic spelling patterns listed in the Appendix to this chapter.

As a comparison with the above spelling, another student had written on the same topic but gained a much higher overall score for writing. There was a clear difference in spelling skill. The student wrote 150–200 words and correctly spelled tricky words like *noticed, issue, captured, statement, habitats, countries, enclosure, forests, argue, government, attempt, fauna, decided, symbolic, inspired, recently, featured, symbolic, destructive, force, supported, activist*, and *integrity*.

Case study 2

This student wrote the following:

> It was nelly the end of the day and the sky was turning a bireliont orange and purple coler. Our holl intier grup set up camp. I whent to bed with a rock under my head, my feet pointing towards the big bondfirer. Enney way as soon as the grup setilled, we could hear noises. I woke up from a horabull sleep. I was awack from listening to the rors of anamills.

The description of the camping trip had 72 words, and there were 15 missed attempts. Put another way, 79% of the words were spelled conventionally and 21% were not.

How would you group the spelling attempts in the above writing? Looking at the missed attempts, many could be avoided using spelling rules.

1. r-affected vowel sounds: *nelly/ne<u>ar</u>ly, rors/r<u>oar</u>s*
2. vowel digraph: *grup/group*
3. final *e* rule: *bondfirer*/bonfire, *holl/whole, intier/entire*
4. final *k* spelling: *awac<u>k</u>/awake*
5. consonant *w: whent/went*
6. suffix *-ible*: *horrabul/horr<u>ible</u>*
7. *-le* and *-ed* at end of word: *setilld/sett<u>led</u>*
8. *-al* suffix: anamills/anim*als*
9. Short vowel sounds: *enny/<u>a</u>ny*

Analysis

The student's strategy for words not known seems to be to spell by sound. Spellings are intelligible but at the cost of accuracy. As is evident from the missed attempts, the student would benefit from a review of basic spelling patterns listed in the Appendix to this chapter.

Case study 3

Imagine a student writes the following piece for a classroom task on the topic of giving a speech to their class:

> I suddenly get my papper and rush up to the spotlight. I nevosly chatter my teeth. I have my classmates stareing at me. I feel the hairs on my arm go stiff. I talk after the end of a masive speech. I sit in a uncomfterbal chair… The light shines apon my face. My frizzeld hair is no longer standing up.

There were seven missed attempts out of 61 words; this is about 11% error rate. It is much better spelling than the other case studies.

What does the student need to do to improve? The missed attempt *uncomfterbal* has its origins in Latin. The student could spell the word in meaning units, with *comfort* as the root word and *-able* as the Latin suffix. Some of the other missed attempts have regular spelling patterns (e.g., *paper, nervous, staring, massive, frizzled*). The student would benefit from revision of the patterns.

14.4 Conclusion

An accurate assessment of spelling skill is best done with a norm-referenced test. Informal assessment can be a window on spelling skill. Observation of missed attempts in spelling has potential to indicate what students need to learn.

Students who need extra help will benefit from the spelling suggestions in the chapter Appendix. They cover useful spelling patterns and will enable students to improve spelling skills.

Appendix

Spelling activities to ensure that students learn to spell well

Scope and sequence: spelling

Students not spelling to their potential, who struggle to spell even basic words, will have a better sense of direction if they follow the learning steps in the *spelling snake* (see Figure 14.3). It starts with basic letter-sounds and moves up to the more complex vowel sounds. For the student, it is like climbing a ladder that has 27 steps (see also Dymock & Nicholson, 2024).

Students who use the spelling snake in their spelling book have a pathway to follow. As they complete each step on the spelling snake, they check it off and move to the next step until finished. Learning to spell is more motivating if students have a scope and sequence to follow. The spelling snake chart has 27 steps from ABC sounds to words from Latin and Greek origins. In every classroom, students will be at different stages on the chart. Some may be at step 15 and others at step 25 or higher. Students will benefit from a scope and sequence to chart their progress.

Steps 1–7: Consonant and short vowel sounds

Each step has four letter-sounds to spell. Read out the letter, and the student spells the sound. As the student covers each step, they can spell words (e.g., in step 1, spell *pat, tap, sat, at, pats, spat*).

By the time they finish step 7, they should be able to spell most CVC (consonant-vowel-consonant) words (e.g., *ran, jump, quack*).

Assessing spelling 191

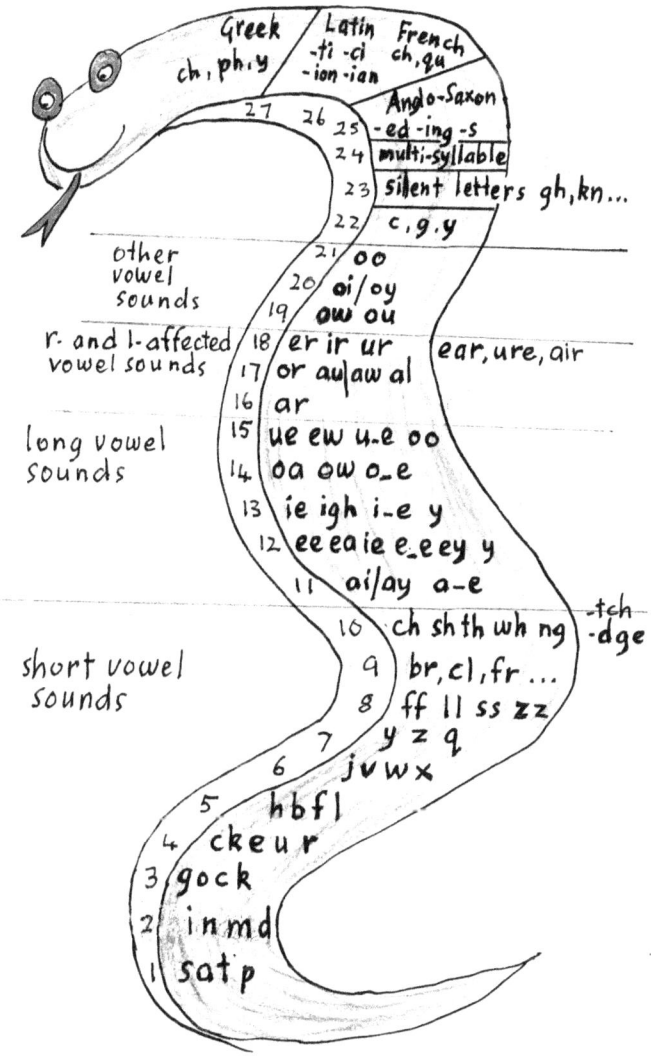

Figure 14.3 Spelling Snake: Levels 1–27.

Step 8: Some letters double at the end of the word

At the end of a one-syllable word, the student should double *f, l, s, z* (e.g., *sell, pill, bass, fuss, buzz, jazz*), but there are exceptions (e.g., *if, gas, this, us, yes, bus, plus, quiz*).

By the time they finish step 8, they should be able to spell (e.g., *bell, will, roll, toll, gull, dull, mass, toss, moss, loss, mess, fuzz, fizz, frizz, whizz, puff, off, cuff*).

Step 9: Adjacent consonants

At step 9, focus on initial clusters first because they are easier to spell and there are more than 20 of them (e.g., cl-); then focus on final clusters (e.g., -nk).

Spell each consonant sound. If there are two sounds, spell both.

There are more examples of adjacent consonants in Figure 2.5.

By the time the student finishes step 9, they should be able to spell words with adjacent consonants (e.g., <u>bl</u>ack, fl<u>eck</u>, <u>spr</u>int, <u>str</u>ess, <u>tr</u>u<u>nk</u>).

Step 10: Consonant digraphs

The consonant digraphs use existing consonants but add an h. They are new sounds to spell. They are ch- *chick*; sh- *ship*; th- *twelfth*; wh- *whisk*; -ng – *gong*.

Steps 11–15: Long vowel sounds

- ai *pain*, ay *foray*, a_e *name*
- ee *street*, ea *steal*, ie *grieve*, e_e Steve, ey *key*, y *hazy*
- ie *pie*, igh *blight*, i_e *deride*, y *decry*
- oa *gloat*, ow *flow*, o_e *slope*
- ue *misconstrue*, ew *sinew*, u_e *absolute*, oo *kangaroo*

Step 16: ar

Main spelling is ar (e.g., charm); there are exceptions but not many (e.g., *heart*).

Step 17: or

There are three spellings: or: *storm*; au/aw: *haunt, saw*; al: *small*.

Step 18: er, ear, air, ure

There are three spellings of er: *verse*; ur: *church*; ir: *whirl*.
Other r-affected vowel spellings:

- ear: *fear, gear, near, clear*
- air: *flair, pair, chair*
- ure: *cure, pure, obscure*

Step 19 : ow

There are two spellings of ow:

> ou (e.g., *mouse*)
> ow (e.g., *cow*)

Assessing spelling 193

Step 20: oi and oy

Spell oi sound as oi in middle of word and oy at end of word.

oi: soil
oy: Troy

Step 21: oo

The main spelling of oo sound is oo.

oo: book

Step 22: Chameleon letters: c, g, y

- c spells s sound before e, i, or y (e.g., *cent, city, cycle, juice, mice, icy*)
- g spells j sound before e, i, or y (e.g., *gem, rage, giant, gym*)
- y and ey spell e sound at end of word (e.g., *hazy, donkey*) or i sound (e.g., *why*)

Step 23: Silent letters

- kn: *knight, knife, knoll, knowledge*
- gn: *gnome, design, impugn*
- st: *listen, whistle, bristle, pestle, castle*

Step 24: Spelling multisyllable words

To spell multisyllable words like chimney, this is what you do:

How to spell *chimney*
1. Draw a line for each syllable ___ ___.
2. Say the first syllable: *chim*.
3. Spell the first syllable: *chim*.
4. Say the second syllable: *ney*.
5. Spell the second syllable: *nee*.
6. Write out your spelling: *chimnee*.
7. Now check your spelling, tick the correct letters: *chimn*.
8. Fix the incorrect letters; change *ee* to *ey*.
9. Write the correct spelling: *chimney*.

Students can use steps 1–9 to spell similar words (e.g., *mag/net, ro/bot, con/crete, gar/den, bub/ble*).

Step 25: Anglo-Saxon spellings

Spell these suffix endings the same way even if the sound is different:

Past tense *-ed*

Present tense ending *-ing*
Plural ending *-s*

Step 26: Latin/French spellings

sh sound for words of Latin origin, spell:

> *ti, ci, si, ssi* (e.g., *suspi<u>ci</u>on, deli<u>ci</u>ous, addi<u>ti</u>on, educa<u>ti</u>on, torren<u>ti</u>al, par<u>ti</u>al, pen<u>si</u>on, mi<u>ssi</u>on*)

sh sound for words of French origin, spell:

> *ch, sci* (e.g., *bro<u>ch</u>ure, para<u>ch</u>ute; con<u>sci</u>ence*)

ay sound for words of French origin, spell:

> *et: ballet, gourmet*

k sound for words of French origin, spell:

> *qu* (e.g., *mystique, antique*)

Step 27: Greek spellings

- f = ph (e.g., *graph, phys-*)
- k = ch (e.g., *chemist, chrono-*)
- i = y (e.g., *gym, gypsy, style*)
- s = ps (e.g., *psych-*)
- r = rh (e.g., *rhythm*)

The Big 8 spelling rules

Students can also benefit from the Big 8 Spelling Rules in Figure 14.4. This chart shows in more detail the steps to follow in learning to spell words from basic letter-sounds to words with Latin and Greek origins.

Review charts for spelling

The charts below give examples of words that match the letter-sounds on the spelling snake up to step 21.

In the charts, the consonant sounds have regular spellings, but the vowel sounds are not like this, especially the long vowel sounds.

Learning suggestions

1. The student reads out all the sounds and words on the chart.
2. Someone asks the student to spell the sidebar words without looking.
3. Spell each word in a spelling book.
4. The student checks their spelling, using the chart.

Assessing spelling 195

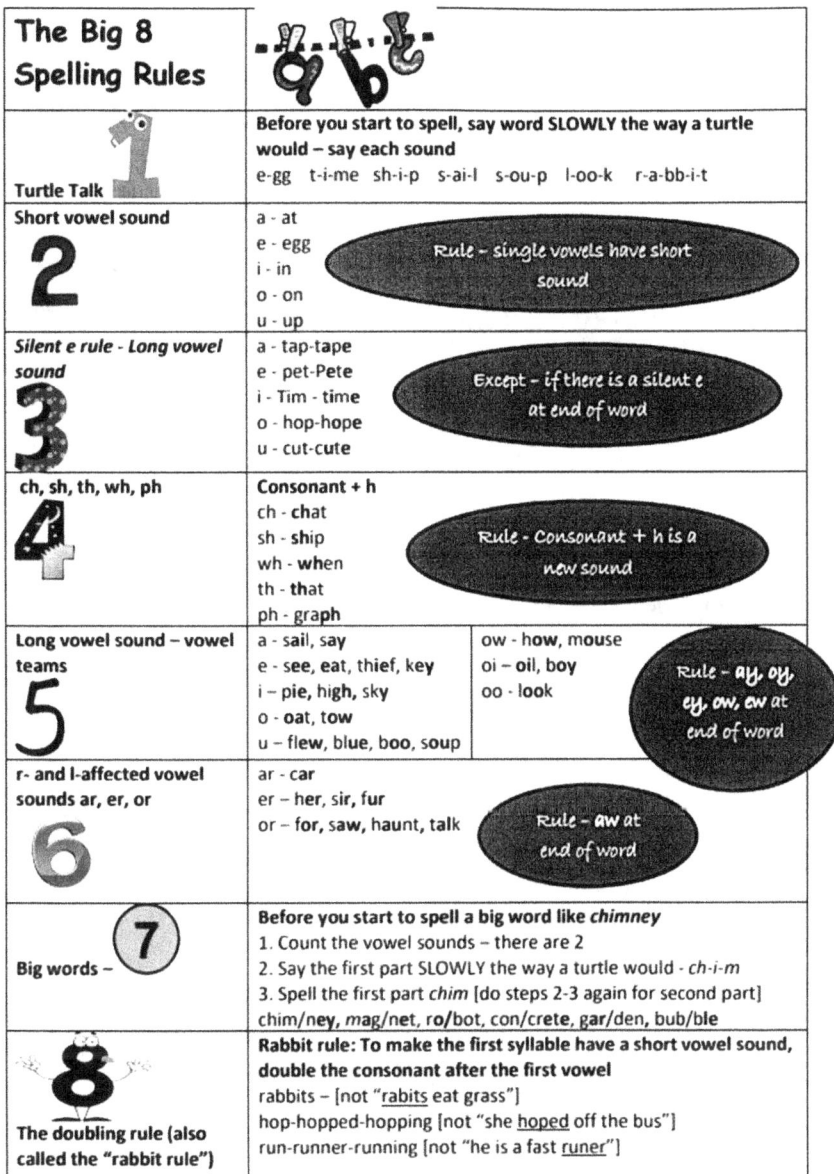

The Big 8 Spelling Rules		
Turtle Talk	Before you start to spell, say word SLOWLY the way a turtle would – say each sound e-gg t-i-me sh-i-p s-ai-l s-ou-p l-oo-k r-a-bb-i-t	
Short vowel sound	a - at e - egg i - in o - on u - up	Rule – single vowels have short sound
Silent e rule - Long vowel sound	a - tap-tape e - pet-Pete i - Tim - time o - hop-hope u - cut-cute	Except – if there is a silent e at end of word
ch, sh, th, wh, ph	Consonant + h ch - chat sh - ship wh - when th - that ph - graph	Rule - Consonant + h is a new sound
Long vowel sound – vowel teams	a - sail, say e - see, eat, thief, key i – pie, high, sky o - oat, tow u - flew, blue, boo, soup	ow - how, mouse oi – oil, boy oo - look Rule – ay, oy, ey, ow, ew at end of word
r- and l-affected vowel sounds ar, er, or	ar - car er – her, sir, fur or – for, saw, haunt, talk	Rule – aw at end of word
Big words – 7	Before you start to spell a big word like *chimney* 1. Count the vowel sounds – there are 2 2. Say the first part SLOWLY the way a turtle would - ch-i-m 3. Spell the first part *chim* [do steps 2-3 again for second part] chim/ney, mag/net, ro/bot, con/crete, gar/den, bub/ble	
The doubling rule (also called the "rabbit rule")	Rabbit rule: To make the first syllable have a short vowel sound, double the consonant after the first vowel rabbits – [not "<u>rabits</u> eat grass"] hop-hopped-hopping [not "she <u>hoped</u> off the bus"] run-runner-running [not "he is a fast <u>runer</u>"]	

Figure 14.4 The Big 8 Spelling Rules.

Chart 1: Beginner chart: all the vowel sounds

Figure 14.6 is a good start to spelling the vowel sounds. It "keeps it simple". Students learn one spelling pattern for each sound. Students will be able to spell most words by using these regular patterns. Some rules for spelling words in the chart are

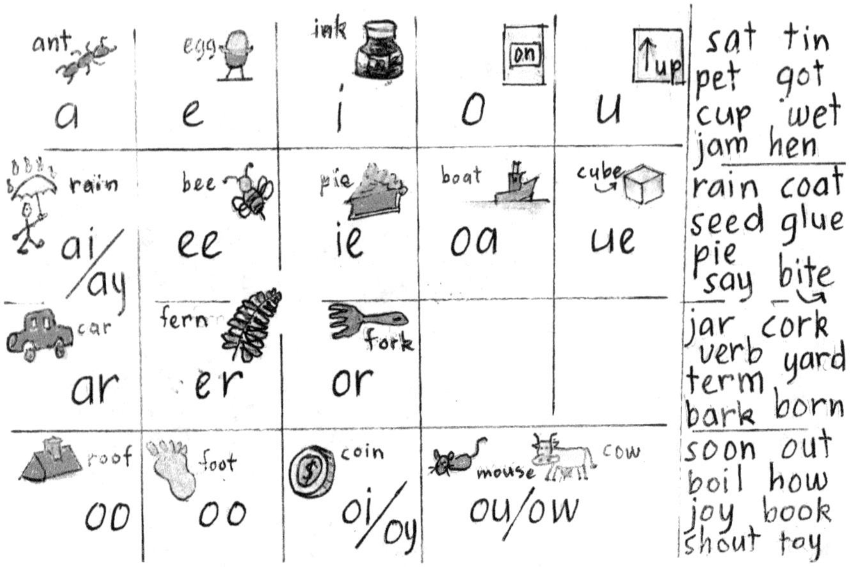

ant	egg	ink	on	up	sat tin
a	e	i	o	u	pet got
					cup wet
					jam hen
rain	bee	pie	boat	cube	rain coat
ai/ay	ee	ie	oa	ue	seed glue
					pie
					say bite
car	fern	fork			jar cork
ar	er	or			verb yard
					term
					bark born
roof	foot	coin	mouse cow		soon out
oo	oo	oi/oy	ou/ow		boil how
					joy book
					shout toy

Figure 14.5 Overview: Common Spelling Patterns.

1. Spell *ai* in the middle of the word and *ay* at the end of the word.
2. Spell *oi* in the middle of the word and *oy* at the end of the word.
3. Spell *ow* at the end of a word (e.g., *how, cow, now, allow*).

Chart 2: Long vowel sound a

Figure 14.6 has common spellings for the long a sound; plus it has a few exception words. Some rules for spelling the long a sound are

1. Spell ai in the middle of the word and ay at the end (e.g., *sprain-spray*).
2. Spell the split digraph pattern a_e with a single *a* in the middle of the word and a silent *e* at the end (e.g., *plate*).
3. Exceptions: *ey: they, obey, survey; et: ballet, bouquet, croquet, gourmet; ei: vein, reindeer, beige; ea: break, steak, great.*

Chart 3: Long vowel sound e

Figure 14.7 has the most common spellings for the long e sound. Some rules for spelling the long e sound are

1. Spell long *e* in the middle of the word with *ee, ea, ie*.
2. Spell *y* or *ey* for long *e* only at the end of the word.
3. Spell the split digraph pattern *e_e* with a single *e* in the middle of the word and a silent *e* at the end.

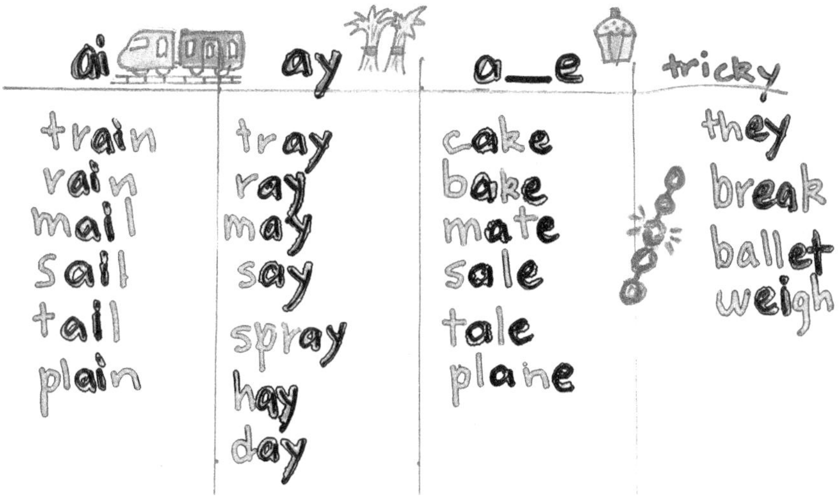

Figure 14.6 Long Vowel Sounds ai ay a_e.

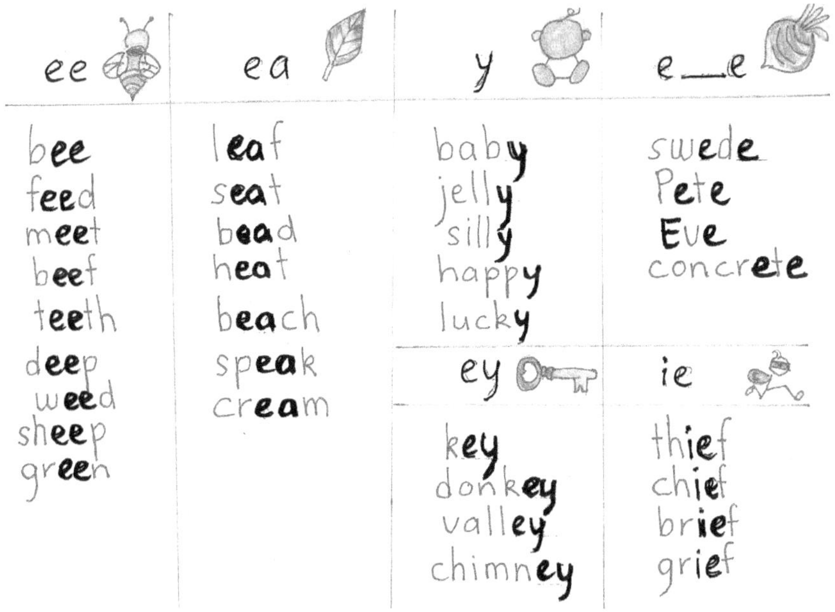

Figure 14.7 Long Vowel Sounds ee ea y e_e ey ie

198 *Teaching Literacy Effectively in Modern Classroom for Ages 9–12*

Chart 4: Long vowel sound i

Figure 14.8 has the most common spellings for the long i sound, plus some exception words. Some rules for spelling the long i sound are

1. long *i* in the middle of the word – *i_e, y, igh* – when followed by *t* (e.g., *plight*)
2. long *i* at the end of the word: *y*, ie, igh
3. Exceptions: *I* and *buy* – only words like this; *eye* – like *dye, rye, goodbye*; *i* – *find, blind, child, behind, alibi*

Chart 5: Long vowel sound o

Figure 14.9 has the most common spellings for the long o sound, plus some exception words. Some rules for spelling words with the long o sound are

1. long *o* in the middle of the word: *o, oa, ow, o_e*
2. *oa* only in the middle of word, not at the end
3. *ow* usually at the end of the word (e.g., *arrow*)
4. Exceptions: *sew*, only word like this; *oe*: *doe, foe, Joe, hoe, floe*; *ough*: *dough, although, though*

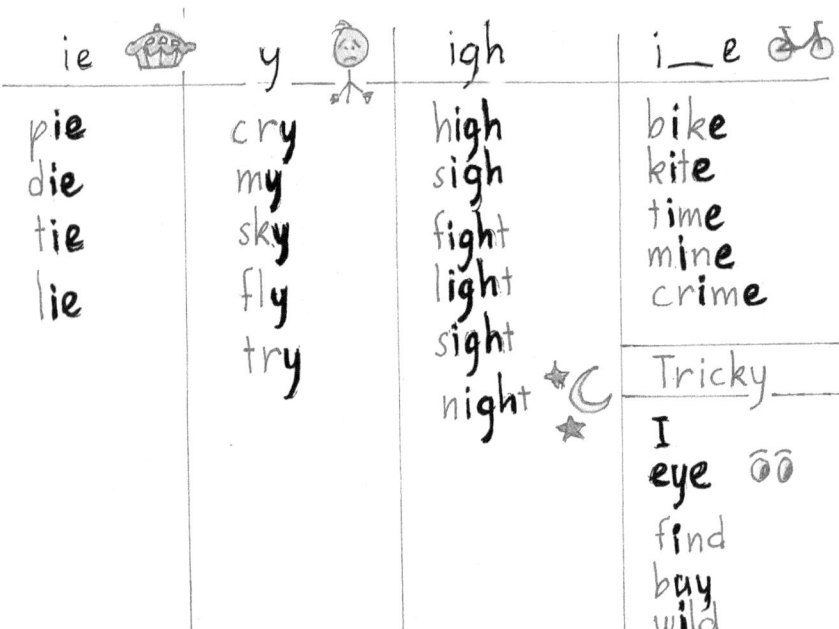

Figure 14.8 Long Vowel Sounds ie y igh i_e

Assessing spelling 199

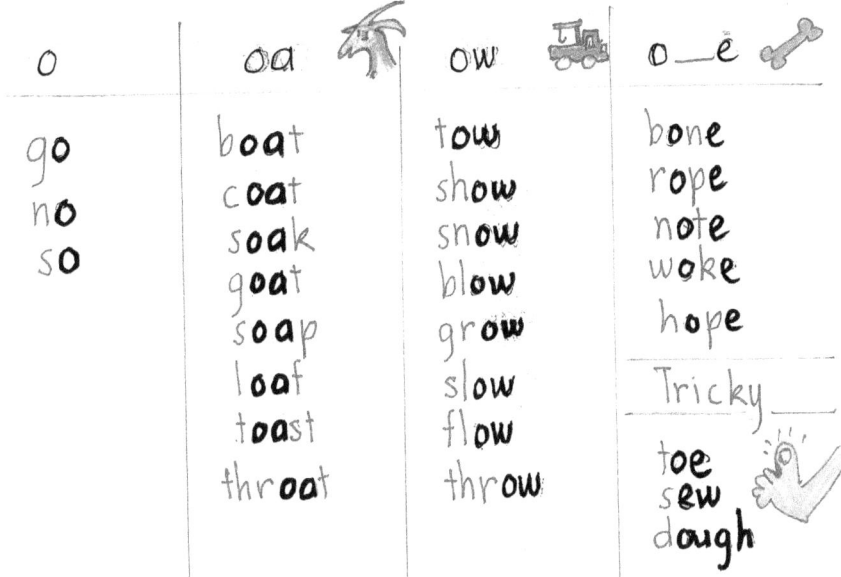

Figure 14.9 Long Vowel Sounds oa ow o_e

Chart 6: Long vowel sound u

Figure 14.10 has the most common spellings for the long u sound, plus some exception words. Some rules for spelling words with the long u sound are

1. long *u* in the middle of the word: oo, u_e, ue, ew, ou
2. *ue* and *ew* usually at the end of the word (e.g., *true, threw*)
3. Exceptions: *ewe, two,* only words like this; *oo_e: goose, loose, ooze, snooze; u: music, funeral, cucumber, Cuba.*

Chart 7: Long vowel sounds ow, ou, oo, oi-oy

Figure 14.11 has common spellings for the long vowel sounds ow, ou, oo, oi-oy, plus some exception words. Some rules are

1. *oo*: for *book, shook,* etc.
2. *ow, ou*: for *clown, mouse,* etc.
3. *oi* in middle of word, *oy* at end (e.g., *avoid, employ*)
4. Exceptions: u: *put, pull, bull, full;* ou: *should, would, could.*
5. Exceptions: ough: *plough* and *bough* – only words like this (note: *plough* is British, *plow* is U.S.)

200   *Teaching Literacy Effectively in Modern Classroom for Ages 9–12*

oo	u_e	ew	ou
boo	flute	flew	soup
zoo	cube	blew	group
too	jute	crew	coupon
food	tube	chew	wound
moon	brute	drew	you
room	juvenile	screw	
tooth	include	threw	"tricky"
spoon			goose
loop	**ue**		music
troop	blue		ewe
pool	glue		two
school	clue		
	true		

Figure 14.10 Long Vowel Sounds oo u_e ew ou ue

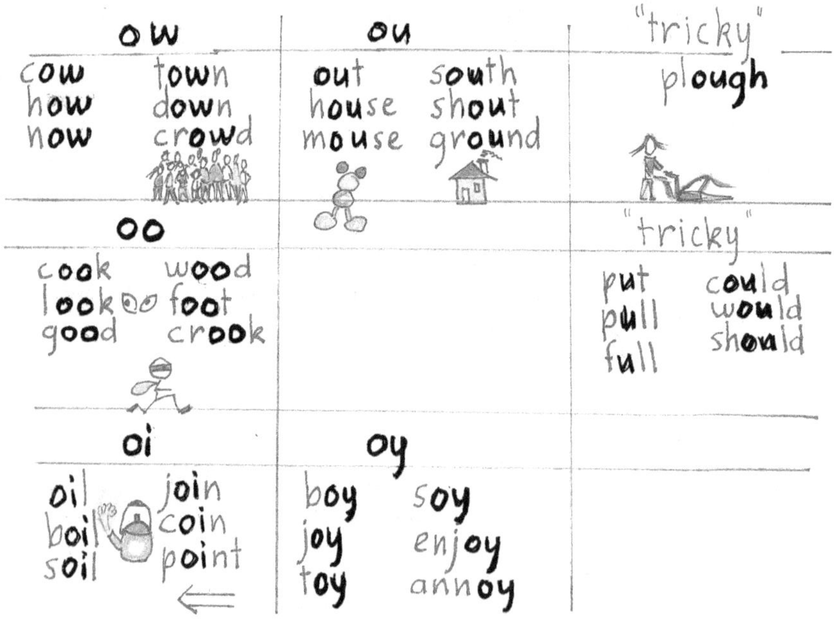

ow	ou	"tricky"
cow town	out south	plough
how down	house shout	
now crowd	mouse ground	

oo		"tricky"
cook wood		put could
look foot		pull would
good crook		full should

oi	oy	
oil join	boy soy	
boil coin	joy enjoy	
soil point	toy annoy	

Figure 14.11 Other Vowel Sounds ow-ou oo oi-oy

Chart 8: r- and l-affected vowel sounds

Figure 14.12 has common spellings for the r- and l-affected vowel sounds.

1. *ar* is the most common spelling of ar sound
2. *or*: *au-aw, al*
3. *aw*: at end of word
4. er: *er, ir, ur*

Exceptions:

ar sound
- *au*: *aunt, laugh, draught*
- *a*: *ask, basket, plaster, grasp, rather, after, France*
- *al*: *calf, calm, almond, embalm*

or sound
- *ar*: *war, quarter, warm, towards*
- *oar*: *soar, coarse*
- *ore*: *more, store, before, snore, explore.*

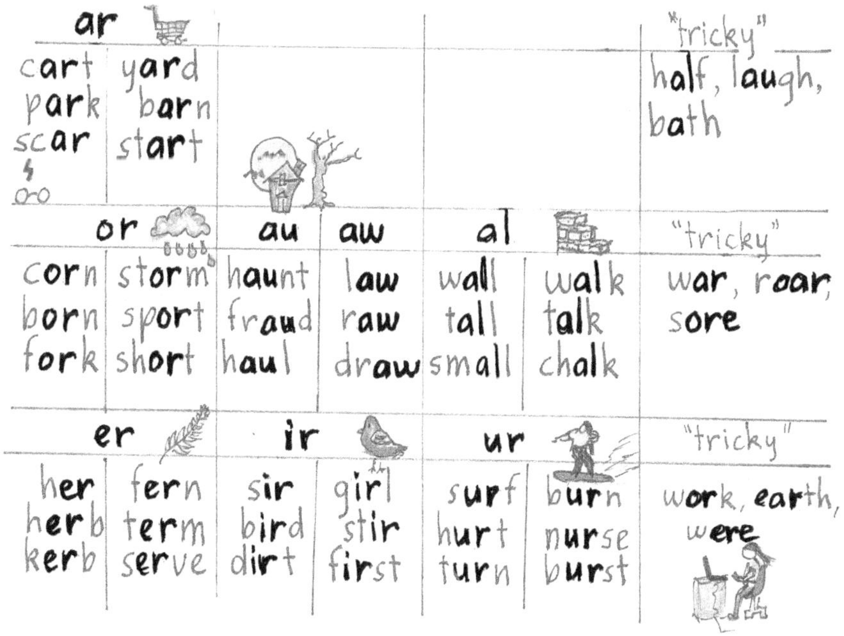

ar						"tricky"
cart yard						half, laugh,
park barn						bath
scar start						

or		au	aw	al		"tricky"
corn storm		haunt	law	wall	walk	war, roar,
born sport		fraud	raw	tall	talk	sore
fork short		haul	draw	small	chalk	

er		ir		ur		"tricky"
her fern		sir	girl	surf	burn	work, earth,
herb term		bird	stir	hurt	nurse	were
kerb serve		dirt	first	turn	burst	

Figure 14.12 R- and L-Affected Vowel Sounds ar or au-aw al er ir ur

Spelling quizzes to check your spelling skills

Spelling quiz 1: Different vowel spellings

Quick review: circle the correct spelling

Short vowels	Split digraphs	r-affected vowels	Long vowels
thump or thamp	tiem or time	yard or yared	train or tran
rent or reent	note or noet	corner or carner	foot or fut
smag or smug	baek or bake	hermit or hrmit	deep or depe
plum or plam	ti or tie	prson or person	joyn or join
	bite or biet		flot or float
			proof or pruef
			shout or showt
			mowse or mouse

Spelling quiz 2: Long Vowel Sounds ee ea y e_e ey ie

Quick review: circle the correct spelling (* = tricky spelling)

coet or coat	shoa or show
croa or crow	drove or droav
towst or toast	groa or grow
throat or throte	*foe or fough
arrow or arroa	*dough or doa

Spelling quiz 3: Long Vowel Sounds oa ow o_e

Quick review: circle the correct spelling (* = tricky spelling)

rain or rane	laik or lake
mayl or mail	snak or snake
tray or trai	whail or whale
trayn or train	*wai or weigh*
stray or strai	thay or they

Spelling quiz 4: Long Vowel Sounds ie y igh i_e

Quick review: circle the correct spelling (* = tricky spelling)

shien or shine	dynamite or dynamite
nyte or night	cieclone or cyclone
knife or knyf	xylophone or xylophone
kite or kight	*eye or ie
cryme or crime	*kynd or kind

Spelling quiz 5: Long Vowel Sounds ai-ay a_e

Quick review: circle the correct spelling (* = tricky spelling)

swiep or sweep	cheaf or chief
theef or theif	cream or creme
acheev or achieve	wheyt or wheat
greet or greyt	concrete or concret
feid or feed	*donkey or donky

Spelling quiz 6: Long Vowel Sounds oo u_e ew ou ue

Quick review: circle the correct spelling (* = tricky spelling)

clue or clew	soop or soup
spoon or spoun	threw or throo
*gouse or goose	inclood or include
wound or woond	rescyou or rescue
snooze or snewze	curfyou or curfew
routine or ruetine	*muesic or music
stoud or stood	*two or tue

Spelling quiz 7: Other Vowel Sounds ow-ou oo oi-oy

Quick review: circle the correct spelling (* = tricky spelling)

house or howse	crook or crouk	boyl or boil
mowth or mouth	woud or wood	ploi or ploy
showt or shout	brouk or brook	voyce or voice
south or sowth	*put or poot	toilet or toylet
*bough or bowgh	*should or shood	poyson or poison

Spelling quiz 8: r- and l-affected Vowel Sounds ar or au-aw al er ir ur

Quick review: circle the correct spelling (* = tricky spelling)

barn or barne	torch or tawch	surf or sirf
park or parke	storm or stalm	cherch or church
sharpe or sharp	cawn or corn	perr or purr
*harf or half	* roar or ror	*erth or earth
*laugh or larf	*sworm or swarm	*world or werld

Punctuation tips

> The spelling teacher teached me about punctuation and what they are called and what they really mean.

Examiner reports on student writing in exams mention that students need to attend to punctuation (e.g., to start the sentence with a capital letter and end with a period/full stop or to use a comma if there is a pause). A comma in the wrong place in a sentence can change the meaning totally. Students need to know how to use punctuation effectively to make their sentences clearer and more effective.

The rule for using punctuation is that less is more; students should use necessary punctuation but not overdo it (e.g., do not sprinkle commas all over the page to make the writing look good). Table 14.1 has the Big 14 punctuation rules for students to review (Samson, 2015).

Students need to learn punctuation because it helps the reader to understand what their sentences mean, it makes them clearer, and readers like it when punctuation is correct.

Table 14.1 The Big 14 Punctuation Tips for Writers

Punctuation marks	Notation	Examples
1. **Uppercase letters**: For the first letter in the word and the first word in the sentence. For the first letter of names of people and places, months, days of the week.	ABC	Detective Gordon woke up in a sweat. Buffy, New York, January, Monday
2. **Period/full stop**: Always put a period/full stop at the end of the sentence.	.	We must investigate.
3. **Question mark**: For questions. Put it at the end of the sentence.	?	Is it a crime?
4. **Exclamation mark**: To show the speaker is saying something with force or loudly. Put it at the end of the sentence.	!	The shelf was still empty!
5. **Comma**: When there is a slight pause in the sentence.	,	You can read it yourself, somewhere in the middle. I ate apples, pears, and plums today. On Sunday, we had chicken for lunch.
6. **Speech marks**: Go around words spoken.	" "	"Toads should not have to look at themselves in the mirror," grumbled Detective Gordon. Mum said, "Hello."
7. **Apostrophe**: For abbreviations and possession.	'	Abbreviation: can't Possession: Ernie's cat. BUT not for plurals (e.g., *I ate five banana's* -is wrong.
8. **Hyphen**: Adds more to the sentence.	-	There were peanuts and a carrot - but no sandwiches.

(Continued)

Table 14.1 (Continued)

Punctuation marks	Notation	Examples
9. **Parentheses**: Goes around some words in the sentence.	( )	The workers at the factory (especially Ernie) were pleased to see him.
10. **Ellipsis**: Words are left out.	…	She hid behind the bushes and waited and waited …
11. **Dash**: To set off non-essential information that might disrupt the sentence	-	The best location – if you have the money to get there – is London.
12. **Semi-colon**: Joins two main clauses	;	Toad's legs were spindly; his flat feet were large and squelchy.
13. **Colon**: To introduce a quotation or a list	:	Detective Gordon suddenly had a terrible thought: imagine if the cake tins were empty!
14. **Quotation marks**: To identify the words of someone else	" "	Shakespeare wrote a famous oxymoron, "Parting is such sweet sorrow." Or to draw attention to a word or phrase – e.g., The word "hopefully" is often used incorrectly.

Note: At the end of a sentence, you can have a period/full stop, a question mark, or an exclamation mark – but only one of these.

Take a quick punctuation test ☺ (answers at end).

1. Which of these sentences has the wrong punctuation in it?
   A. This question isn't easy
   B. Is this the right answer?
   C. "I hope I get this one right," she said to herself.

2. Which of these sentences has the wrong punctuation in it?
   A. "That's John's apple!" he shouted.
   B. All shop's are closed on Christmas day.
   C. My cat's name is very silly.

Answers:
1A
2B

15 Teaching spelling

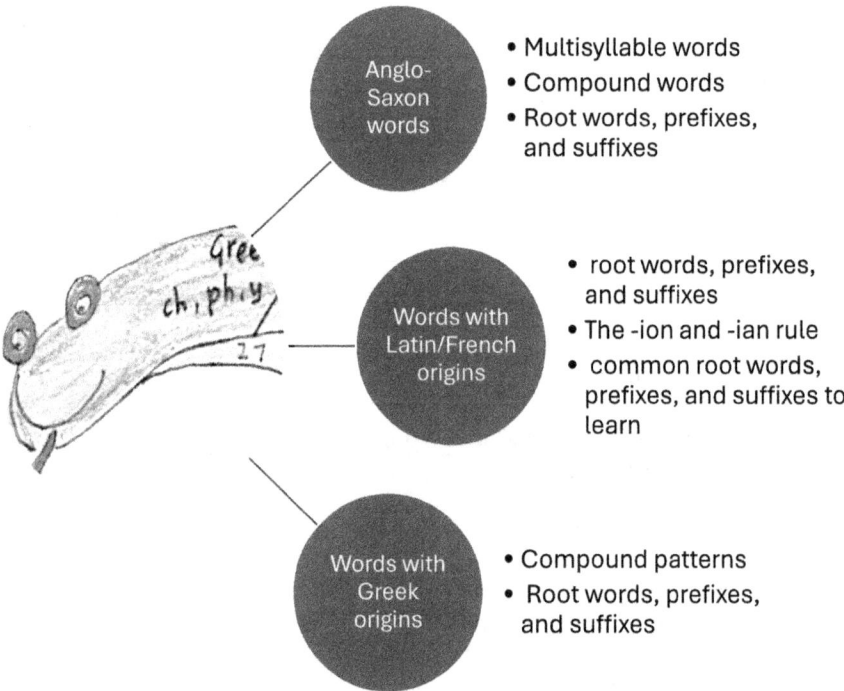

Figure 15.1 Overview of Chapter 15: Teaching Spelling.

15.1 Introduction

> I can't spell properly or anything.
> I need the most help with how to spell hard words and how to know what the rule is.

DOI: 10.4324/9781003130789-20

Students learn what they are taught. If a student fails to acquire spelling skills, then we should first examine the instructional approach. Studies show that spelling instruction does work for words taught and tested in the classroom, but the problem is there is little transfer of the taught skills to the spelling of new, untaught words that students face in tests and exams.

If spelling instruction is not working well, it is because the spelling curriculum lacks coherence. Students need to learn to spell in a systematic way. They also need to be taught directly, not in a multitude of little ability groups where there is little or no learning. Spelling should be taught to the whole class at the same time in the same way. If we have high expectations for students, a belief that they can spell well, they will step up. They cannot do that if we have some in the "monkey" groups and others in the "eagle" groups. We can teach spelling better than we do.

Spelling is a Cinderella in the classroom. Although schools teach spelling it does not seem to be of high priority. When you visit schools, each one seems to teach spelling differently. It is a mish mash. In school reports, spelling does not have its own category but is subsumed under writing. It should have its own place in the sun, so parents know how well their children are doing.

Critics of spelling say that spelling instruction is not a good use of class time. They argue that 20% of students do not need spelling instruction, and that those who do need instruction do not improve, even with help. They argue that schools are obsessed with spelling correctness, ignoring the fact that nearly one in three students are spelling below standard.

Critics say that the science and linguistics of spelling has turned spelling lessons into a nightmare of alphabet soup. There may be something in this. Some spelling curricula and manuals on teaching spelling seem to get carried away with linguistics and overuse technical terms when there are simpler replacements: phonemes (sounds), morphemes (small chunks of meaning), and so on. The present chapter has tried to keep terminology to a minimum. There are some technical terms but only necessary ones, and when they are mentioned, there are definitions of them.

Spelling is important. The ability to produce spelling of words fluently is a sign of an educated person and it may have other advantages in that it helps to build vocabulary and general knowledge. It certainly helps with writing. Fluent spellers write more and use a wider range of vocabulary. Spelling is an important part of being literate.

The present chapter will cover the following spelling topics:

- Anglo-Saxon spellings
- Latin spellings
- Greek spellings

15.2 Anglo-Saxon spellings

Learning to spell Anglo-Saxon words is the students' first spelling challenge. This is what they must do to spell correctly:

1. They must know how to use Turtle Talk (i.e., saying the word slowly, phoneme by phoneme) to segment the sounds in words (e.g., c-*l-o-ck-s*).
2. They must know the sound-to-print rules – a BIG job but critical.
3. They must know statistical patterns (e.g., spell a for o after w: *was, watch, waddle*).

Spelling compound words

Many Anglo-Saxon spellings are compounds (e.g., *buttercup, footsteps, nightcap, downright, humbug, piggybank, downstream, honeysuckle, meadowsweet, forehead, sundown*).

Compounds are two words combined to create a new meaning. In Anglo-Saxon, this was a common way to create new meanings.

The core meaning of a compound spelling is usually in the second part. For example, in *raindrop*, the core meaning is *drop*, a *drop* of *rain*. In *rainbow*, it is a *bow* of *rain*. In Old English, *bow* described the curved shape of the *rainbow*.

Table 15.1 is a list of compound spellings that follow this pattern. List 1 has *rain* at the beginning (e.g., *raincoat* is a coat for rain), and List 2 has *fish* at the end (e.g., *jellyfish* is a fish made of jelly).

A student can benefit by reading the lists in Table 15.1, dividing each spelling in two, working out each meaning, spelling them several times, and writing them in sentences. These are all routine rote-learning strategies, which is good, but the crucial learning point is, can the student explain the logic behind this way of creating new meanings (i.e., combining existing words)?

Do they know that each part of *raincoat* is a real word, that *rain* and *coat* have real meanings? While students may know how to spell *rain* and *coat*, they may not be able mentally to combine them spell a new word like *raincoat*. It is a cognitive leap. It is not obvious to the beginner that *raincoat* is composed of two words. The teacher asks the student to spell rain and coat. The student spells them correctly. The teacher asks them to spell raincoat. To the surprise of the teacher the students says, "I don't know how to spell that word." Once they understand how compound words work, however, they will be better equipped to spell words like *raincoat*. This is the purpose of the lists below, to learn the logic of compound words. It is logical thinking. Students need to know what they are doing and why.

Table 15.1 Anglo-Saxon Compound Spellings

List 1	List 2
raindrop	catfish
rainbow	kingfish
raincoat	goldfish
rainfall	jellyfish

Spelling root words, prefixes, and suffixes

A root word meaning can be almost any real word (e.g., *get, bid, red, like, slow*). Prefixes are mostly prepositions that alter the meaning of the root word (e.g., *by, for, in, un, over, under, with, be*). Suffixes change the tense of the root word (e.g., *-ed, -ing*). Or the form class (e.g., from a verb to an adverb, by adding *-ly*). Suffixes can change the root meaning from singular to plural: *-s, -es*. Suffixes can add meaning (e.g., *-hood, -dom, -less, -ship, -able, -ful*).

15.3 Latin-based spellings

Learning to spell Latin-based words, the sophisticated words, that were imported into English is the student's second spelling challenge. This is what they must do to spell them:

- Learn to dig out the morphemes and spell them: prefixes, suffixes, root words.
- Learn the Latin spelling of the sh sound: ti - *action*, ci - *magician*, si - *mission*.

The suffixes -ion, -ian

The suffixes *-an, -ian* tell us this is a person (e.g., *barbarian, equestrian, Australian, historian, physician, Roman, American, Shakespearean*). In contrast, *-ion* tells us that the noun is not a person (e.g., *action*). In Table 15.2 are examples of *-ion* and *-ian* words.

Table 15.2 Spelling Examples of -ion and -ian

-tion: state of	-sion: state of	-cian: having a skill
vacation	compression	magician
distraction	depression	musician
construction	impression	politician
subtraction	progression	physician
addition	confession	statistician
direction	admission	electrician
expedition	pretension	mathematician
nutrition	compulsion	tactician
repetition	repulsion	
superstition	apprehension	
partition	comprehension	
ignition	tension	
notification	transmission	
detention		

A possible lesson for -ion and -ian might be

Today the class is learning about Latin words. You can usually tell a Latin word because it has a special beginning called a prefix and an ending called a suffix. The suffix is important because it tells the part of speech of the word. Let's look at these two suffixes. This one is *-ion* and this one is *-ian*; see Figure 15.2.

> Here is *state* in this column, but to add *ion* to *state*, it means dropping the *e* at the end of *state*. What does it spell now?
> Statin
> Let's have a closer look. In spellings with Latin origins, you spell the sh sound with a *ti*.
> Station
> Yes, that's it. Is there a station near where you live, a railway station? (pause)
> Is there a petrol station?
> Yes
> Great. Now let's work on this column. Look at this spelling – teacher writes *magic*.
> Magic
> What's magic?
> People do magic, play magic
> Yes, they do tricks, pull rabbits out of hats, that sort of thing.
> Look, now -ian is attached to *magic*. What have I spelled now?
> Magikan
> Here is a clue. In Latin you spell the sh sound with *ci*.
> Magician

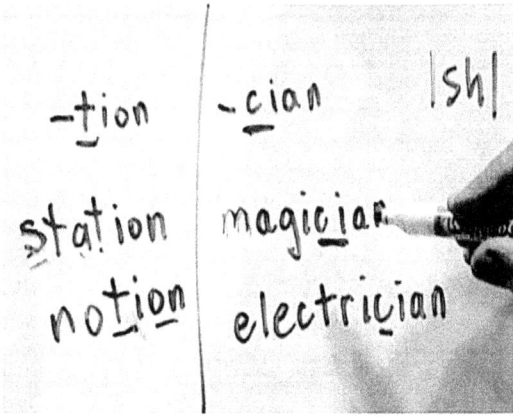

Figure 15.2 Spelling -ion and -ian.

Look at this spelling [writes *electric*]. What will the spelling be with -ian attached to the end of it?
Electran
Here is a clue, *ci* makes the sh sound – it says *electrician*
Electrician
Great. What you learned today was that when you spell *-ian* at the end of the spelling means a person – a *magician* is a person who does magic. In this column, *station* ends with the *-ion* which means it is not a person. If what you want to spell is not a person, the suffix is *-ion*.

15.4 Greek-based spellings

Learning Greek-based spellings is the student's third challenge. This is what they must do to spell:

- In Greek spelling, the sound k = ch - *chemist*, the sound f = ph - *graph*, the short vowel i = y - *myth*, the long vowel i = y - *cyclone, xylophone, hydraulic*.
- Other Greek spellings: the sound r = rh - *rhododendron*, the sound s = ps - *psychology*.

Greek combining forms

Many Greek spellings have two parts. Each part has meaning. For example, *astronaut* = *astro* (star) + *naut* (sailor), meaning *a sailor of the stars*; *dinosaur* = *dino* (terrible) + *saur* (lizard). A dinosaur is a *monstrous lizard*. Splitting Greek spellings into two parts makes them easier to spell.

Greek spellings combine two meaning parts, but each part may not necessarily have an independent meaning (e.g., *agoraphobia* is a fear of public places. It combines the independent meaning units, *agora* and *phobia*). Other spellings are different (e.g., *thermometer* is a measure of heat, but thermo is not an independent meaning).

Some meaning units act like root words (e.g., *chrono, graph, phono, phys, psych, thermo*). Others act like prefixes (e.g., *micro-, auto-, biblio-, hemi-, hydro-, octo-, tele*). Others act like suffixes (e.g., *-cracy, -ology, -phobia, -scope*).

One way to think about these spellings is that the student must break them into parts to make them easier to spell.

There are two meaning units in *seismograph*. Spell *seismo* first, then *graph*. In this spelling, both parts have meaning: *seismo* means shake, *graph* means writing. A seismograph measures earthquakes by "writing" seismic wave patterns.

There are two meaning units in *monograph*: *mono* means one, *graph* means writing. A *monograph* is written on one topic.

There are two meaning units in *graphology*: *graph* means writing, and *-logy*, meaning study of, acts like a suffix. Graphology means the study of writing.

Exercise: Greek words

1. Divide each spelling into its parts (e.g., *psycho/logy*).

List 1	List 2
microscopic	microcosm
psychology	psychic
philosophy	sophisticated
chronology	chronometer
thermometer	thermodynamics
monochrome	monologue
dinosaur	megalosaurus

2. Divide each spelling into two parts and in list 2 write its meaning.

List 1	List 2
telepathic	
biography	
autocrat	
zoology	
biology	
democracy	
metropolis	
archaeologist	

3. How would you explain to someone who does not know about foreign spellings in English the meanings of these Greek spellings?

aerodrome
atmosphere
autograph
bibliophile
biography
hydrant
catalogue
octopus
tripod

15.5 Conclusion

After digesting this chapter, the reader may think it is too hard for students to learn to spell. There are too many rules, so thank goodness for spell checkers!

Yes, spellcheckers are helpful, but they are not yet foolproof. When a word is spelt incorrectly, the spellcheck offers a list of alternative words. Which alternative is correct? Even more confusing, correctly spelt words are often identified as incorrect. Spellcheckers miss some mistakes. For example,

- *The knight rode the hoarse into the distance.*
- *I had a refreshing swim in the see.*
- *I could not swim for long because my ant had just arrived.*

Teaching spelling 213

Students do not need to rely on spellcheckers. There is a systematic spelling code for English, and they can learn this code. It is true that to spell well takes time, practice, and persistence, but this is worth it. Even if spellcheckers were perfect, there are reasons why students should be good spellers rather than having to rely on spellcheckers. The main benefit is the wellbeing factor. To know that they can spell well is very motivating when it comes to tasks that require writing skills. Spelling is important for exams. Spelling well adds credibility to a person's work and is a positive boost to self-esteem.

Finally, for the older student who is behind in spelling and would like to brush up on basic English spellings such as long vowel sounds and so on, the Appendix to the present chapter provides 18 mini quizzes. Chapter 14's Appendix also has a 27-step scope and sequence chart, eight spelling charts with examples of the various spelling rules, and some practice yes/no spelling quizzes.

Appendix: Quiz resources to use for spelling practice (Figures 15.3–15.20)

Circle the correct letter   y   w   j   z   ck

1		y	u
2		y	w
3		g	j
4		z	s
5		ck	k
6		k	x

Figure 15.3 Spelling Quiz: Consonant Sounds.

Write the correct vowel sound -

a e i o u

1		d_g
2		m_p
3		k_g
4		p_g
5		d_ck
6		b_g

Figure 15.4 Spelling Quiz: Short Vowel Sounds 1.

Write the correct vowel sound -

a e i o u

1		_gg
2		s_n
3		t_n
4		p_t
5		n_t
6		g_n

Figure 15.5 Spelling Quiz: Short Vowel Sounds 2.

ch   sh   th   ng

1	 (chick)	__ick
2	(shrek)	__rek
3	(ring)	ri__
4	(fish)	fi__
5	(three)	__ree

Figure 15.6 Spelling Quiz: ch sh th ng.

Circle the correct spelling

	a e i o u

1	🐕	ap	ape
2	🎩	hate	hat
3	🐎	mad	made
4	🏠	home	hom
5	🌲	pine	pin
6	📌	pin	pine
7	🎵	not	note
8	🧴	tube	tub
9	🔥	fir	fire

Figure 15.7 Spelling Quiz: Long Vowel Sound: Silent e Rule.

Write the correct spelling -

ar   or   ur

1	 🏚 b__h	b__n
2	 🌽 c__n	c__n
3	 🏄 s__f	s__f
4	 🌳 p__k	p__k
5	 ☁️ st__m	st__m
6	 ⛪ ch__ch	ch__ch

Figure 15.8 Spelling Quiz: ar or ur.

Write the correct spelling

-all   -ell   -ill   -oll   -ull

1		b__
2		p__
3		d__
4		b__
5		g__

Figure 15.9 Spelling Quiz: all ell ill oll ull.

Write the correct spelling

ai - ay

1		m__l
2		tr__
3		t__l
4		tr__n
5	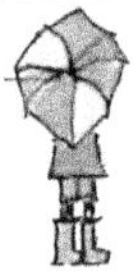	r__n

Figure 15.10 Spelling Quiz: Long Vowel Sounds ai ay.

Write the correct spelling

ee ea e_e

1		sw _ d _
2		sh _ _ p
3		l _ _ f
4		s _ _ t
5	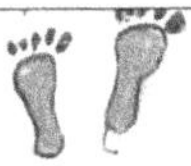	f _ _ t
6		qu _ _ n

Figure 15.11 Spelling Quiz: Long Vowel Sounds ee ea e_e.

Write the correct spelling

igh　　　ie　　　i_e

1	 (moon)	n __t
2	 (pie)	p__
3	 (kite)	k_t_
4	 (light)	l__t
5	 (eyes)	s__t

Figure 15.12 Spelling Quiz: Long Vowel Sounds igh ie i_e.

Write the correct spelling -

oa   ow   o_e

1		t__
2		b__t
3		g__t
4		sn__
5		h_m_
6		l__f

Figure 15.13 Spelling Quiz: Long Vowel Sounds oa ow o_e.

Write the correct spelling

ou   ew

1		s__p
2		fl__
3		gr__
4	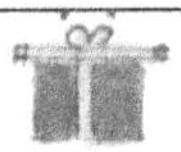	n__
5		gr__p
6		scr__
7		vi__

Figure 15.14 Spelling Quiz: Long Vowel Sounds ou ew.

Write the correct spelling -

oo   ew   u_e   ue

1		m__n
2		sp__n
3		fl_t_
4		scr__
5		t_b_
6		bl__
7	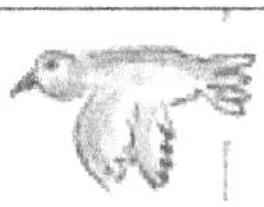	fl__
8		c_b_

Figure 15.15 Spelling Quiz: Long Vowel Sounds oo ew u_e ue.

Circle the correct spelling -

au   aw

1		haunt - hawnt
2		saw - sore
5		dinosaur - dinosor

Figure 15.16 Spelling Quiz: Long Vowel Sounds au aw.

Write the correct spelling

oi   oy

1		b__
2		__l
3	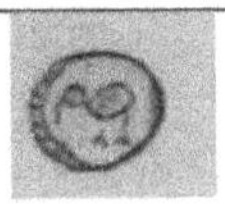	c__n

Figure 15.17 Spelling Quiz: Long Vowel Sounds oi oy.

Circle the correct spellings

1		hay	hey
2		son	sun
3		tale	tail
4		sore	saw
5		sale	sail
6		flee	flea
7		reign	rain
8		purr	per
9		blew	blue
10		hare	hair

Figure 15.18 Spelling Quiz: Homophones.

Circle the correct spelling

-s   -ed

1	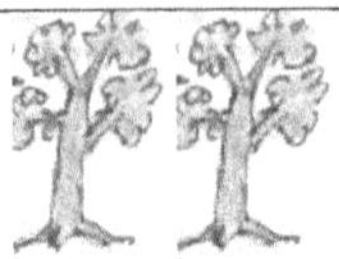	treez	trees
2	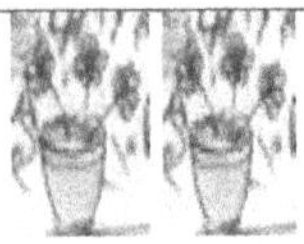	potted	pottd
3		moppt	mopped
4		cowz	cows
5		cars	carz

Figure 15.19 Spelling Quiz: Suffixes -s, -ed.

1		magician	magicion
2		statian	station
3		musicion	musician
4	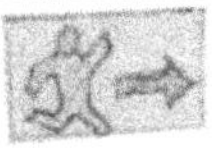	direction	directian
5		optician	opticion

Figure 15.20 Spelling Quiz: Suffixes -ian, -ion.

Part 6

Countdown to the classroom

Chapter 16, *Countdown to the classroom*, explains the need for a 3-month countdown to plan lessons and to find out the school's policy on teaching, on student conduct, and on how to handle problems. A happy classroom will learn more, and sail to success, but poor student conduct can destroy a lesson. You must teach in a businesslike way, use routines, try out each lesson first, teach the whole class, say no to ability grouping, be calm, never get angry, give praise for good conduct, make simple changes to avoid chaos, be like a lighthouse with a spotlight looking to nip problems in the bud, use strong body language, and do not let chatter take over. You are not a dictator, but you must be the boss.

16 Countdown to the classroom

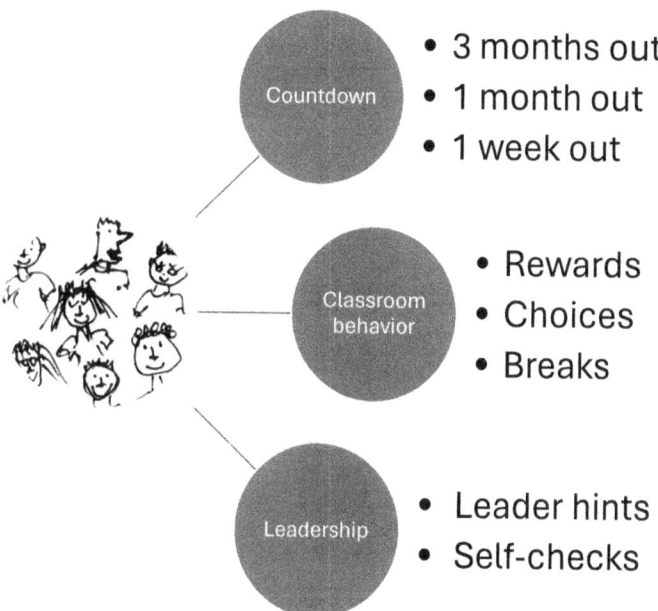

Figure 16.1 Overview of Chapter 16: Countdown.

16.1 Introduction

> You spend most of your life in here, in school, and you come here every day. I think it should be better than this, and I like the teachers to be a bit more friendly than what they are. Closer to the kids would be better.
>
> You come to this place all bright and cheery in the morning, you step inside the gate, and the atmosphere just dulls you. You just break down and wish you hadn't got up this morning.

Today's schools are complicated, perhaps more than in the past. There has always been diversity in classrooms, but it seems greater now. It can seem overwhelming; there are so many pressures, so many needs.

It seems complex, but some would say that there are a few simple ideas that will make all the difference. One thing that is true in life and in the classroom is the power of routine – and stability.

The key points to think about in planning:

- Routine: Every lesson starts the same way, with a warmup, and ends the same way.
- Students like predictability and stability, minimal change, expecting the same.
- No surprises. Give lots of warning if something new is on the horizon.
- Never raise your voice. Always be calm, like a stone in the river.
- Explain each lesson to students, what its purpose is and why they are doing it.
- Do one subject at a time and do it well. Avoid jumble. Cover one skill, then another.
- Use formal language, but do not overdo it (e.g., polysyllabic, plot, metaphor).
- Give praise (e.g., "Good job", "High five", "I like the way you …").
- Enjoy each lesson (e.g., "What a great day we had!" "This class is doing so well!").

The present chapter will cover these topics:

- Countdown to the classroom
- Expertise and credibility
- Leadership

16.2 Countdown

What is most important is planning. Everything works better if it is prepared ahead of time. The Chinese saying is "win at the starting line." It means be so prepared beforehand that you always do the task required, you hit the ground running, and everything goes well.

Planning is the key to everything, right down to the bread-and-butter things like the state of the classroom and the resources you will need to survive each day, each term, and the whole year.

Rule #1 is to make sure your planning and ideas are consistent with the policies of the school you will be in. Schools have their own systems for student learning. These ways make sense to the school and are the result of much prior experience.

Three months out

When you arrive at a school for a first look-around, find ways to understand how it works. Visit the classroom; be sure to check that the classroom has enough tables and chairs, internet connections, and other relevant resources. Is there technology? Is it working? Do you have internet access? Think about how to make the room work. Can you request furniture you need?

One month out

Are there any meetings planned at school? Will you have a mentor? Check resources: Are there up-to-date textbooks? What does the school expect in terms of planning?

Two weeks out

Make lesson plans. The plans can be sketchy at first, and add detail later, but they will show the big picture of what you are trying to achieve over the school term. Rules for every lesson are (Ashman, 2018)

- Stay business-like. Be friendly but it in a professional way. Give the class the impression that you have a job to do, that there are things they need to learn.
- Routines. Start with the same activity each lesson. No surprises (e.g., students have their homework out ready for you to look at). Have a warm-up activity (e.g., a vocabulary quiz, handwriting practice, a spelling test, a poem to read chorally, a decoding chart to recite).
- Practice every lesson on yourself.

What to include in a lesson

✓ Warm-up activity, something familiar and easy (e.g., spelling quiz).
✓ There should be structure: an opening that explains the purpose of the lesson, a middle that focuses on content, and a close that explains what was learned.
✓ Reminder list with all things needed for the lesson (e.g., laptop, whiteboard, pens, charts, watch, timer). Check these off before you head to class. Put up a daily timetable on the board in the classroom, for you as well as the students, so everyone knows where the boat is going.

Day 1

Some "neutral" opening activities could be

- Introduction: students say their name and talk about what they did in the vacation.
- Explain the class routine, how each day will work, and what the class will do. Write the details on the whiteboard.
- Explain class rules.
- Explain homework requirements but first check the school's homework policy.

16.3 Equity – why it is important

What matters more than anything in moving literacy levels forward in the classroom is to give explicit lessons. Explain content to the class. Do not go on for 10 minutes and then spend the next hour in small groups. Research on classroom grouping has found that breaking the class into ability groups for literacy lessons, with eagles, butterflies, tigers, and crows, does not give students instruction according to their needs. Instead, meta-analyses of multiple studies have found that lower-ability groups get treated unequally (Bolick & Rogowsky, 2016).

Whereas the top readers do the exciting stuff, read the interesting books, do high-level comprehension and vocabulary, the bottom groups languish, consigned to low-level tasks, given easy-to-read books and simplistic activities that do not push them forward.

Some may think that having small groups and easy readers will help the lower readers, but this only pushes them back. One meta-analysis of many studies on this topic pleaded to "consider ways to ensure that students within the lowest reading groups receive equal access to rigorous instruction and materials" (Patrick, 2020, p. 631).

Putting high and low readers into separate small groups may be a major reason why there is such disparity in literacy achievement in classrooms and schools. For most of each lesson, they are not listening to ideas or new information content or seeing how to use new skills but instead are spending most of the time doing out-of-seat work in small groups – to what end? It does not help the lower readers.

Students learn when the lesson conveys information to them, but if they are spending most of their time doing stuff in small groups, they are not learning from anyone.

This does not mean that students must be always listening to information and looking to the front of the class. The class can break into small groups, there is nothing wrong with this; they should all be working on the same task, not higher learning for the top group and lower learning for the bottom group. Having small groups with some doing complex work and others doing simplistic work is not equitable. Having small groups in the classroom, like streaming in high school, is not fair on the lowest readers. The rich get richer, the poor get poorer.

The key point is that everyone in the class should do the same work; students should all have access to the same content and the same lessons. There should not be literacy segregation in the classroom. Small groups are a form of segregation. They are not necessary.

16.4 Planning for good conduct in the classroom

Some classrooms are a joy to work in; students are attentive and focused and enjoy coming to class. Other classrooms are a jungle; the students wear you down, little by little, niggling and testing you all the time. Some give up with the constant pressure from students and do not last. There must be a balance between students feeling free to express themselves and a productive classroom where work gets done.

Calm

The most important thing, when the classroom is falling apart, is to be calm. If a student is disruptive, do not let it continue; it will not fix itself. Act quickly and focus on de-escalation rather than reprimand.

Some students need time out to calm down. Reiterate the class rules. In some classrooms, it will take only a moment to get the class on track, but in other classrooms, it will take longer.

Imagine you are a stone in the river: let the emotions wash over you, do not react. Always reiterate the task, that it must be done. You can reason but never give in to bullying or threats. You are not anyone's friend. You are not a parent, but you are someone students should listen to. This is the main reason students go to school: to learn from an expert, from you.

It is easy to get upset with students when their conduct is unacceptable, but this never works. Never yell and never make a threat. Always stay calm. If overwhelmed, seek immediate advice.

Praise

Use specific praise that is related to the actions you want to encourage in the classroom, like paying attention, sitting quietly, and being helpful. Give praise when the class quiets down or when a disruptive pupil calms down and re-joins the group (e.g., "Glad you are back, well done" or "I like the way you look so focused, ready to get the work done").

Reduce task difficulty

If the task is difficult, like a long novel with dense prose to read or a complex science topic, break it into small chunks. Do one or two pages each lesson. Students can help. Assign small groups a page a day to sum up, that they must explain to the class, and each day one more page gets explained to the class, by the class.

Keep it simple. Do not swamp the class with work that is too hard. They will resent it, and they will not make any progress. Do not say to yourself, "We must do this, we cannot stop, we will never finish the curriculum if we slow down."

These are silly words. What good will it do if you finish on time but the class knows nothing and resents it. The best solution is breaking the work up into small chunks. If it is a decoding chart, fold it in half. Do one half today and the other tomorrow. If it is a comprehension lesson, with 20 questions, break them into four sets of five and do one set each day. If it is a writing task, give out planners to work on, discuss what to do, then finish the writing tomorrow. These strategies reduce student panic and confusion.

Rewards and points

Give points for good conduct – but never deduct points; students will think it is not fair. A point is a point. Students like getting points. It is a visible sign of achievement.

The class gets points for sitting up straight, being in their seat, attempting the lesson, and not shouting or being disruptive. If they get ten points, they get a small reward such as three minutes of free time or even simple but honest praise like "good job."

Choices

Give the class a choice of two activities. Let students choose which one they would like to do first.

Breaks

Sometimes, to settle the class, it helps to take mini breaks, but it must be the right kind of break (e.g., you read the class a poem, a short story, a picture book, show a short video, or the class can all sing a song). There are many exciting, action poems that students will like you to read to them.

Engagement

The class will learn only if they are engaged. If the class is not on-task or if everyone is talking at once, learning will not happen. Even if you keep talking, ignoring the noise, it will not work out; students will not learn anything.

Studies show that the class is more engaged when the learning task is something that they can understand and do (e.g., if the book or worksheet or handout is something they can read easily for themselves). If students think they can do the task, there is less frustration, more engagement, better comprehension, and more creativity.

You may want to try a new idea with the class, but it will never work unless it is signposted early and explained early and students get some easy practice with it.

If the literacy task is too far above student ability levels, they will be frustrated. There is no need for students to read or write when the task is too hard for them. If there is no choice, because it is a required text or required in the curriculum, then break it into small chunks and coach them through it.

Avoiding descent into chaos

When the lesson has gone completely wrong, when you feel you have lost control, sometimes it helps to change tack completely.

A simple change will work. In some classes, it is not uncommon to see a noisy rabble quieten down when you read them a book. In some classes, it is a routine, the reading of a chapter of the book every day. It has a calming effect. Even the toughest students will calm down and sit and listen.

Another idea is a spelling test but do not give a hard test; use words they are familiar with. Start with very easy words. It quietens the room as they get out their spelling books and write the numbers one to 20 down the page and get ready for the first word. Every class likes a spelling test. Students like to see what score they get. At the end of the test, they can mark their work as you spell out the answers. These seem like mundane tasks, but studies show that they increase engagement and improve learning.

Self-observation

Sometimes it is good to stand back and observe your interactions with the class. Observe how you talk to them, how you present as an educator, how the school would like you to present, and its expectations of you.

One suggestion is to audio-record 15 minutes of one lesson (e.g., with a smart pen). It is unobtrusive and can sit on the desk during the lesson. Of course, before trying this idea out, check with your team leader if it is possible to do it. Listen to parts of the lesson later and think of what to do to improve.

16.5 Leadership

> I do some stupid things to stir teachers up, but if I put my mind to it, I can work ... I have mucked it up now for my future, but oh well. Big deal. I have mucked it up that much now I might as well muck it up the rest of the way.

Three components of leadership

These suggestions are from Elliott (2009). Leadership depends on three factors: the students, who are the ones presenting challenges; the classroom leader, yourself; and the school's climate, regulations, and rules for correct conduct.

An effective leader is someone who responds to poor conduct but more importantly makes sure that poor conduct does not happen in the first place. The effective leader is aware of everything going on around them, like a lighthouse with a spotlight continually circulating.

The effective leader exhibits actions that on the surface do not seem important but students recognize them and will behave correctly. What are these?

Awareness

An effective teacher leader is constantly scanning the class and can send subtle signals (e.g., looking at the student, moving slightly towards them). It is not nipping problems in the bud but being vigilant, looking for possible signs of things that might go wrong.

Body language

An effective teacher leader can project control non-verbally. A strong voice is important. Be loud and clear, loud enough for students to hear. Never shout. The voice must convey strength. Any hesitation will be seen as weakness. Body posture must be relaxed, not rigid or tense. Always keep hands at the side; do not wave hands or cross arms. Students will see this as a sign of fear.

Be the boss

An effective teacher controls what students talk about in class and how much talk is allowed. Students will nitpick you, looking for weak points, by asking questions, making unnecessary requests, ignoring instructions, and paying no attention to what you are saying. Handling this is a key skill.

The novice will engage with students, respond to their questions, and try to be their friend, but students will see them as weak, lacking expertise, and not a "proper" teacher.

A teacher leader needs a confident voice and a face and body that exude calm and control. If you are not confident, students will sense fear or anxiety in your voice, your actions, and your looks. The leader must always be in control. You are not the students' friend, but at the same time, nor are you a dictator or bully.

16.6 Conclusion

Helping students to achieve their potential is challenging. There are difficult headwinds and turbulence. A safe landing for everyone depends on effective learning in the classroom. The classroom is the student's best chance of success. They can gain the expert help they need.

A calm, happy, productive classroom can happen. The secret to success is routine. On every day of school, there should be no surprises. Students need predictability and trust. If students feel overwhelmed, they will rebel.

Front-end planning is essential. It is best to start planning well before meeting the class for the first time. Try to anticipate possible turbulence and headwinds and what to do about these.

Lastly, if you are happy, the class will be happy. Have fun!

References

Apel, K., Masterson, J. J., & Brimo, D. (2012). Writing. In A.G. Kamhi & H.W. Catts (Eds.), *Language and reading disabilities* (3rd ed., pp. 226–243). Pearson.

Ashman, G. (2018). *The truth about teaching: An evidence-informed guide for new teachers.* Sage.

Australian Curriculum, Assessment and Reporting Authority. (2013). *NAPLAN 2013 persuasive writing marking guide.* ACARA.

Ayroles, J., Potocki, A., Ros, C., Cerdan, R., Britt, M. A., & Rouet, J.-F. (2021). Do you know what you are reading for? Exploring the effects of a task model enhancement on fifth graders' purposeful reading. *Journal of Research in Reading*, *44*(4), 837–858. https://doi.org/10.1111/1467-9817.12374

Binder, K. S., Ardoin, S. P., Mellott, J. A., Nimocks, E., & Moss, C. (2024). Reading Comprehension Tests: Students' question reading and responding behavior. *Educational Assessment*, *29*(3), 182–205. https://doi.org/10.1080/10627197.2024.2356200

Bolick, K. N., & Rogowsky, B. A. (2016). Ability grouping is on the rise, but should it be? *Journal of Education and Human Development*, *5*(2), 40–51. https://doi.org/10.15640/jehd.v5n2a6

Broc, L., Joye, N., Dockrell, J. E., & Olive, T. (2021). Capturing the nature of the spelling errors in developmental language disorder: A scoping review. *Language, Speech, and Hearing Services in Schools*, *52*(4), 1127–1140. https://doi.org/10.1044/2021_LSHSS-20-00086

Bryant, D. (1975). *Bryant test of basic decoding skills.* Teachers College, Columbia University.

Carney, R. N., & Levin, J. R. (2008). Conquering mnemonophobia, with help from three practical measures of memory and application. *Teaching of Psychology*, *35*(3), 176–183. https://doi.org/10.1080/00986280802186151

Cervetti, G. N., Fitzgerald, M. S., Hiebert, E. F., & Hebert, M. (2023). Meta-analysis examining the impact of vocabulary instruction on vocabulary knowledge and skill. *Reading Psychology*, *44*(6), 672–709. https://doi.org/10.1080/02702711.2023.2179146

Chetail, F. (2024). Reading books: The positive impact of print exposure on written word recognition. *Cognition*, *251*, 105905. https://doi.org/10.1016/j.cognition.2024.105905

Colenbrander, D., von Hagen, A., Kohnen, S., Wegener, S., Ko, K., Beyersmann, E., Behzadnia, A., Parrila, R., & Castles, A. (2024). The effects of morphological instruction on literacy outcomes for children in English-speaking countries: A systematic review and meta-analysis. *Educational Psychology Review*, *36*(4), Article 119. https://doi.org/10.1007/s10648-024-09953-3

Cushing, I. (2023). Word rich or word poor? Deficit discourses, raciolinguistic ideologies and the resurgence of the 'word gap' in England's education policy. *Critical Inquiry in Language Studies*, *20*(4), 305–331. https://doi.org/10.1080/15427587.2022.2102014

Cushing, I. (2024). Tiered vocabulary and raciolinguistic discourses of deficit: From academic scholarship to education policy. *Language and Education*, *38*(6), 969–987. https://doi.org/10.1080/09500782.2024.2308824

Dickens, C. (1850/1981). *David Copperfield*. Oxford University Press.

Dymock, S., & Nicholson, T. (2024). *Teaching literacy effectively for ages 5–8*. Routledge.

Dymock, S., & Nicholson, T. (2016). *Talking about text: Unpublished data*. Faculty of Education, University of Waikato.

Dymock, S., & Nicholson, T. (2017). To what extent does children's spelling improve as a result of learning words with the look, say, cover, write, check, fix strategy compared with phonological spelling strategies? *Australian Journal of Learning Difficulties*, *22*(2), 171–187. https://doi.org/10.1080/19404158.2017.1398766

Elleman, A. M., Lindo, E. J., Morphy, P., & Compton, D. L. (2009). The impact of vocabulary instruction on passage level comprehension of school-aged children: A meta-analysis. *Journal of Research on Educational Effectiveness*, *2*, 1–44.

Elliott, J. G. (2009). The nature of teacher authority and expertise. *Support for Learning*, *24*(4), 197–203.

Gough, P. B. (1983). Context, form, and interaction. In K. Rayner (Ed.), *Eye movements in reading* (pp. 203–211). Academic Press.

Gough, P. B. (February 1996). *A pox on both your houses*. Paper presented to *symposium on integrated direct instruction, sponsored by the Language Arts Foundation of America and Oklahoma Schools*, Oklahoma City.

Gough, P. B., & Hillinger, M. L. (1980). Learning to read: An unnatural act. *Bulletin of the Orton Society*, *30*, 179–196. https://doi.org/10.1007/BF02653717

Graham, S., Collins, A. A., & Ciullo, S. (2024). Evidence based recommendations for teaching writing. *Education 3–13*, *52*(7), 979–992. https://doi.org/10.1080/03004279.2024.2357893

Graham, S., Collins, A. A., & Rigby-Willis, H. (2017). Writing characteristics of students with learning disabilities and typically achieving peers: A meta-analysis. *Exceptional Children*, *82*(2), 199–218.

Graham, S., & Eslami, Z. R. (2020). Does the simple view of writing explain L2 writing development? A meta-analysis. *Reading Psychology*, *41*(5), 485–511. https://doi.org/10.1080/02702711.2020.1768989

Graham, S., Harris, K. R., & Hebert, M. (2011). It is more than just the message: Analysis of presentation effects in scoring writing. *Focus on Exceptional Children*, *44*(4), 1–12. https://doi.org/10.17161/foec.v44i4.6687

Graham, S., Kim, Y.-S., Cao, Y., Lee, J. W., Tate, T., Collins, P., Cho, M., Moon, Y., Chung, H. Q., & Olson, C. B. (2023). A meta-analysis of writing treatments for students in grades 6–12. *Journal of Educational Psychology*, *115*(7), 1004–1027. https://doi.org/10.1037/edu0000819

Graham, S., & Santangelo, T. (2014). Does spelling instruction make students better spellers, readers, and writers? A meta-analytic review. *Reading and Writing: An Interdisciplinary Journal*, *27*(9), 1703–1743. https://doi.org/10.1007/s11145-014-9517-0

Hammill, D. D., & Larsen, S. C. (2009). *TOWL 4: Test of written language*. Pro-Ed.

Harley, T. (2017). *Talking the talk. Language, psychology, and science.* (2nd ed.) Psychology Press.

Harris, C. (2024, January 25). Students at a loss for words, experts say. *Sydney Morning Herald*, 17.

Hasbrouck, J., & Tindal, G. (2017). *An update to compiled ORF norms* (Technical Report No. 1702). Behavioral Research and Teaching, University of Oregon.

Hoover, W. A., & Tunmer, W. E. (2020). *The cognitive foundations of reading and its acquisition*. Springer.
Hunter, I. (2008). *Write that essay! A practical guide to writing better essays and achieving higher grades*. McGraw Hill.
Joye, N., Broc. L., Marshall, C. R., & Dockrell, J. E. (2022). Spelling errors in French elementary school students: A linguistic analysis. *Journal of Speech, Language, and Hearing Research*, 65, 3456–3470. https://doi.org/10.1044/2022_JSLHR-21-00507
Juel, C., & Minden-Cupp, C. (1999). One down and 80,000 to go: Word recognition instruction in the primary grades. *The Reading Teacher*, 53(4), 332–335.
Levin, J. R. (1993). Mnemonic strategies and classroom learning: A twenty-year report card. *The Elementary School Journal*, 94(2), 235–244. https://doi.org/10.1086/461763
Nation, P. (2020). The different aspects of vocabulary knowledge. In S. Webb (Ed.), *The Routledge handbook of vocabulary studies* (pp. 15–29). Routledge.
New Zealand Qualifications Authority. (2024). *NCEA interim assessment report*. NZQA.
Nicholson, T. (2005). *Phonics handbook*. Wiley.
Nicholson, T., & Dymock, S. (2023). *The New Zealand dyslexia handbook* (2nd ed.). NZCER Press.
Nilsson, U. (2015). *Detective Gordon: The first case*. Gecko Press.
Nilsson, U. (2016). *Detective Gordon: A complicated case*. Gecko Press.
O'Neill, S. (May 2, 2016). Gradgrind Morgan is sucking the joy out of learning. *The Times*, 30.
Patrick, S. K. (2020). Homogeneous grouping in early elementary reading instruction: The challenge of identifying appropriate comparisons and examining differential associations between grouping and reading growth. *The Elementary School Journal*, 120(4), 611–635. https://doi.org/10.1086/708666
Pei, M. (1967). *The story of the English language*. Lippincott.
Petersen-Brown, S., & Kromminga, K. R. (2024). Systematic review and meta-analysis of the implementation and effectiveness of spelling instruction and intervention. *Psychology in the Schools*, 61(8), 3315–3338. https://doi.org/10.1002/pits.23223
Pinnell, G. S., Pikulsi, J. J., Wixson, K. K., Campbell, J. R., Gough, P. B., & Beatty, A. S. (1995). Listening to children read aloud: Data from NAEP's integrated reading.
Radaker, L. (1963). The effect of visual imagery upon spelling performance. *The Journal of Educational Research*, 56(7), 370–372. https://doi.org/10.1080/00220671.1963.10882958
Richards, M. A. (2022). *A history of words for students*. Thames & Hudson.
Sabatini, J., Wang, Z., & O'Reilly, T. (2019). Relating reading comprehension to oral reading performance in the NAEP fourth-grade special study of oral reading. *Reading Research Quarterly*, 54(2), 253–271. https://doi.org/10.1002/rrq.226
Samson, D. (2015). Teaching punctuation. *The Virginia English Journal*, 64(2), 23–37.
Schonell, F. J., & Schonell, F. E. (1960). *Diagnostic and attainment testing* (8th ed.). Oliver & Boyd.
Shaughnessy, M. F. (2003). An Interview with Joel R. Levin. *Educational Psychology Review*, 15(3), 297–309.
Stanback, M. L. (1992). Syllable and rime patterns for teaching reading: Analysis of a frequency-based vocabulary of 17,602 words. *Annals of Dyslexia*, 42, 196–221.
Standards and Testing Agency. (2018). *Teacher assessment exemplification: End of key stage 2 English writing*. https://www.gov.uk/government/publications/2018-teacher-assessment-exemplification-ks2-english-writing
Toste, J. R., Clemens, N. H., Filderman, M. J., Chandler, B. W., Rodrigo, S., & Moore, C. (2025). Investigating the contribution of spelling practice to the multisyllabic word reading skills of upper elementary students with dyslexia. *Learning Disability Quarterly*, 1–13 (preprint) https://doi.org/10.1177/07319487251327223

Townsend, S. (1983). *The secret diary of Adrian Mole, aged 13¾*. Methuen.

Treiman, R. (2018). Tutorial: Statistical learning and spelling. *Language, Speech, and Hearing Services in Schools*, 49(3), 644–652. https://doi.org/10.1044/2018_LSHSS-STLT1-17-0122

Treiman, R., & Altmiller, R. (2021, May/June). What science tells us about learning, the nature of written language, reading, and reading instruction. *The Reading League Journal*, 2(2), 22–31.

Treiman, R., & Altmiller, R. (June 2025 in press). Statistical learning in spelling and reading. *Trends in Cognitive Sciences*, in press. https://doi.org/10.1016/j.tics.2025.05.002

Trudgill, P. (2023). *The long journey of English: A geographical history of the language*. Cambridge University Press.

Wang, Z., Sabatini, J., O'Reilly, T., & Weeks, J. (2019). Decoding and reading comprehension: A test of the decoding threshold hypothesis. *Journal of Educational Psychology*, 111(3), 387–401. https://doi.org/10.1037/edu0000302

White, S. et al. (2021). *The 2018 NAEP oral reading fluency study*. U.S. Department of Education.

Wilkinson, G. S., & Robertson, G. J. (2017). *Wide range achievement test 5*. Psychological Assessment Resources.

Wong, B. Y. (1986). A cognitive approach to spelling. *Exceptional Children*, 53(2), 169–173.

Author index

Pages in *italics* refer to figures

Apel, K. 173
Ashman, G. 235
Australian Curriculum, Assessment and Reporting Authority (ACARA) 141, 186
Ayroles, J. 74

Binder, K. S. 74
Bolick, K. N. 236
Broc, L. 186
Bryant, D. 19, *26*

Carney, R. N. 119
Cervetti, G. N. 100
Chetail, F. 100
Colenbrander, D. 176
Cushing, I. 104

Dymock, S. 129, 175, 190

Elleman, A. M. 100
Elliott, J. G. 239

Gough, P. B. 5, 7, 71
Graham, S. 129, 131, 142, 176, 178

Hammill, D. D. 134
Harris, C. 103
Hasbrouck, J. 8
Hoover, W. A. 68
Hunter, I. 156

Joye, N. 174
Juel, C. 100

Levin, J. R. 117, 119

Nation, P. 100
New Zealand Qualifications Authority (NZQA) 139
Nicholson, T. 19, 68, 129, 175, 190
Nilsson, U. 114, 122, 149

O'Neill, S. 4

Patrick, S. K. 236
Pei, M. 9
Pinnell, G. S. 7

Radaker, L. 176
Richards, M. A. 152

Sabatini, J. 7
Samson, D. 204
Schonell, F. J. 68, 186
Shaughnessy, M. F. 117
Stanback, M. L. 10
Standards and Testing Agency xiv, 136–137

Toste, J. R. 10
Treiman, R. 174
Trudgill, P. 9

Wang, Z. 7
White, S. 7
Wilkinson, G. S. 186
Wong, B. Y. 172

Topic index

Page numbers in **bold** denote tables, page numbers in *italics* denote figures.

countdown to the classroom: achieving good conduct in the classroom; avoiding chaos 238–239; breaks 238; calm 237; choices 238; keeping the class on task 238; need for balance 236; praise 237; reduce task difficulty 237; rewards 238; self-observation 239; equity–say no to ability grouping 236; features of good teaching 235; leadership: awareness 239; be the boss 240; body language 240; key points 239; planning ahead: first day 235; key points for planning 234; one month out 235; three months out 234; two weeks out 235

decoding: assessment of decoding skills; case study with error analysis 23; decoding revision charts: adjacent consonants *29*; Anglo-Saxon words *35*; chameleon sounds of c, g, y *32*; consonant digraphs *30, 31*; Greek words *37*; Latin words *36*; multisyllable words *34*; r-and l-affected vowels *31*; silent letter words gn, kn, st, etc. *33*; VC and CVC words *28*; VCe words-split digraph/silent e rule *31*; vowel digraphs/vowel teams *31*; diagnostic tests 19, *26*; norm-referenced tests 18; scope and sequence for poor decoders: student step-by-step guide: "reading snake" *27*; teacher overview **25**; trouble shooting diagnostics: consonant clusters–e.g., g<u>r</u>od 22; consonant digraphs–e.g., <u>ch</u>o *19*; CVC patterns, e.g., gik *19*; multisyllable patterns, e.g., bimdop 22; prefix-root word-suffix patterns, e.g., bomdactious 22; r-and l-affected vowels, e.g., gr<u>or</u>· *19*; split digraph pattern, e.g., nev-n<u>eve</u> *20*; lesson example 20; vowel digraphs, e.g., pl<u>ou</u>t *19*; lesson example *21*; teaching decoding: age 9 phonics targets; multisyllable words 40–45; closed syllable pattern *40*; -le syllable pattern 44, *45*; open syllable pattern *41*; r-and l-controlled syllable pattern *42*; split digraph syllable pattern *43*; vowel team syllable pattern *44*; age 10 phonics targets: Anglo-Saxon words 45–47; compound pattern 45, **46**, 47; prefix-root word-suffix pattern 47; age 11 phonics targets: Latin/French words **47**, 48, **49**; common prefixes 48, **49–50**; common root words 47–48; common suffixes 48, **49**; age 12 phonics targets: Greek words; examples 49–50; practice charts: Latin root word structures: dict 55; form *51*; greg *52*; jec 56; ped *52*; port *53*; rupt *51*; scrib 55; struct 54; spect 54; tract 56; vent *53*; what is decoding?: cracking the code: what the student must do 5–6; decoding– what is it? 5; definitions of terms: consonants 4; graphemes 4; morphemes 4; phonemes 4; syllables 4; vowels 4; fluency speed of reading 6–8; *speed targets for each age level* **8**; newletter-sounds in foreign words: French 14; Greek 15; Latin 14; polysyllabic words: how they work 9–11;

Topic index   247

six syllable types 10; *syllable breaking rules* 10; *what are syllables?* 9–10; prefix-root word-suffix structure 11–16; Anglo-Saxon 11–12; Greek 15–16; Latin/French 12–14; story of English: a short history *8, 9*; structure of compound words 11

reading comprehension: assessment of comprehension; age-level comprehension expectations: ages 9–10 read between the lines etc. 67; ages 11–12 assess credibility etc. 67; difference between good and poor readers: at or above expectation 68–69; below expectation 69; closing the gap 69; norm-referenced tests 68; question-answering skills: critical thinking 69; question analysis 69; simple view of reading 68, 71–72; using the simple view–data from four students **72**; test-taking strategies: *answering questions* **70**; *following directions* **70**; teaching comprehension: argument/persuasion; claim 85; example–"climate change" 85; supporting arguments 85; comprehension difficulties: what not to do 85–86; what to do 85; nonfiction/expository: descriptive; lesson example–"bears" *83*, **83**, *93*; list 78; weave 79, sequence 79; lesson example "poverty cycle" *84, 94*; web 79; lesson example 1 "snails" 79, *80, 90*; lesson example 2 "dogs" *81, 91*; lesson example 3 "cockroaches" *82, 92*; question-answering skills 74–76; church story: what can go wrong 75–76; practice examples 87–88; answers to practice examples 76; church **87**; farming rice **88**; rubber **87**; scratched knee **88**; skin diving **88**; two crows **88**; text structure explained fiction/narrative/story: components: setting, characters, plot, theme 76; lesson example–"hare and tortoise" 76, 77; story web 77; story graph–plot 77; practice lesson *89*; what is reading comprehension?: defining comprehension: cognitive 60–61; in-depth 60; simple 60; differences between fiction and nonfiction 62–63; fiction/narrative: what is it?: definition: imaginary, made-up 63; story structure: setting, characters, plot (graph of timeline) 63; non-fiction: what is it?: definition: real, factual, not stories 64; descriptive structures: list, etc. 64; sequential structures: linear string, etc. 64; persuasion: what is it?: examples: podcasts, advertisements, speeches 65; purpose: to persuade 64; structure: claims and supporting arguments 64; theories of reading comprehension: bottom-up theory 61; interactive theory 62; top-down theory 62

spelling: assessing spelling; big 8 spelling rules 194, *195*; error analysis: case study 1–48% error rate for *Animals getting cewd* 186–188; case study 2–21% error rate- 189; case study 3–11% error rate 189–190; norm-referenced tests 1; schonell spelling test 186; wide range achievement test 18, 186; punctuation tips–general rule, "less is more" 203–204; apostrophe **204**; colon **205**; comma **204**; dash **205**; ellipsis **205**; exclamation mark **204**; hyphen **204**; parentheses **205**; period/full stop **204**; practice test 205; question mark **204**; quotation marks **205**; semi-colon **205**; speech marks **204**; uppercase letters **204**; revision spelling charts: chart 1-beginner chart-common vowel sounds *196*; chart 2: long a sound ai, ay, a-e *197*; chart 3: long e sound ee, ea, y, e-e, ey *197*; chart 4: long i sound ie, y, igh, i-e *198*; chart 5: long o sound o, oa, ow, o-e *199*; chart 6: long u sound oo, u-e, ew, ou *200*; chart 7: other vowel sounds ow, oo, oi *200*; chart 8: other vowel sounds ar, er, or *201*; scope and sequence spelling chart: *student copy of 27 step "spelling snake" 191*; *27 steps explained* 190–194; spelling quizzes: quiz 1–mixed patterns **202**; quiz 2–ai-ay a_e **202**; quiz 3–ee ea y e_e ey ie **202**; quiz 4–ie y igh i_e **202**; quiz 5–oa ow o_e **203**; quiz 6–oo u_e ew ou ue **203**; quiz 7–ow-ou oo oi-oy **203**; quiz 8–ar er or sounds **203**; teaching spelling: Anglo-Saxon words: compound pattern 208; prefix-root word-suffix pattern 209; Greek words: ch, ph, y, rh, ps, pn 211; combining forms 211;

practice exercises 212; Latin words: examples of suffixes-ion,-ian **209**; lesson plan *210*, 211; quizzes: basic spelling rules 8; consonant sounds: digraphs ch sh th ng *216*; single letter sounds *213*; homophones *227*; Latin suffixes-ian-ion *229*; long vowel split digraph rule *217*; r-and l-affected vowels: all ell ill oll ull *219*; ar or ur *218*; short vowel sounds *214–215*; simple suffixes-s,-ed *228*; vowel teams: ai ay *220*; au aw *226*; ee ea e_e *221*; igh ie i_e *222*; oa ow o_e *223*; oi oy *226*; oo ew u_e ue *225*; ou ew *224*; what is spelling?: classifying words for teaching: no transfer value *177*; transfer value 177; exception spellings: combine rules with practice 175; learn regular rules first 174; regular rule knowledge predicts exception spelling *175*; faces of spelling: morphemic 171, 173; morphophonemic 171; orthographic 173; phonemic 171, 173; how the early printers made new rules: other letter-sound rules 171; silent e rule 171; words ending in i, u, v 171; imagery training: helps with tricky words e.g., aorta 176; painting on mental billboards 176; morphemes: bound 172; free 172; quirky spellings: handy tips: look for relatives 176–177; *other spelling tips* 180–182; over-pronounce tricky bits 176–177; spell kw as qu 176–177; spell "ve" at end of word 176–177; research on teaching spelling: lessons may not transfer to untaught words 176; lessons work for taught words 176; spelling "bee" winners-what makes top spellers 179; spelling debates 178; statistical spelling-how it works: -ead 174; -ic 174; *other patterns* 174; -tch 174; wa- 174; teaching Latin words: answers to spelling grid **179**; examples of prefixes, suffixes, root words 181–182; spelling grid method for teaching Latin words **173**

vocabulary: assessment of vocabulary; are student vocabulary scores declining? 103; assessment: rationale 103; curriculum expectations for vocabulary: figurative meanings 104; literal meanings 103; multiple meanings 104; examples of different vocabulary knowledge: figurative: allusion 109; cliché 108; connotation 108; euphemism 108–109; hyperbole 107; idiom 107–108; metaphor 106–107; onomatopoeia 107; oxymoron 107; paradox 108; personification 107; pun 108; rhetorical question 109; simile 106; literal: dictionary definition 104–105; morphemes 105–106; synonyms/ antonyms 105; multiple meanings: homographs, e.g., bass (music, fish) 209; homonyms e.g., bark (tree, dog). 109; homophones e.g., hare, hair 110; norm-referenced tests: British Picture Vocabulary Scale 104; Language comprehension 104; Reading vocabulary 104; test scores and stereotypes: avoid labels like "below average" 104; be sensitive to personal identity and culture 104; teaching vocabulary: bookmarking *122–123*; concept diagrams 113–116; sequence: definition 114; life cycle for *amphibians* 114–115; thermometer 115–116; diagram for *fear* emotions 119; weave 113–114; matrix diagram for crime suspects **118**; weave diagram for alligator, lion, bear *118*; web/concept wheel 113–114; web diagram for chameleons *117*; web diagram for fish *116*; web diagram for state of california *115*; web diagram for tigers *114*; context clues 112; dictionary/ thesaurus 113; keyword method: definition 117–119; examples of keyword method: *lachrymose* 119, *121*; *obsequious* 118; *phobias* 119, 122; Spanish words, e.g., *gata* 118, 121; structural analysis 116–117; morphemes 116; practice exercises **120–121**; word hunting 123; what is vocabulary?: breadth and depth 98–99; distinctive feature theory **99**, 100; English vocabulary: a polyglot 101; number of words students must know 100; what does not work: ability grouping 100; "easy" texts 101; what works to some extent: extensive reading 100–101; vocabulary lessons 100

writing: assessment of writing; examiner checklists on writing quality: above expectation checklist 142; below expectation checklist 142–143; examples of national assessments of student writing: *Applause*: above expectations 137–139; *Cruel to keep animals*: above expectation 141–142; *Good leader*: at expectations 139–140; *Jim Jarvis*: below expectations 136–137; expectations and targets **135**; features of good writing 135–136; norm-referenced tests of writing 134; personal checklists for students to use when writing: argument/persuasion 144; fiction 143; nonfiction 144; teaching writing: grammar-sentence structure: 12 kinds of sentences: adverb at front 156; alliteration 157; colon 157; em dash 156; metaphor and simile 157; oxford comma 157; paired double 156; prepositional phrase 157; repeating pattern 156; verb at start 157; very short sentences 156; W start 156; sentence combining technique: defined 155; example 155; practice exercises 156; sentence devices: phrases, clauses, passive voice 155; sentence diagramming technique: defined 155; example 155; sentence structure: subject, verb, object 155; fiction writing: definition: not real, made up 147; example of a story opening–*The First Case* 149; examples of narrative prompts in exams 147–148; planning the narrative 148; non-fiction writing: *definition: real, factual* 149; *descriptive writing*: list structure 149–151; weave/Venn structure 150–152; web structure 150–151; sequence writing–process, step-by-step: cause-effect 153; continuum 153; cyclical 153; linear string 151–152; problem-solution 153; persuasive writing: features 153–154; practice exercises-national test examples 154; writing planners: fiction/narrative: advanced *159*; proficient *158*; nonfiction: description: list planner *160*; weave planner *162*; web/concept wheel *161*; nonfiction: sequence: linear string *163*; problem-solution *164*; persuasion: debate *165*; what is writing?: defining the elements of effective writing: skill in generating ideas, putting them on paper 128; skill in persuasion 129; skill in spelling, grammar, punctuation 128; *reasons for writing* 128; research on teaching writing: little transfer to untaught topics 131; taught topics work 131; simple view of writing *129–130*; ideas and spelling both necessary *130*; students with writing difficulties *130*, 131; writing = ideas x spelling 129; strategies for writing well: ideas/creativity 131; planners 131; presentation skills (e.g., spelling, punctuation) 131; text structure 131; targets for long term writing: few or no errors 132; personal writing voice and style 132

For Product Safety Concerns and Information please contact our EU
representative GPSR@taylorandfrancis.com
Taylor & Francis Verlag GmbH, Kaufingerstraße 24, 80331 München, Germany

www.ingramcontent.com/pod-product-compliance
Lightning Source LLC
Chambersburg PA
CBHW070314240426
43661CB00057B/2639